To renew this book, phone 0845 1202811 or visit
our website at www.libcat.oxfordshire.gov.uk
You will need your library PIN number
(available from your library)

OXFORDSHIRE
COUNTY COUNCIL
SOCIAL & COMMUNITY SERVICES
www.oxfordshire.gov.uk

For Jyoti, who is everything

Contents

List of illustrations

'Humanity has taken to monoculture once and for all, and is preparing to produce civilisation in bulk, as if it were sugar-beet. The same dish is to be served to us every day.'

Claude Lévi-Strauss, *Tristes Tropiques*, 1955

1

Citizens of Nowhere

If you don't know where you are, you don't know who you are.

Wendell Berry, *The Gift of Good Land*, 1982

Reculver Beach, Kent
11 May 2006

It's ten to eight. The sun was just beginning its descent as we walked down the cliff path an hour ago, sacks of sea bass, sea beet, sea purslane, dulse and bladderwrack slung across our shoulders. Behind us the twin towers of the ruined cliff top church of St Mary, which stand sentinel over the remains of the Saxon shore port of Regulbium, were framed by the late evening light.

Now I sit cross-legged beneath the cliffs, piling driftwood onto a stuttering fire. Above me, hundreds of darting, chattering sand martins ride the evening breeze, shooting in and out of slits in the sandy face. Out to sea, framed by the dipping sun, are the rusting steel remains of wartime anti-aircraft tripods. Further out, a new windfarm stalks the horizon like some distant approaching army.

My fingers are encrusted with sea salt and ash. The crimson sun is behind me, the square stone towers up ahead. You can smell this place in the air. The evening silence is broken only by the crackling of the burning wood, the nattering of the martins and, now, the shifting of the gravel beneath Fergus's feet as he makes his way back up from the shoreline.

'I gutted the fish,' he says. 'How's the fire going?'

Fergus Drennan is one of England's few professional foragers. He makes a living – just – by hunting down, seeking out and selling wild food. Take Fergus to a wood, a patch of waste ground, the edge of a railway line or an empty evening beach, and it's likely he can feed himself, and probably you, and feed you well. He's been doing it since he was young, and it's never going to make him rich. He says it makes him free, though, as far as that's ever possible.

Our evening at Reculver brings to a close a day spent together in the Kent countryside, where Fergus has been inducting me. He's taken me to the woods and showed me how to find morel mushrooms, how to cut nettle tops, when to pick ash keys and how to track down the giant yellow bracket fungus known as 'chicken of the woods'. He's shown me how to make nettle soup, what to do with wild garlic, sorrel and hairy bittercress and what type of seaweed to harvest at low tide. Now, below the red cliffs and under the red sun, we're ending the day with the fruits of our labour: baked sea bass, dulse soup and fried sea beet, offset by strong sloe gin.

'The thing is,' says Fergus as he unwraps one of the bass from its foil and pokes it experimentally with a stick, 'that we're just so cut off now. Very few people understand the land, or even know what grows in their gardens or on the bit of wasteland behind their back fence. But once you do know, you start to understand the place you live in, and feel part of it. It's about culture, as much as anything. Remember those St George's mushrooms we picked earlier? They got the name because they start to appear around St George's Day, the 23rd of April. You hear people all the time moaning about how the traditions of this country are disappearing, we're not in touch with our heritage, nobody celebrates St George's Day any more, blah, blah. But most of these old traditions, when they were living, they came

2

from the land and from people's attachment to it. These days we don't know where we are, or what happens in our landscape, so we can't create new ones. Traditions come from places – from the land, from our relationship to it. Once that's gone, so has that living culture.'

The fish is done. We unwrap one each and poke around in the shingle for our forks.

'So many of my friends are constantly criticising this country,' says Fergus. 'You know, "I've got to get out, it's all going to the dogs" – all that. But for me, this is what I do. Foraging... it's not even about food, really – it's kind of about belonging. I feel such a part of it through this that I could never leave. I suppose it ties me to England. This is my place.'

Bluewater Shopping Centre, Kent
12 May 2006

I have never seen anything like this.

Or have I?

I'm driving down a slip road from the A2, following the white words painted on the road, and the white arrows painted above them in case there was any doubt at all about where I was headed.

↑
BLUEWATER

It opens up below me suddenly and to the left. It is stunning; it stuns me to the extent that I swear to myself out loud above the music from the CD-player.

Clawed out of the Earth, a mile, surely, in diameter, is what looks like a giant, abandoned quarry. Its sides are sheer white chalk cliffs, ringed with slip roads, roundabouts, junctions and pylons. The road I am now following sweeps round to the left in an arc, passes between two giant white stone pillars, as if into some ancient amphitheatre, and leads me down.

In the centre of the quarry is a quite remarkable construction. It is a huge, spreading complex of enormous buildings, steel grey, topped with curious angled towers. I've seen their shape before, and recently. It puzzles me for a moment, and then I have it: oast houses. For the past hour, driving through Kent, I've passed dozens of them; shells mostly, now, their old weatherboarded wooden towers topping house conversions or offices. These giant, steel approximations scream their separateness as they try, simultaneously, to belong.

As I get closer, I can make out more. The vast complex, linked together by covered walkways, is surrounded by a sea of white-lined asphalt. Regiments of trees and black steel lampposts separate lines of parked cars.

I get out of the car and lock it. If the world ended today – if this place were covered in ash for a thousand years and then excavated by some future civilisation – what would it say about who we were?

It seems to be designed to make you crane your neck and gasp. Its scale and its pomposity – the stone pillars, the towers, the lakes… it could be a colosseum, a palace, a cathedral. It is none of those things. It contains not courtiers, relics or kings, but KFC, M&S, Top Man. Just shops – and yet, not just shops. This is the biggest shopping centre in Europe. It attracts 27 million shoppers every year. There is parking space for 13,000 cars. There are 330 shops, 16 restaurants, 14 cafés, 9 fast food outlets and a 13-screen cinema. There is a bar, a car valet, a crèche, several hairdressers, a spa, a putting green, a go-kart track, a boating lake and a climbing wall. There is a multi-faith chapel with fifteen attendant chaplains of different religions.[1] This is not just a shopping centre. This is an *experience*.

As I walk from the car park towards the sliding glass doors that will grant me entry to the 'Wintergarden', I pass two drinks machines, selling cans of Coca-Cola products. They aren't simply standing there as they would be in any other mall or sports centre or cinema. They are encased in what look like steel sheaths, pointing like cathedral towers to the sky. On the side of each is a logo: a blue horse rising from a foaming sea. BLUEWATER, it insists.

It's then that it hits me.

I look around me. Everything here is controlled. Everything is part of an overall plan. From the trees to the spires, the pillars to the litter bins, the lakes to the drinks machines. Everything fits.

Inside the Wintergarden, the first thing I see is a statue. Rising perhaps 20 feet high, dominating all around it. It is a statue of a Coke bottle. Affixed to its sides are four telescreens, silver and rounded, beaming out Coke adverts and Sky news. Behind the statue rise six imposing white stone pillars, holding up a high atrium of glass and steel. On top of every pillar is a brace of CCTV cameras. Everything I am doing is being monitored.

From nowhere, now, comes a hidden voice. Female, mellifluous, well-elocuted, it advises me to keep my belongings with me at all times. And now I know what this is. It just seems so obvious, so clear.

This is totalitarian.

And it is, in the original sense of that often abused word. Bluewater is a total experience. Every aspect of it is planned, controlled and monitored by authorities who you never see but who only ever have your welfare at heart. Their authority here is absolute, but unless you abuse their trust, break their rules, you will never see them. You are here to consume, and as long as you do so you will be left alone.

Planned, focus-grouped, monitored, maintained, private. Here I am, in somebody else's kingdom, disturbed and slightly sickened and yet also somehow excited. The abundance is breathtaking. Thousands of people in caps, shorts and open shirts mill around me with children, trolleys, Burger King cardboard cups. Bring me your poor, your huddled masses yearning to breathe free, and I will *sell them things*.

Welcome to everywhere. Welcome to nowhere.
Welcome to the Pleasure Dome.

Two places. Separate, distinct, divided by 50 miles of England and half a world. Two ideas of what a landscape can be. Two visions of the future. Two sets of assumptions about the world and what it is for. Which is more recognisable to most of us? Which is most representative of the country we live in, the world beyond? I would like it to be Reculver. But Bluewater wins every time.

There is a bit of Bluewater in every town in England. And not just in the towns; in the villages too, and even in the fields. On the motorways and the A roads, the coastal towns and the conurbations, the fens and the forests. There is a bit of that manufactured, placeless, corporate landscape almost everywhere you go, and it is getting bigger. Spreading out. Digging in. It is the story of our age. It is the future, if we allow it to be.

The things that make our towns, villages, cities and landscapes different, distinctive or special are being eroded, and replaced by things which would be familiar anywhere. It is happening all over the country – you can probably see at least one example of it from where you're sitting right now. The same chains in every high street; the same bricks in every new housing estate; the same signs on every road; the same menu in every pub.

The meaning of England is different for everyone who lives in it. Its physical reality – its actual and emotional landscape – resonates at different frequencies for all of us. But whatever tone we hear, it is increasingly drowned out by the louder but flatter sound of landscapes being levelled, colour being drained and character being driven out by money and self-interest and over-development. Whether the real England, for you, is the local newsagent or the local church, the thatched cottage or the city terrace, the hardware store that clings on in your high street, the struggling street corner pub, the patch of overlooked waste ground, the chaotic street market, the hedgerows or the downlands, an old farm or an urban canal: you can be sure that if it is not sufficiently profitable or obedient, then it is not safe from the accelerating forces of homogenisation and control. It, too, will be Bluewatered in time.

We are far from alone in this. Anyone who has travelled – anyone who has been on holiday beyond these shores, which is most of us – has seen similar things happening elsewhere. We've seen the same two dozen global chains take over the streets of cities as previously distinct as Bombay and Brighton, Stockholm and Sydney. We've sat in those identical airport departure lounges, drunk the same canned produce on different continents, driven the same cars in different hemispheres.

Perhaps we've seen kids on Pacific islands, in South American jungles or on African savannahs wearing the same clothes, listening to the same music, watching the same TV. Perhaps we've felt, if we stopped to feel, a dullness descend upon us; harboured a suspicion that the world used to be – could be – a more diverse, colourful, interesting place.

What ties these experiences together is this: in each case, something distinctive has been replaced by something bland; something organic by something manufactured; something definably local with something emptily placeless; something human scale with something impersonal. The result is stark, simple and brutal: everywhere is becoming the same as everywhere else.

The small, the ancient, the indefinable, the unprofitable, the meaningful, the interesting and the quirky are being scoured out and bulldozed to make way for the clean, the sophisticated, the alien, the progressive, the corporate. It feels, to me, like a great loss – a hard-to-define but biting loss, which seems to suck the meaning from the places I care for or feel I belong to. It matters.

Why? Because in the name of economic efficiency, investment, growth, development, or just simply money – whatever words are used – the complex web of intimate relationships between people and communities and the landscape they inhabit is being dismantled, with nobody's permission. Because our landscape is being rapidly and thoughtlessly remoulded to meet the short-term needs of a global economy that is built on sand. And because what we are losing in the name of progress is being replaced, in most cases, with things which are not better, but worse.

Within and between nations, at local and national level, the world is being cleaned up and flattened out. What is happening all over England is no coincidence. Vanishing identities, vanishing cultures, homogenising landscapes: these are part of a global trend – unintended, no doubt, but an inevitable result of our choices as a society and a civilisation.

We live in the age of the ascendant global market – the driver, we are told, of all that is good, modern, progressive; creator of wealth, destroyer of want. But we have encountered a flaw in the program. We are discovering that a global market requires a global identity; that not just goods, but landscapes and cultures must be branded and made safe for the universal act of consumption.

We are discovering that a global market requires global tastes – that it needs us to want the same things, feel the same things, like or dislike the same things, see in the same way. Only that way can demand cross, and break down, cultural boundaries. And we are discovering that an advanced post-industrial economy is symbiotic with mass production, the smoothing-out of edges, uniform and characterless development – the standardised manufacture of places as well as things.

In order for this global consumer economy to progress, we must cease to be people who belong to neighbourhoods, communities, localities. We must cease to value the distinctiveness of where we are. We must become consumers, bargain-hunters, dealers on a faceless, placeless international trading floor. We must cease to identify with our neighbourhood, our landscape and our locality, or to care much about it. We must become citizens of nowhere.

Talking like this often brings on a barrage of pre-emptive aggression from people who assume that the speaker must be a nostalgic reactionary or a tiresome romantic, fuelled by loathing for a whole range of things – Europe, America, globalisation, progress. But this is no paean to the past, or simple reaction against change. Neither is it an invitation to shore up the stockades of Little England. It is about promoting and defending cultural distinctiveness and the power of people and communities to define it. My landscape and its associated cultures – my England, if you like – has a real and living meaning. It matters to me. I do not want to see it destroyed for nothing. And I know that I'm not alone.

Over the last decade I've spent a lot of time exploring these issues on a bigger, perhaps more glamorous scale. I've written a book and countless articles about the impact of the voracious global economy on people and places all over the world. I've travelled to Mexico to live with Zapatista rebels. I've climbed the fences of farms occupied by rural squatters in Brazil. I've lived with anti-globalisation thinkers in the Himalayas and painted banners with anti-privatisation protesters in South Africa. I've trekked through the forests of New Guinea with tribal warriors and been blinded by tear gas on the streets of Genoa, at the largest ever demonstration against corporate globalisation in 2001.[2] I've had some exciting times.

But exciting is easy. Ordinary is much harder, and what I haven't done enough of is stopping and looking around me. What I haven't seen enough of is what this process is doing to my country, my culture – my place. This lack of local, human perspective has been mirrored in most of the critiques of 'globalisation' we've seen in recent years. You'll hear a lot about global inequality, climate change, sweatshops and Third World debt – and quite right too. But all this is Big Picture stuff. It happens somewhere else: in Africa, in Thailand, in Seattle, in the troposphere. It all adds to an impression that this is that most nebulous of things – a 'global issue'. Something inhuman:

something that happens to other people; something that doesn't affect you, or that you can't easily change.

This book is about what happened when I stopped and looked around me. It is about what happened when I took my eyes off the horizon and focused them on the ground beneath my feet. It is about the sort of country I live in, and the sort of people who inhabit it. It is about the ongoing homogenisation of that country, the wiping out of its culture and character: why it's happening, why it matters, and what can be done about it. It is both an incomplete, and unashamedly partial, document attesting to the state of England and a call to arms.

It is about something which is uniquely, exquisitely small, local and hard to pin down: a sense of place. It is a sense of place that binds healthy communities together, and distinguishes living cultures from dead ones. Globalisation is said to have confined this to history. Our evolution into citizens of nowhere is supposed to be A Good Thing; an opening up, a casting off of our narrow, parochial past, our petty local differences. Communities are no longer geographical but communities of interest. Barriers are broken down by mass media, technology and trade laws. Rootless, we gain freedom. Placeless, we belong everywhere.

But this is nonsense. Placelessness and rootlessness do not create contentment but despair. Ask a tribal family whose land has been stolen for a mine or a logging concession; ask an alienated twenty-something working in a bank in any of the world's mega-cities; ask a pensioner who no longer understands the country they live in; ask a post-modern novelist. We are building ourselves an all-consuming global civilisation of malls, asphalt, brushed aluminium and sliding doors. The rising tide of this global progress, we are told, will lift all boats. But some of our boats are anchored; anchored by place, identity, a sense of belonging. Anchored boats are not lifted by rising tides; they are overwhelmed, and sunk with all hands.

In one sense, this is nothing new at all. Here, for example, is J. B.

Priestley, in his book *English Journey* in 1934. Priestley is looking out of the window of a coach near Southampton, and he's not impressed with the view:

> This road, with its new lock-up shops, its picture theatres, its red-brick little villas, might have been anywhere: it is the standard new suburban road of our time, and there are hundreds of them every-where, all alike. Moreover, they only differ in a few minor details from a few thousand such roads in the United States, where the same tooth-pastes and soaps and gramophone records are being sold, the very same films are being shown.[3]

Gramophone records. Picture theatres. It's another world, and yet a recognisable one. By the time Priestley was writing, the obliteration of landscape character and local distinctiveness in the name of progress and development was already advanced. More and more people were noticing. Here is the writer H. J. Massingham, just over a decade later in 1946:

> The suburb, the building estate, the factory, the cinema, the govern-ment office, the department store... these have no frontiers... Manchester might as well be Montreal, Stalingrad Sunderland... They are populations rather than persons. They do what their indus-trial economy tells them to do.[4]

And here is architecture critic Ian Nairn eleven years on, fresh from his own English journey, angrily writing up his findings in a special issue of *The Architectural Review*. Nairn had coined a new term – 'subtopia' – for what he had seen, and his findings were an uncanny echo of Priestley's two decades before, even down to the location he choose to illustrate his point:

> Subtopia is the annihilation of the site, the steamrollering of all indi-viduality of place to one uniform and mediocre pattern. Its symptom will be that the end of Southampton will look like the beginning of

Carlisle; the parts in between will look like the end of Carlisle or the beginning of Southampton.[5]

'The end of Southampton will look like the beginning of Carlisle...' It is eerily prescient, and fifty years on Nairn's predictions have come resoundingly true. Today, all over England, the consequent loss of landscape- and place-identity seems to remain both widely felt and curiously unspoken.

In local papers and local pubs, in community centres and shopping centres, you'll hear people talking about the individual components of this machine: this new housing development, that new megastore, this street market closing down, that pub disappearing. People feel that something is wrong; they just don't know quite what, or why, or what to do about it or how to bring it all together. They don't have the language, or the permission, to discuss it.

If they do bother to complain, it is usually patiently explained to them that these are small, insignificant local issues, of no import in the grand scheme of things. They are told to think about something more important: economic growth, perhaps, or the War on Terror. And if they persist, they are called 'Luddites' or 'nimbys',[6] pigeonholed as reactionaries or nostalgic grumblers. No one, runs the subtext, has the right to take up arms in defence of their place, their sense of belonging, their attachment to a locality. We should all have better things to do.

Well. I have come to believe that there are few better things to do. I have come to believe that this matters, a lot. So, in a bid to find out what is erasing the detail from our national canvas, I set off on a series of journeys around England. This book is the result.

Why England? Why not, say, Britain? Because England is a nation; Britain is a political convenience. And, though it's unfashionable to say so in polite company, England matters to me. Not because I am a 'patriot' in the old-fashioned sense of the word. Not because I think it's better than everywhere else. Not because I don't like foreigners or have a visceral desperation to win the World Cup. Simply because it is my country. It is the place I was born and grew up in and it is the place I belong. I know its landscapes and its history, and feel connected to both. I couldn't write about Scotland or Wales in anything like the same way, because I am not part of them and they are not part of me. For better or for worse, I am English. And I think that gives me the right to speak out.

What I found on my travels made me want to speak out, loudly and urgently. I discovered that the real England is being eroded by three forces, which are meshing together to form a uniquely destructive whole: a powerful alliance of big business and big government; an unspoken, twenty-first-century class conflict, in which every nook and cranny is being made safe for the wealthy urban bourgeoisie; and a very English reluctance to discuss who and what we are as a nation or to stand up for our places, our national character and our cultural landscape.

The first of these three forces is probably the most conspicuous. In the high streets and saloon bars and marketplaces of England, the omnipresence of chain store and supermarket is striking. Giant multinational companies dominate almost every area of national life, from finance to farming. They do so with the full and enthusiastic encouragement of the State, whichever political party happens to be managing it. Meanwhile, the same State busies itself enacting or enforcing laws, from Health and Safety legislation to EU hygiene directives, which crush the life out of the small, the independent and the local. Those on the right who blame an over-mighty State for our national woes and those on the left for whom the villain is the over-mighty corporation are both right, and both wrong. These days, as I hope to show you on my journey, they are increasingly one and the same.

Secondly, there is the rise of the class missionaries who are aggressively paving the way for a new England: a smoke-free, health conscious, well-dressed designer nation whose values are those of its new ruling class, the city bourgeoisie. As I travelled around the country I stumbled upon something that I had not really expected to see in our supposedly egalitarian twenty-first-century society: a growing class divide and, as a result, an increasingly antagonistic class conflict. The country is being remodelled and made safe for urban 4x4 drivers, gastropub diners, the owners of investment properties, the wearers of clean wellies and fashionable scents. Everywhere I went I saw their advance: local pubs turned into wine bars or expensive private houses; villages hollowed out by second homes; farm buildings bought up by city investors; inner city communities fighting off the advance of the sharp-suited regenerators. Before them scatter those whose values are different; perhaps older, certainly less profitable, less controllable, less tamed.

This pincer movement is rapidly changing the face of the nation. Whether the nation as a whole wants these changes is a separate question, and one which is quite deliberately never posed. These changes are the work of elites, and elites never ask permission. But England is not only being eaten – it is also eating itself. These first two forces have taken hold so successfully because of a third element: a problem that the English people themselves have long had.

Put simply, we are terrible at talking about who we are. As a nation we are almost comically reluctant to discuss our identity, our culture or our sense of nationhood. For decades we have been told that to do so is to cede the debate to racists or to 'offend' somebody somewhere. Our intellectual classes have drummed into the heads of generations the message that the English are uniquely dangerous, historically nasty, somehow unsound. It is nearly seventy years since George Orwell wrote that 'England is perhaps the only great country whose intellectuals are ashamed of their own nationality'.[7] England may no longer be a 'great country', but the rest of that comment still stands, and very firmly. Few other nations can have imposed upon themselves such a sophisticated form of cultural self-loathing.

And it has left us powerless. Because we won't talk about what makes up our culture, we find it hard to argue against its destruction. Because we won't discuss our national identity, we can't discuss its loss, or seek to rekindle it based on where and who we are now. Our consequent lack of commitment to local distinctiveness and regional diversity has led, as we will see, to the cloning of our entire environment – from our living rooms to our landscapes. Commitment to place and to culture can provide a bulwark against the advance of the global consumer machine. Without that bulwark, we are left exposed.

The 'triple whammy' of these three forces goes largely unexamined in the media and in the debates and discussions held by our governors in London. Out in the country at large, though, its effects are seen every day. And people are furious about what is happening.

All over England the bleaching out of character, community, place and meaning in the name of growth, investment and global competitiveness is causing ripples, resentment and resistance. I have discovered, joyfully, that there are many people out there who refuse to lie down before this juggernaut, who refuse to sacrifice the landscapes and places that matter to them for the benefit of a global economy which is beyond their control.

I have discovered, too, that their reaction is not, as it is often portrayed, the whining of reactionary snobs worried about their house prices collapsing. It is something much more deep-seated and valuable; something which should be celebrated rather than dismissed. It is the sound of people who care about the place they live in – who feel they belong to it, who understand why it matters and who are prepared to fight for it. It is the sound of political engagement.

Drinkers fighting to save their local from a corporate makeover. Multi-ethnic communities in the inner cities defending their streets from private predation. Countryside campaigners fighting for farms and rural traditions. Respectable Middle Englanders battling superstores and power companies. Activists taking a stand against airport expansion or motorway building. Councillors and MPs obstructing profiteering developers or crazed government directives. These are the minutemen in an ongoing guerrilla campaign – a drawn-out series of skirmishes with those who would clean up, tie down, sterilise and organise everything that makes the country worth living in.

As the globalised, placeless world spreads, and as progress is increasingly defined as the ability to look out of a hotel window in any city and see the same corporate logos lit up in familiar neon, it could be that the most radical thing to do is to *belong*. Belonging is a human need – see how we replace our fading localities, where we know our neighbours or live near to our families, with online communities, sharing interests, jokes, gossip, arguments. We need to be part of something. Yet true belonging surely needs place as well as people. It means belonging to a piece of land, a community – and being prepared to defend it. It means standing up for the real against the fake, the particular against the general, the human scale against the colossal. In today's bland, commercial and increasingly unreal world, these have become almost revolutionary acts.

All over England, every day, there are people doing just this. People who are fighting the cause of the real England that still lives and breathes beneath the spreading plastic of the consumer machine. People who know what it means, and what it is for. This book tells some of their stories, explains why they matter to them, and explains, too, why I think they should matter to you.

The next seven chapters invite you along on this journey of discovery. Each focuses on a type of landscape or a particular place which, to my mind, is a key part of the fabric, the character, the history and the essence of the country. The last chapter steps back for a wider look at what has been discovered and exposed, and what we might be able to do to change things for the better.

The peculiar, personal whole which emerges is a sketchy outline of my own private England. It is not everything, of course: but it is something. It is something which matters, has meaning and will last, if we let it. It is something which makes us who we are, and which we would do well to pay attention to while we still can. It is, I think, something worth fighting for.

'There is nothing in front but a flat wilderness of standardisation, either by Bolshevism or Big Business. But it is strange that some of us should have seen sanity, if only in a vision, while the rest go forward chained eternally to enlargement without liberty and progress without hope.'

G. K. Chesterton, *The Outline of Sanity*, 1926

2

Drown Your Empty Selves

There is nothing which has yet been contrived by man, by which so much happiness is produced as by a good tavern or inn.

Samuel Johnson, in James Boswell, *Life of Johnson*, 1791

Blackdown Hills, Devon
November 2004

It's 10.30 on a Friday night and the place is packed. I'm leaning on the bar, deep sediment in my refilled jar, listening to the conversation. That's conversation singular: the place isn't big enough for more than one at any one time. Tonight the place is full – perhaps a dozen strong, most of them local dairy farmers. They've had a few pints of Otter Head beer and their faces are red and beaming. The room is a rolling sea of Devonian accents. The talk is of fertiliser, somebody called Mr Pissley, the stupidity of the Cornish and a local dog which may or may not be part wolf. Outside, winter rain is battering onto the tin roof of the unlit outhouse which doubles as the toilet.

Fix the words 'traditional English pub' in your head. What do you see? A thatched roof, perhaps. A Grade II listed building. Polished horse brasses. A big flagstone fireplace. Rows of hand pumps. Inspector Morse. The Luppitt Inn has none of these, and yet it is more of a traditional pub than most you will find in the tourist guides or the coffee table books about Olde England.

The Luppitt is owned and run by 85-year-old Mary Wright. It has been in her family for over a hundred years. Mary's husband ran it before he died, and his father before him. It has long been the only watering hole in this little village in the Blackdown Hills, but these days the village, like the pub, seems to be on its last legs. Only a few regulars come to Mary's taproom now. When she goes, the pub will probably go too.

You would miss the Luppitt if you weren't looking for it. The pub sign that swings lazily by the roadside is faded and peeling, and the only thing that distinguishes Mary's farmhouse from any other is a small wooden sign above the front door which, if you look closely, turns out to be the announcement of a licence. Little more than the front room of her farmhouse, the inn is only open in the evenings. There is no food on sale, apart from the odd packet of peanuts. There are no hand-pumps, no till, no price list, no slot machines, no music, no telephone, no bar staff, no spirits. Only one type of beer is on offer; brewed in a small brewery at the top of the valley, it sells at a rate of about ten gallons a week.

Mary has run the pub all her life, and has rarely left it, or the village. She once went to Edinburgh, she tells me, but she's never been to London. 'Never been further than the pig's trough,' she says. Behind the bar she has a set of pint glasses which date from the reign of George VI. They're not used much, in case someone breaks them. She charges locals £1.70 a pint, but outsiders like me pay more. She's probably responsible for a list of Health and Safety breaches as long as your arm. A committed bureaucrat would be horrified, but the regulars don't seem to mind.

The Luppitt Inn is a telling time capsule. There was a time when every village in England would have had a small informal alehouse like this. Mary's is the last. Leaning on the bar, listening to and occasionally being ribbed by the circle of farmers sitting around the

Luppitt's only table, I am acutely aware that I am bearing witness to a way of life that was once common everywhere but has now retreated, holed up here. Somehow, the Luppitt Inn has remained unchanged as the rest of England has moved on.

'The village has changed, of course,' says Mary, as she refills my glass. 'There used to be dairy farms all round here. Not any more. A lot of new people moved into the village and they don't come in here. There's no living in it. It's more like an old car. You put in more than you get out. I do it for the regulars, really.'

Grahame Smith, a Luppitt local, leans across the bar towards me. 'You come here if you want a hedge trimmed or some weeding done, there'll be someone here who can help,' he explains. 'It's about Mary, the locals, getting together... It's a little bit of forgotten Devon. We are some of the last to see what rural England used to be, before it's lost forever.'

The Oxfordshire Cotswolds
November 2004

A hundred and thirty miles away, up a twisting, hedge-lined lane on the edge of an Oxfordshire village, I stand looking up at the yellow stone and dark wood of a Victorian tower brewery as it belches clouds of beery steam across the fields. Carts full of malt lean against the asymmetrical, Gormenghastian tower. The brewery's two shire horses graze in a nearby field. An early winter mist hangs around the malt-stained stone.

The Hook Norton brewery is the only steam-powered brewery in England. It has been here since 1849 and has somehow survived as its competitors, one by one, have fallen away. Now this 150-year old business, with its horse-drawn drays, steam-driven brewing engine, mash tuns, spurging pipes, fermenting rooms, grist mill and malt loft, must steer a path through the new and ruthless world of the global drinks industry.

So far, says Jerry Vallance, they are just about managing it. Jerry – white-haired, red-faced, wearing a suit and tie with a reflective yellow waistcoat over the top – is giving me a private tour of the brewery. Jerry is Hook Norton's Retail Manager. He has been conducting public tours of this place for decades. 'Health and Safety don't like the public coming in here,' he says. 'But people want to, and we want them to.'

Jerry runs me through the history of the brewery in such detail that I'm lost within a couple of minutes. Then he walks me around the labyrinthine building, stopping every few yards at some feature he thinks I should know about. I've seen the inside of a few breweries in my time, but I've never seen anything like this. It's like a working museum. It's like being inside Willy Wonka's chocolate factory but with beer, which at this stage of my life I somehow prefer.

At the very bottom of the complex stands an 1899-vintage steam engine, all polished brass, wheels, pistons and shafts. A system of belts and gears runs up through six floors, powering the machinery that brews the beer. Further along, the malting room is home to a vast 'copper' – an outsized wooden barrel, in which water and hops are boiled up. Then there's a huge metal vat for straining the wort.

'The copper can boil up to 4000 gallons,' says Jerry. 'A big brewer could do much more, of course. Doesn't mean it's worth doing, though. I remember when Ruddles was a small brewery like this. We bought their mash tun from them when they closed down. They were bought by Grand Met and they – excuse the language – fucked it up. Water's crucial, you see, and they moved the brewery, so the taste changed. If we tried to brew Old Hooky in Burton-on-Trent it would taste completely different.'

We move on, Jerry telling me about cracked malt and what the spurging pipe does. I'm taking in the Horlicksy smells and the rooms that look like old school chemistry labs, full of test tubes and cylinders, or old barns, full of split sacks of Fuggles and Goldings hops. Jerry picks up a handful of them and gestures to me to do the same.

'Rub them between your fingers,' he instructs. 'You'll get a bit of oiliness and a lovely sharp aroma. I can remember when all beer was cask, like ours. This was before lager. Before the yellow stuff. When it was thundery, you had to drape wet cloths over the barrels to keep them dry. There were no refrigerated cellars.'

At the very top of the brewery, up a sequence of wooden ladders, beyond the malt loft, the grist mill and the yeast store, is a square room the width and length of the entire tower. Taking up all of the floor space, apart from a thin strip around each edge, is a copper cooling tray, filled with immature beer. A man in a white coat stalks around it, periodically dipping a long paddle into the froth that floats on its surface. Hook Norton is the only brewery in the country still using one of these, says Jerry, proudly.

'When our water tanks are full,' he says, 'you've got 40 tons of water up here and the tower will sway slightly. It'll move about 3 to 4 inches each side.'

On all four sides of the room, wooden louvre windows let steam out into the winter air. Through them I catch a glimpse of hedges, rooftops, bare trees, medieval field patterns on the opposite hill.

By the time this book is published, Jerry Vallance will have retired as Hook Norton's Retail Manager. Whether his successor will make it through to retirement has to be open to question. Thanks to good management, good beer and undoubtedly a dose or two of luck, the Hook Norton brewery has so far managed to survive in a world very different to the one it was born into. But it is one of just thirty-eight traditional, independent regional breweries that do[1] – the remnant of a time, not so long ago, when every region of England could be identified by its beer; when the country was a tapestry of tastes woven from its national drink, ale. Hook Norton, like the Luppitt Inn, is a remnant of the past in a world where the future looks dangerously uncertain.

A century ago there were more than six thousand breweries in Britain;[2] now there are around 600.[3] The names of the fallen make up an elegiac, melancholy roll-call which grows longer by the year. The last decade alone has seen the end of Morrells of Oxford (founded 1782), Brakspear of Henley (1799), Castle Eden of Hartlepool (1826), Morland of Abingdon (1711), Gales of Horndean (1847), Ruddles of Rutland (1857), Courage of Bristol (1702), Ridley's of Chelmsford (1842), Redruth of Redruth (1742), Strangeways of Manchester (1778) and Mitchells of Lancaster (1871) – names that were sources of national heritage, regional pride and local employment, sold off, shut down or converted into housing. There have been, and will be, more.

Then there are the pubs which the breweries serve. A stunning fifty-six of them close every *month*[4] – usually demolished or converted into housing. Over half of those that remain are in the hands of ambitious and rapidly expanding pub corporations which have set about remaking them with the help of loans from Japanese banks and marketing techniques developed in pizza and sandwich chains.

In the countryside, rural pubs are disappearing with unprecedented speed, leaving over half of the villages of England 'dry' – publess – for the first time since the Norman Conquest.[5] In towns, six urban locals close every week,[6] often replaced by giant town centre binge-drinking sheds, known in the trade as 'high volume vertical drinking establishments'. These contain no chairs (the more you sit, the slower you drink), few tables or flat surfaces (if you can't put your drink down, you're likely to drink it faster), and music so loud you can't hear yourself speak (so you drink instead).

The last decade has witnessed an explosion of these, accompanied by a rise of identikit chains – O'Neill's, All Bar One, the Slug and Lettuce, Wetherspoons – in a whirlwind 'McDonaldisation' of pubs in which, according to the Campaign for Real Ale, only 254 of the most historically significant pub interiors have survived.[7] Finally, there is the beer itself, which is declining with the local patchwork of breweries and pubs. Today's multinational brewers and stock market-floated pub companies find a handful of brands of lager, alcopops, wine and slickly marketed bottled beers, ciders and mixers easier, more profitable and much less trouble than dangerously awkward – and definably local – real ale could ever be.

To put this in context, try and imagine that it's happening in France. Imagine that classic grape varieties – Pinot Noir, Riesling, pink Muscat – are no longer being grown; that the chateaux which produced them are being converted into luxury flats for wealthy Parisians. Imagine that you can no longer buy Veuve Clicquot, Mouton Rothschild or Sancerre. Imagine that, instead, people are drinking a few heavily marketed varieties of imported Australian or Californian wine distributed by a handful of drinks corporations. Imagine the riots on the streets of France, and the outrage in the dining rooms of middle-class houses all over England.

Substitute 'beer' for 'wine' and you get some idea of the cultural significance of what is happening here. If you think this is an exaggeration, then hear it from a Frenchman; Hilaire Belloc, the poet who made England his adopted home in the early twentieth century and spent much of his time here quaffing flagons of ale in various taverns. Among all the guff about Empire, cricket and the playing fields of Eton, Belloc thought he had pinned down where the heart of his adopted nation really lay: in the ordinary, unglamorous, communal institution of the common people. 'Change your hearts or you will lose your inns,' he warned, famously, 'and you will deserve to have lost them. But when you have lost your inns, drown your empty selves, for you will have lost the last of England.'[8]

Belloc knew what plenty of English people seem to have forgotten: the history of this country is a history written in beer. And not just any beer, but one which is produced only here – a dark beer made from malted grain, hops, water and yeast and known originally by its Saxon name, *ealu* – ale.

The Romans imported the *taberna*, the ancestor of the pub, in the first century AD, and the English never looked back. By the tenth century, beer-drinking was such a popular national pastime that King Edgar initiated the first government campaign against binge-drinking. In a fit of legislation of which New Labour would be proud, he issued a law limiting the number of pubs in each village to one, and decreed that all drinking vessels should be a standard size: 4 pints, divided into eight parts by pegs set inside the tankard. Drinkers were officially limited to one peg's worth at every visit. Tragically for Edgar, his attempt at controlling the appetites of the masses backfired, as every self-respecting drinker regarded the new law as a challenge rather than a limitation, and competed to literally take each other down a peg or two, or three, or four.[9]

A century later, King Harold's army lost the battle of Hastings, according to one observer, because they were 'no better than drunk when they came to fight'.[10] Over the ensuing centuries breweries, many the work of monks, and inns – originally developed as watering holes for medieval pilgrims – sprang up all over the country, and embedded themselves in its cultural fabric.

But beer and the twentieth century, with its red tape, licensing laws, globalisation and mass production, were set for a collision. After World War II, the big national brewers became more ambitious, and by the 1980s the country's six biggest brewers owned over half of the country's pubs and produced 75 per cent of its beer. Over the same period, they began to turn their backs on cask ale, focusing instead on newly developed 'nitro-keg' beers – pasteurised versions which were cheaper to brew, travelled better and lasted longer – and heavily promoted lagers.

But the big brewers had pushed things too far and Margaret Thatcher, who hated both monopolies and brewers (whom she correctly regarded as part of the old establishment; curiously they were also significant donors to the Tory party), swooped. In 1989, acting on a recommendation from the Monopolies and Mergers Commission, the Conservative government introduced sweeping legislation to end the 'complex monopoly' of the big six. The 1989 Beer Orders, as the legislation became known, decreed that no brewer could own more than 2000 pubs. Furthermore, they would now have to give their landlords the option of selling at least one 'guest beer' produced by a rival.

The idea was simple: the smashing of the monopoly would see a flowering of smaller brewers, more varied pubs and more choice for drinkers. Everyone – except the big brewers – would win.

St Albans, Hertfordshire
October 2004

Roger Protz looks slightly uncomfortable when I ask him what happened next. Protz, probably the best-known beer writer in Britain (certainly the one with the most awards), is a leading light in the Campaign for Real Ale (CAMRA), which was founded in the 1970s to fight the corner of traditional beer and pubs. Big, bearded and, well, CAMRA-esque, he sits on a threadbare swivel chair in CAMRA's head office in St Albans – a shrine to beer which incorporates its own bar – and considers what went wrong.

'Basically, I think we were tremendously naïve,' he says. 'We were very optimistic. The Beer Orders said that the big brewers couldn't own more than 2000 pubs, and we thought "They'll be happy with that". They weren't happy, because they weren't prepared to open their pubs up to other brewers' beers.'

The Beer Orders did not, after all, break up the monopoly of pub ownership and beer-brewing: all they did was to shift it sideways. Rather than sell off some of their pubs and keep the rest, the big brewers created something new – stand-alone pub companies – to which they sold all their pubs. Because they didn't brew beer themselves, the companies – known as PubCos – were exempt from the legislation.

'There were a lot of sweetheart deals,' explains Protz. 'The brewers would say to some of their management team, "Here's a golden hand-shake, go off and start a pub company. Buy a tranche of pubs and in return, only take our beers." And that was what happened.'

Today it is the PubCos, not the brewers, who call the shots. In 1989, the three biggest brewers owned around twenty thousand pubs – about a third of the UK's total.[11] Today, the three biggest PubCos own… around 20,000 pubs.[12] Meanwhile the six biggest brewers, who now own no pubs at all, are actually more powerful than they were before the Beer Orders. In 1989, the six biggest brewers produced 75 per cent of all the beer drunk in Britain's pubs. Today, they produce 84 per cent.[13] The difference is that whereas in 1989 they were all national companies which owned pub estates, today they are multinational conglomerates with no particular attachment to anything except their shareholders.

'My own personal feeling is that the situation is worse,' says Protz. 'We were offered this great Shangri-La of choice and it hasn't happened. Choice is just as restricted under pub companies as it was under brewers. I think the worst thing that's happened is that the relationship between pub owner and tenant is much worse than it used to be, and the attitude to customers is much worse than it used to be. Customers are quite blatantly referred to as "traffic". You don't want old Charlie going in and sitting all night over a pint of mild and bitter. You want people coming in, having a few drinks and going, and being replaced by somebody else.' He looks frustrated.

'What was once my local has closed,' he says, by way of example. 'It passed from being owned by Watneys to Grand Met to Scottish Courage. Then it was bought by Noble House Leisure who turned it into something called "Jim Thompson's Oriental Bar and Restaurant", which is a chain theme thing. It only lasted eighteen months before it folded. Now it's a pub again, and it's owned by Ember Inns, which is a subsidiary of Mitchells & Butler, the third biggest PubCo in the country. It's perfectly pleasant, but it's identical to a pub on the other side of St Albans, called the Three Hammers. They have this kind of jelly mould…'

He sighs. I wonder why I didn't suggest meeting him in a pub. He looks like he could do with a drink. I certainly could.

'Everything is about profit now,' he says. 'Of course the old brewers were there to make money too. But they understood that pubs had a community role. The modern pub companies just couldn't give a stuff about that.' He shakes his head.

'The corporatisation of pubs,' he says. '… I really have no idea what to do about it.'

Leeds, Yorkshire
December 2004

Tony Jenkins knows what he'd like to do about it, but he thinks it may be unprintable. In the dark depths of a January evening he is standing in an alley in central Leeds outside the local branch of Mook, a national chain of bars aimed at hip young dudes. Tony is not a hip young dude. He is the chairman of the Leeds branch of CAMRA; a large, jovial man wearing a fleece with the words 'Tetley Bittermen' emblazoned on it. He shivers in the cold and sticks his hands into his pockets.

'I'm not going in there,' he says. 'It's a matter of principle.'

Mook, until recently, was a backstreet local called The Whip. It was, says Tony, 'the sort of place where the bar staff were professionally rude to you. I remember when I was sat in there once and this bloke came in and asked for a gin and tonic. All you could hear was the door swaying in the wind. It was that sort of pub.'

It's not that sort of pub any more, and hasn't been since it was bought by the Spirit Group, one of the country's most ambitious PubCos. 'It was really quite sad,' says Tony, 'because there were people who'd been there every week for fifty years, you know. And Spirit came along and just trashed it. Where did those people go? It's not that I object to bars like this, but Leeds is full of them. We didn't need another' – he wrinkles his nose and spits out the word – '*Mook.*'

A few hundred yards away, down another alley off a shopping street, lies what Jenkins calls 'the last real city centre pub in Leeds'. Whitelock's is something of an institution. The 300-year old tavern has been hymned by the likes of John Betjeman, Peter O'Toole and Keith Waterhouse for its atmosphere, its beer and its regional cuisine. Its Yorkshire puddings and jam roly-polys are, apparently, notoriously good.

Or they used to be. That was before the Spirit Group got hold of Whitelock's too. You won't find jam roly-polys or Yorkshire pudding on its menu now. You'll find nachos, penne and Kashmiri chicken. You'll find, in fact, the sort of food sold in other Spirit Group pubs up and down the country.

Tony and I squeeze into the long, narrow bar and order a couple of pints. The interior, which has hardly changed since the 1890s, is a riot of carved wood, old tiles, brass, decorated mirrors and very low beams. Tonight's customers range from a white-haired old man slowly rolling cigarettes in a corner to a pair of twenty-something lovebirds gazing into each other's eyes over pints of Staropramen.

The homogenising of the Whitelock's menu caused a minor storm in Leeds. In August 2004, a journalist on the *Yorkshire Evening Post* got hold of an internal memo that had been sent to the pub's staff. It described two imaginary customers who represented the sort of clientele that the PubCo now wanted Whitelock's to attract.

'Mick and Ruth' were two work colleagues: he was a manager who drove a BMW and drank beer; she was an office worker who ate pasta and drank Pinot Grigio wine. They were both busy, modern, business-minded people and neither of them, apparently, was interested in Yorkshire pudding. Soon after the memo went round, the menu and wine list were changed by head office. Fearing that the Spirit

Group wanted to do to Whitelock's what it had already done to The Whip, over fourteen hundred people signed a petition urging the PubCo not to touch 'this gem of the north'. Spirit promised that it had no intention of inflicting any wholesale changes, and so far it has kept its word. But many people, Tony Jenkins included, are still nervous.

'I emailed Spirit to ask it to clarify its plans,' says Tony, conspiratorially, 'and I got a reply from a woman who described herself as Business Development Manager for "The Whitelock's". She didn't even know the name of the pub. If you dredge through its website you discover that the Spirit Group has chains within chains. It has "Spirit locals", "city day pubs" – all these "concepts". I think it decides what to do with its pubs by using postcodes. Whitelock's is in LS1, and somewhere in the Spirit Group manual it will say "a pub in the city centre has to be an alcopop bar for fourteen-year-olds". What it wanted to do was make Whitelock's fit its brand.' He takes a large gulp from his pint.

'But,' he says with satisfaction, 'it got caught.'

The story of the Spirit Group is a neat metaphor for the fluidity, ambition and ruthless business focus of the PubCo industry. In 1992, the new PubCo Punch Taverns divided its 'portfolio' into two tranches: tenanted pubs – run by landlords who hired their premises from the PubCo – and managed pubs, run by managers directly answerable to head office. They sloughed off their 1000 managed pubs into a new company, Spirit Group.

Spirit's CEO was the dressed-down, Bransonesque Karen Jones, founder of the Café Rouge chain, who had brought her particular brand of expertise to bear on Spirit's pubs. She made Spirit the largest managed PubCo in the country, with 2,400 pubs, each of them directly answerable to her. So successful was her £500 million company, in fact, that Punch began to regret having disposed of it. In early 2006 it made a successful takeover bid, and the Spirit Group was back where it started.

Spirit, like other managed pub chains, has always been a centrally controlled operation, and it remains very big on demographics – or 'market leading concepts', as it calls them. There are 800 'Spirit Locals', which themselves are divided into smaller groups with names like 'great locals' ('big-hearted community pubs'), 'young and classics' ('where the community live'), and 'sports'. There are 600 'City Spirits', which include 'Bars and Clubs' ('the place to be seen') and 'City Night' ('the best night out in town'), and 500 'Spirit Foods' with brands like 'Chef and Brewer' and 'Two For One'. Then there are their other brands – John Barras, Wacky Warehouse, Q's, Bar Room Bar.[14] Each grouping targets different markets – and every time it is head office, not the pub itself, that decides which customers it will attract, and how.

This, in a nutshell, explains what happened to Whitelock's and The Whip. They didn't fit into the blueprint. PubCos work to attract the 'consumer demographic' that will give them the highest returns. If you don't fit into it – well, tough. A traditional local pub, whatever its flaws, provides a genuine community space. A PubCo pub provides year-on-year increases in shareholder returns, and if it doesn't it will have to go. The Spirit Group has made the stock market very happy by applying the operating techniques of chains like Pizza Express and Café Rouge to the traditional pub. It makes perfect economic sense. Which may well be the problem.

I sometimes wonder why any of this matters to me. I wonder why I care about the fate of pubs which, in some cases, I've never even drunk in. Until recently I lived in the Oxford suburb of Jericho. A warren of two-up-two-down terraces, Jericho was thrown up in the nineteenth century to provide housing for employees in the nearby ironworks. By the beginning of the twentieth century it was said to have 'a pub on every corner'. On Saturday nights it could sometimes be too risky for the police to venture in. It was avoided conscientiously by Oxford's genteel classes.

Most of Jericho's pubs are now gone, though it has just enough left to keep it humming. Walk the streets and you'll see, on many of the corners, buildings which were clearly hostelries some time in the past. They have over-wide front doors or places where signs once hung. Some of them still have little plaster tiles embedded in the walls, displaying the name of a long-defunct brewery.

There was one such place a couple of streets away from my house. It was a corner building that presumably used to be a pub, though no one I've spoken to can remember it. It was a charming, odd little place, whitewashed, with a door set into the corner of the building. Above the door was an old, black coaching lamp, slightly bent out of shape. Along each wall, both fronting onto different streets, was a tall, wide, lattice-work window.

The windows – tall, light, redolent of Dick Turpin to me, for some inexplicable and probably ridiculous reason – were the building's highlight. Then, one day, I walked past it to see them covered with sheets of plywood. My heart sank. The next day, a skip sat outside the building. A week or two later, I cycled past to see the plywood gone, and the windows gone too. Two dusty blokes in saggy jeans were bricking up the gaps with grey breeze blocks. A week later they put in some standard sash windows; the ones every other building in the street already had. It wrenched my gut to see it, but I wasn't quite sure why.

Up in the Chiltern Hills, between Oxford and London, is a little village called North End. It's surrounded by silent, ancient beech woods which are stunning in the autumn, with the crisp brown leaves falling as the year ends, and in the spring, when the bluebells are in bloom and the trees are born again, their translucent leaves clear against the new blue sky.

A few years ago I was walking in those woods with a group of friends. It was autumn. We'd been wandering around for a couple of hours, climbing stiles and damming streams and generally regressing to childhood while we still had the chance. At about lunchtime we came upon the village of North End, and piled, with relish, into its one pub, the White Hart.

The White Hart was a tiny little two-room place; a real, local pub, which served good food. It was packed with people, eating and drinking and talking. There was a fire in the grate and through the window, in the beer garden, we could see a strangely oversized bird table, strewn with great chunks of meat. A few years back, the near-extinct red kite had been reintroduced into the area as an experiment – it was so successful that they now seem to be as common as starlings. The landlord told us that if we were lucky, we might see one land and feed. We didn't.

A year or so later, I visited North End again with my girlfriend, who hadn't been with me on the previous occasion. I remembered the pub fondly, and wanted to take her there. I knew she'd like it. We drove around for a while, but couldn't find it. I knew where I thought it was, but there was only a house there. The second time we drove past, I looked more closely. I could see what used to be the front door, now a window, and where the sign used to hang. The pub – the village's last and only – was gone. I pretended to be annoyed, but I felt much more than that.

Why? Things change, all the time. People move on, tastes alter. Pubs open, pubs close. Big deal. Why should such small, singular things matter to me so much? Am I just being sentimental? Would it matter if I was?

I think I can identify a number of reasons why I might feel like this. Take those lattice windows. In one sense, I think, they *belonged* to me. I didn't own them, I didn't know the people who did, and in one sense it was none of my business. I had no right to expect them to stay the same just because I liked them. Yet in a wider, maybe deeper, sense, they were mine. They were part of my everyday life, part of the architecture, both physical and mental, of my community and my neighbourhood – my living space. That someone could fail to see all the things that were special about them – could fail to see what set them apart, how lucky they were to own them, their duty to cherish them – felt like a personal betrayal. It was none of my business, and yet it was.

As for the White Hart; I was only there once, for maybe an hour, and yet its passing hit me hard. This time, I can see the reasons perhaps more clearly. Pubs like that are a part of our history – a history that lives, and which we still inhabit. The institution of the English pub is not replicated exactly anywhere in the world. Every time another one goes, another connection to our past is lost. Another communal gathering space is shut off, enclosed, privatised. Another opportunity for a community to be a community is lost.

Something small, meaningful and, in its very ordinariness, special, is gone for ever. In the case of somewhere like North End, what had been a village with a central, open, gathering point became instead a collection of dwellings, fenced off from each other, separate, isolated. A location, but no longer a place. Rural pubs, in particular, are central to our national myth. The image of a thatched inn, with smoke curling from its chimney in a 'timeless' English village, is one of the great tourist clichés. But rural pubs are being hit hard as villages and rural areas cease to be connected to the land around them and become, instead, playgrounds for wealthy commuters.

A traditional village local can make its owners a decent enough living, but this will never be as profitable as converting it into an upscale house, like the White Hart, or a 'gastropub' – a pricey rural restaurant with the odd gourmet ale on tap and wealthy urban customers who drive there for Nigella-style Sunday lunches in their BMW 4x4s.

Real pubs are some of the last human-scale spaces we have which remain more or less uncontaminated by marketing, centralisation, homogenisation and the mores of the office-bound, the health-conscious, the bureaucratic and the over-wealthy. A year or two ago I was writing an article on this subject for a national newspaper. I was already having enough trouble with the editor, who was elegantly missing the point ('Is a beer, any beer, really comparable to a fine burgundy?' she had written in an email to me; my heart had sunk). I visited the giant, city centre branch of Wetherspoons in Leeds, with the photographer I was working with, to get a few shots of the Friday night crowd in this giant, two-storey drinking factory, lit up with neon and pastel shirts. We thought it would make our point for us.

Adrian had his camera at the ready when we were approached by the young manager.

'Hello', she said, nicely. 'Can I help you?' Adrian explained what we wanted to do. Would it be all right, he asked, if he took a few shots?

'Do you have permission from head office?' she inquired.

'Er,' he said. 'Well, no.'

'I'm sorry then', she replied. 'I'd have to have an email from head office in London before I could give you permission to take photos. If you want to try calling the media team when the office opens on Monday, you can talk to them about it.'

This is what a PubCo is, and what it represents. Distance, hierarchies, managers, media teams, emails from head office. It is the polar opposite of what a pub should be – which, in the case of Wetherspoons, is something of an irony.

In 1946, in one of his grouchy, nostalgic moods, George Orwell subjected readers of the London *Evening Standard* to an essay on his favourite pub, The Moon Under Water. Complaining that a decent pub was increasingly hard to find, he explained the character that made his local what it was:

> The cast-iron fireplaces, the florid ceiling stained dark yellow by tobacco-smoke, the stuffed bull's head over the mantelpiece – everything has the solid comfortable ugliness of the nineteenth century. In winter there is generally a good fire burning in at least two of the bars, and the Victorian layout of the place gives one plenty of elbow-room. Upstairs, at least six days a week, you can get a good solid lunch...[15]

The Moon Under Water had no 'glass-topped tables or other modern miseries… no sham roof-beams, inglenooks or plastic panels masquerading as oak'.[16] It had no piano or radio, and was quiet enough for conversation without being boring. It had a garden and was two minutes from the nearest bus stop. Best of all, the staff knew the regulars and served them real ale in 'proper' pint mugs, with handles.

In 1979, a young entrepreneur called Tim Martin opened a pub in London, which he called, in tribute to Orwell, The Moon Under Water. These days, Martin runs a chain of 650 pubs, under the Wetherspoons banner. Fourteen of them are called The Moon Under Water. They all look, feel and taste virtually the same, many of them have the same name, and all of them are as far away from Orwell's ideal as it is possible to be (though admittedly none has a piano). The Manchester Moon Under Water is reputed to be Britain's biggest pub: it can wet the whistles of up to 1800 drinkers at once from its three bars, and not one of them has any chance of getting their beer in a 'proper' glass.

At the end of his essay, Orwell revealed what 'the discerning and disillusioned reader will probably have guessed already' – his favourite pub wasn't real. It was a composite, made up of all the features that Orwell thought the perfect urban pub should have. The Moon Under Water did not exist.[17] These days, he might consider this a blessing.

At this stage it might be worth stepping back a bit. The wider view is often the clearer one, and brings with it a breath of clean air. It's easy to get grumpy about 'modern miseries', after all; and if glass-topped tables were all Orwell had to contend with, he didn't know how lucky he was. Try slab-shouldered bouncers, Bacardi Breezers and vomit-stained, Friday night no-go zones, George. Get some perspective.

What perspective shows us is that the pub, the tavern, the inn, the alehouse – whatever you call it – has been with us for two millennia in its various forms. It has survived King Edgar, Oliver Cromwell, the

Victorian abstinence movement and, so far at least, early twenty-first-century health hysteria. Pubs have been through phases which would make them unrecognisable to us today. They have been private houses, religious institutions (early breweries were owned and run almost exclusively by monks), gin palaces, travellers' hostels and estate owners' cash cows. Their clientele has varied as much as the drink they sell. However hard times get, it's unlikely that the pub as an institution will ever die.

Pubs have also survived a far more recent threat to their character and existence. Pop down to your local library and root out, if you can find it, a 1973 book called *The Death of the English Pub*, by someone called Christopher Hutt. This landmark publication, the cover image of which shows a pair of hand-pumps encircled by a funeral wreath, was a powerful blast against the big brewers who, almost forty years ago, were threatening the life of the local as the PubCos are today.

It's a telling read, full of examples of shallow corporate branding, the 'gimmicky' remodelling of buildings, the harassment of landlords and the watering-down of pints. Sometimes the reader feels a sense of *déjà vu*. Take this extract from a report in the *Daily Telegraph* in 1970, about the activities of the now-defunct Watney's Brewery:

> Dozens of village pubs have been shut in recent years and sold for conversion. Dozens more are being threatened with it in the near future. Some villages have a second pub to fall back on, but most are left beerless... Watney's policy of rationalisation has been strongly attacked by local councils, magistrates and in the press. Critics also say that redecoration, modernisation and the installation of managers instead of licensees has ruined the atmosphere and character of many pubs.[18]

It's tempting, reading it, to conclude that some things never change, among them the tendency of beer drinkers to whinge about things changing. But this isn't quite right. Hutt's book led to the foundation of CAMRA, of which he later became Chairman. The 1989 Beer

Orders were the eventual result of the campaign which the book began and which CAMRA continued. Enough people took an interest, and began to resist the destruction, to ensure that the big brewers didn't, in the end, have it all their own way.

Had they done so, things might look very different now. *The Death of the English Pub* is full of unintentionally hilarious predictions by the corporate visionaries of the time, which should, if nothing else, give us pause for thought whenever we hear today's equivalents come up with a bit of 'blue sky thinking'. Take this, for example, from the then director of Scottish & Newcastle Breweries:

> It may be that you will be able to travel round cities in a Hover Bar in which one can have a drink while travelling from point to point. Managers will more than likely be running automated pubs with no barmaids.[19]

The point to be drawn from all this is not that change in itself is a problem. The problem comes when change is initiated by distant, over-powerful forces, in the interests of their profit margins rather than of the people that change will affect. I could come up with my own Orwell-like list of what would make up my ideal pub, but that wouldn't be the point. I don't want to live in a country where every pub is part of a branded chain, but neither do I want to live in a country where every pub is the sort of place I like to drink in.

What I'm after is the diversity and character which is created when people are given the freedom and the power to express themselves without interference from deskbound, rulebound profit-watchers in some distant business park. What I'm after is the chimera which the ever-expanding consumer economy promises us constantly, but rarely seems to deliver: choice.

This is the great irony of modern capitalism. 'Choice' is the Holy Grail of the global consumer economy. It is the justification used for much of the ongoing destruction of the institution of the English pub by corporate power. But it is a myth. Just as the 'choice' provided by the supermarket giants is actually limiting – you can no longer choose not to shop in supermarkets, because they have destroyed the local economy – so the 'choice' offered to drinkers by PubCos is often a bad joke. Real choice, in the context of the pub, comes from a local landlord responding to the needs and desires of the regulars and the wider community of which he or she is part. PubCo 'choice' is defined in advance by brand managers, multinational brewers and the need to satisfy shareholders.

Today, a combination of corporate power, soaring property prices and often absurd over-regulation is hoovering up colour and character and spitting out conglomeration and control. The fact that this is not unprecedented does not mean that it isn't real. What precedent tells us, in fact, is that if we want real, characterful, local pubs to survive the current onslaught we are going – again – to have to fight for them.

Notting Hill, London
January 2005

Mike Bell knows this well. Mike is landlord of the Portobello Gold, in Notting Hill. A world away from either the Luppitt Inn or The Moon Under Water, in either of its incarnations, the Portobello Gold is a very modern London watering hole. Light, contemporary, open plan, it is all tiled floors and fresh wood. It incorporates a palm-hung dining room, an art gallery and an internet café. For all that, though, it is still recognisably a pub, and Mike intends it to stay that way. The problem is that it's not entirely up to him.

It's four in the afternoon, and the Gold is quiet. We're sitting around a table by a fire. 'My Boy Lollipop' is playing so loudly through the speaker above us that we can't hear ourselves talk. Mike tells the bar staff to turn it down. He is white-haired, red-faced and determined, like Christopher Hutt before him, to bring down the corporate behemoths who he insists are ruining the institution of the pub.

'You need to understand the way the PubCo model works,' he says. Once you get him going on this subject, I am discovering, he can be hard to stop. And he speaks of what he knows: the Portobello Gold is owned by Enterprise Inns, Britain's second-biggest PubCo. At the time of writing, Enterprise owns almost 8000 pubs. By the time you read this, it may well own more.

'The PubCo model has to be based on constant expansion,' says Mike, 'or there are no growing returns for shareholders. How can they achieve that? They can buy up more pubs, which they've been doing, but there will be a limit. A decent, well-run pub can provide a living for its tenants, but it's not going to be some ever-expanding profit-machine. So what does a PubCo do? Maybe they run it down so that they can persuade the local authority to let them sell it off for quick-buck housing. A pub, a hotel, any licensed premises is never going to make you as much, or as quickly, as a private house. I can quote you several examples of pubs that have been deliberately run into the ground by PubCos. They employ useless tenants, or they charge such a high rent that no one can make a go of it. Then they turn round to the local council and say, "Sorry, the pub's not viable, can we turn it into flats please?" Where they do keep the pubs going they will squeeze the landlords dry. And I mean dry.'

Squeezing the landlords dry is Mike's main concern. So concerned is he that he has set up an organisation called Freedom For Pubs, which has taken up cudgels on behalf of landlords, and aimed them at the PubCos. Since Mike set up Freedom For Pubs he has received 'toe-curling, stomach-churning' testimonies from hundreds of unhappy landlords, many of them sent anonymously for fear of reprisals. The flood of fury and despair that has landed on his desk has shed a grim light on how the biggest PubCos really make their money.

'The problem is what's called the "beer tie",' he explains. 'I pay my rent to Enterprise but I also have to buy all my beer from them. It's in my contract, and that of all their tenants. If I was buying my beer free of tie, I'd be getting it £20,000 a year cheaper. They are raising the rents constantly, and their beer prices are much higher than on the open market, plus they restrict what we can sell. You can have a really full-on, successful pub, in a good location, run well, and still do badly, because of being squeezed by the PubCos. They just want everything from you. The PubCos are actually uncompetitive whole-salers, and they're driving pubs into the ground.'

Mike is a man with a vision. He wants the beer tie gone. In an ideal world, he would like PubCos gone too, or at least cut down to size, as the big brewers were before them. Mike has a vision of what a pub should be – a vision tinged with nostalgia and a certain romance, it's true, but no less enticing for it.

'The PubCos have single-handedly destroyed the whole ethos of the pub,' he laments. '"Mine host's" should theoretically be like a pri-vate house. Pubs are private houses in a way. That's how they began – someone inviting people in for a drink. There should be no pressure at all on a publican, because they give up their lives to welcome people into their homes. A lot of them live above their pubs. If we had genuine free trade, if the PubCo model went, if every pub was a free house, people could run them exactly how they liked – that would give you such fantastic variation. Just imagine! None of this branding and targeting and promotions and all that rubbish. Free pubs, genuine character, a living for landlords...' He has a glint in his eyes.

'Why not?' he asks.

PubCos have an answer to that. This sort of talk is all very nice, they imply, but you might like to try, well, getting real. This is what Francis Patton is telling me, though he's putting it a bit more tactfully than that.

Patton is Customer Services Director of Punch Taverns, the country's biggest PubCo. Inside its corporate HQ, in Burton-on-Trent, he shows me around its call centre. If you're one of Punch's 9,304 landlords, and you want to contact your employer, this is where they answer the phones. There are banks of cubicles staffed by young, keen, customer service types. One of the walls bears the instruction BE POSITIVE in big yellow letters. A digital display board shows the number of calls waiting and the number of agents available to answer them.

Patton, who is friendly, professional and slightly harried, can wax lyrical too. Punch loves its pubs, he tells me. It takes care of its tenants, because that is its business. It spends a lot of money ensuring they are as happy as can be. It employs 'business relationship managers' who visit landlords regularly to discuss any problems with them. They organise community events and fundraise for charity. People like Mike Bell, he suggests tactfully, have simply got it wrong.

'It's not in our interests to make life difficult for our tenants,' he insists. 'We're only as successful as the people we have running our pubs. You've got to understand the way the model works... if you want to own and run your own pub as a free house, it will cost you about £450,000. With us, you can be trained and up and running your own business for about £20,000. In what other industry can you do that? If you take a lease with us, the deal is that you pay a lower than market price rent on your property, and you buy all your beer from us. Therefore, we take part of the risk. If your trade does well, we do well. If your trade doesn't do well, we suffer with you.'

Precisely how well Punch, or any other PubCo, is doing from this model is hard to tell – it refuses to say how much it pays for beer and how much it sells it for, claiming that such information is commercially confidential. Talk to some of the landlords themselves, though, and a different story begins to emerge.

And landlords are beginning to talk, though to do so is to take a big risk with their employment prospects. Since Mike Bell put his head above the parapet to challenge the might of the PubCos, others have followed. One of them is Andrew Hall, who has run the Rose and Crown pub in Oxford for twenty-two years. Hall looks like a traditional English landlord should: he's round and bearded, smokes cigarettes and enforces a 'no dogs or politicians' rule on his premises at all times.

The Rose and Crown is a well-liked, popular, old-style community pub. It has two wood-panelled rooms and a covered garden, open fires, good beers and a collection of resident locals. It sells pistachio nuts by the pint and – joy of joys – beer in 'real' glasses, with handles. I've been drinking there, on and off, for years and seen Hall many times, holding forth or holding court, barring people for using mobile phones or leaning on the bar, deep in conversation with some regular or other. He's often the worse for wear. It's part of the charm.

Today, though, its lunchtime, and he's sober as a PubCo auditor. He's invited me over to tell me how PubCos are ruining his living. Since Punch took over his pub, he says, he is in financial trouble.

'I'm not singling out Punch,' he says, quickly. 'My criticism is of PubCos in general. The basic problem is simple. When pubs were run by brewers they charged us very low rents and we had to buy all our beer from them. Now they're run by PubCos who are charging high rents, and we still have to buy all our beer from them. As a result, this is now a business where you can't make money.' All he wants, he says, is 'a fair deal'.

'In simple terms,' he explains, 'my income has been cut by a third since the 1980s. I was paying £12,000 rent in 1987. Now I'm paying £26,000 but I'm paying the same sort of prices for my beer. If I buy a case of Becks from Punch, it costs me £28. I could get the same case from Oddbins for £16, but I'm not allowed to. When my wife and I started as tenants here we were doing very well. Trade hasn't gone down since then – if anything it's increased – but we're heading towards bankruptcy. The PubCos have got us up against the wall.'

On the table between us, in the Rose and Crown's front room, sits

a folder of documents. From it, Andrew Hall pulls a newspaper clip-
ping from early 2004, detailing how Punch's 37-year-old chief executive, Giles Thorley, has pocketed £3.6 million from selling some of his
Punch shares. In total, says the article, Thorley is estimated to be
worth around £20 million.

'Look at this,' says Hall, gesturing with his cigarette. 'Giles Thorley.
The man's a great entrepreneur. I don't want to discourage great
entrepreneurs in our society. But he's made his money by taking my
living away from me. And that I find hard.'

Whether Mike Bell, Andrew Hall and the other troops who are beginning to mass at pub level to take on the might of the PubCos will succeed remains to be seen. But it may be that the PubCos will not have
things their own way for ever. It may be that, like the brewers before
them, they will overstep the mark and be reined in.

Small rumblings have already begun at high level. In 2004, following complaints from the Federation of Small Businesses, the House of
Commons Trade and Industry Committee instigated an investigation
into PubCo practices. They took evidence from a wide range of witnesses, including CAMRA, the Federation of Licensed Victuallers
Associations, the Society of Independent Brewers (who complained
that big PubCos acted like supermarkets and made it almost impossible for them to sell their beer to many pubs), the Office of Fair
Trading and the PubCos. Their final report, produced at the end of
2004, recognised that landlords were facing problems, and suggested
giving the PubCos more time to improve the way they dealt with
their tenants. But it also recommended that the government 'should
not hesitate' to impose new laws on them if they failed to do so.

The government, however, shows no signs of doing so. Quite the
opposite, in fact: since its accession to power in 1997, the Labour
Party has governed very much in the interests of corporations like the
PubCos, and with a studied lack of interest in small businesspeople
like Andrew Hall and Mike Bell. It has certainly unleashed a firestorm

of new pub-related legislation; but it has hit the landlords, not the corporations.

Andrew Hall gave me an example as we left the Rose and Crown. 'Look at this door,' he said, as we walked through it. 'We have to have it widened and put a ramp in for wheelchair users, because the Disability Discrimination Act says so. It's going to cost us fifteen grand, and it's me who has to pay for that, not the PubCo. We're a community pub. We've had customers in wheelchairs coming in for years. We get together and lift them over the step. But apparently that's not good enough now, because some politician has decided that one size fits all.'

This kind of thing is a common feature of conversations with pub landlords across England. The last decade has seen a blizzard of laws which either target or – like the above example – threaten to clumsily crush the spontaneity and community enjoyment that defines the traditional local. Health and Safety legislation has forced drinkers with dogs away from pubs which serve food. The smoking ban has done the same for smokers. A new licensing act has done away with the rule that allowed landlords to have a couple of live musicians in their pub without State permission. A pub now needs a licence even to have someone playing a piano or strumming a guitar in the corner (though no licence is required if it wants a wide-screen telly or a jukebox).

Meanwhile, the PubCos seem to have interpreted the Trade and Industry Committee's conclusion, and the government's nonchalance about their power and influence, as a green light to carry on as before. Evidence of this came in an extraordinary set of letters written by an anonymous PubCo insider over the course of several months. Describing himself as 'a senior manager working in one of the largest Pub companies' (one of Punch's 'Business Development Managers', perhaps?), he wrote, among others, to the Select Committee expressing disappointment at its mealy-mouthed conclusions:

It was hoped that the publication of your report would yield the start of a new period of hope and fairness within the business. However, my employers and other PubCos have taken your report as a ringing endorsement of the way in which they do business... I think the general consensus of opinion is that PubCos feel they have room to push the boundary a little further... At the coalface, 4 of my 500+ tenants have attempted suicide since Christmas... I have mentioned before that in my professional opinion 80 per cent of my tenancies are unprofitable for the tenant...[20]

But while government sits on its hands, some think that economic logic will overtake political expediency. Brian Jacobs, an accountant and expert on the economics of PubCos, who gave evidence to the Select Committee inquiry, is one of them. He is convinced that the PubCo as a business model is heading for a fall.

'The PubCo model is based on the promise of guaranteed income and guaranteed profit,' he told me, when I phoned him in his Birmingham office. 'They're also in the happy position of being able to drop a lot of the operating costs onto the tenant.' He, too, brings up the Disability Discrimation Act. 'How many pubs do you frequent with disabled toilets?' he asks. 'Well, the Act requires all pubs to have them installed. That's going to cost anything between ten and seventy-five thousand, and it's the tenant, not the PubCo, who has to pay.'

It sounds to me, I say to Brian, as if the PubCos have themselves a nice little earner. Why does he think there's a problem?

'I actually think the writing is on the wall for the PubCos,' he says. 'They have overvalued their portfolio. They've got tranches of pubs worth about £60,000 which they've valued at £500,000, based on the inflated amounts they're bringing in from the beer tie. Inflating value inflates their ability to borrow, you see. But that's not the true value of their assets. They're artificially inflating the value of their property year on year, but profits are actually falling year on year. They're storing up trouble for the future.'

Select Committees. Accountants. Valuations. Property portfolios. It's all a million miles away from what a pub is actually about. And the more I think, the more I write, and the more, perhaps, I drink, the more I think I can begin properly to pin down what it *is* about.

The pub is one of the most definably *local* institutions there is. You can't clone a real pub, and when you try – and many have – the results are horrific: all fake road signs and a corporate version of conviviality. The atmosphere in a good pub comes from a peculiar and entirely un-reproducible mix of the people who drink there, the décor, the attitude of the landlord and his staff (surly, cheerful, under the table – every pub has its own style) and the general ambience.

It also, of course, comes from the beer. A traditional beer is probably the ultimate local product. Its taste will depend on the precise blend of ingredients used: the variety of hop, the flavour of the malt, the type of water. The brewery itself – the equipment it uses, the recipes it has developed over the years – will be the key to its uniqueness, which is why the death of so many traditional brewers is such a cultural tragedy. And because a real ale 'lives' and continues to brew in the barrel, it cannot be transported far before it goes off – unlike the dead, gassy multinational brands which are designed specifically to be freighted across continents.

In other words a good local pub, serving good local beer, is the ultimate antidote to placeless globalisation. At its best, it can be the perfect representation of a rooted, human scale institution serving good-quality local produce, which results in good-quality local enjoyment. It's hard to know what more to ask for.

Caldbeck Fells, Cumbria
June 2006

Hesket Newmarket is a pretty little Lake District village – neat stone and whitewash houses, an oak tree standing sentinel over the village green, a small shop and post office. In the village centre stands what looks like a pleasant, unremarkable pub. It may be more than that though. The Old Crown could, if all went well, be an example for others to follow. It could even perhaps become something of an alternative to the PubCo model.

The Old Crown is a small, two-room affair, with a log fire burning in the stone fireplace, lines of silver tankards hanging from the roof beams, three old men sitting on bar stools discussing the weather and ten separate beers advertised on a chalkboard behind the bar. So far, so unsurprising. What is unusual about this place, though, is that it is owned not by a PubCo, not by a brewery, not even by the landlord, but by the community. The Old Crown is Britain's first, and so far only, co-operatively owned pub.

Sitting by the front window with a pint of Blencathra (all the beers sold here are named after local mountains) Julian Ross explains how it happened. Julian, a local resident and pub enthusiast, was one of the driving forces behind the Old Crown's transformation from a pub under threat to a pub under community control.

'The previous landlord, Kim, decided to sell up in 2001,' he explains. 'His wife had died and he didn't want to run the place on his own. The worry was that it would be bought by a PubCo, or that it might even go for housing. Enough people were concerned about it for us to get together and discuss what we could do as a community to safeguard it.' The Old Crown is the only pub in the village. The locals knew that if it went, a key part of their community would go too.

So they did something about it. After much discussion they came up with a business model that would give control of the pub to the community, and ensure it was safeguarded for the future. They set up a co-operative, and appealed for people to buy shares. Rules were strict – only one share could be bought per person, and no one could sell their share to anyone except the co-op itself. This way, the possibility of any kind of unwanted takeover was avoided, and community control was retained. One hundred and twenty-five people bought shares initially – some from as far afield as Australia and the US, who had visited it on holiday and wanted to help save it. The share issue was a success, and the co-op bought the pub.

Julian gives me a tour of the place to show me the fruits of their labours. The co-op employs the current landlord and bar staff. Their success at running the pub has also allowed them to build a bright, new dining-room extension out the back, which has only just opened. It still smells of paint.

But the *pièce de résistance* is outside. Julian walks me through a sea of steel barrels and garden furniture into an old barn behind the pub. The smell of malt and steam hangs in the air. This is the Old Crown's microbrewery, the Hesket Brewery. It, like the pub, is owned by the community. All the beers sold in the pub are from the brewery here, and it sells them, too, in other pubs and shops countrywide. The brewer, Mike, who has decades of expertise behind him in bigger breweries, shows me the bottling machine they have just bought, with which they intend to step up trade.

'To me,' says Julian, as we stand in the doorway of the brewery, 'it was like saying, "Thus far, but no further." So many things are now cloned, McDonaldised, you know. We were saying – whatever else you've got, you're not having our pub. And now they can't. We've taken it out of the market-place, and it will be very hard to get it back on.' Outside, someone starts rolling steel barrels around on the concrete. The sound is sharp and satisfying.

'It's easy to look at the whole advance of homogenisation and corporate control and think, "It's too big, there's nothing we can do,"' says Julian. 'But you can do it. My wife has a saying – if you want to eat an elephant, you don't try to do it all at once. You do it bite by bite. That's what we're doing at the Old Crown – biting the elephant. If enough of us do it, you know – well, it's eaten.'

3

A Secret, Special Place

When you work with water, you have to know and respect it.
When you labour to subdue it, you have to understand that
one day it may rise up and turn all your labour to nothing.

Graham Swift, *Waterland*, 1983

Osney Lock, Oxford
July 2005

Ferd marches past the lock cottage, hefting a wooden chair on his
shoulder. A roll-up hangs from his lower lip. Usually he stops to talk
– he's the one who does most of the talking – but today he's in a
hurry to get back to his boat. *Under Milk Wood* is moored a couple of
hundred of yards downstream, where it shouldn't really be.

'Heavy,' he says, as he walks. 'Later.'

Summer 2005, and I'm working as an assistant lock-keeper on the
river Thames. A parallel world has unfurled before me. I live less than
a mile from this river – I've walked by it many times, swum in it,
kayaked on it, passed endlessly over its bridges. Yet I've evidently
never really seen it. It is a whole new channel of human life, and the
work it does, the people who live on it, live from it, work it and know
it are a whole world of their own.

The lock-keepers themselves, for example. A cynical bunch of old buggers, most of them, but beneath the dismissive veneer is a centre that knows the river and the people on it, feels for it, belongs to it in some way. I wouldn't say this to them, of course, because they'd think I was unbearably pretentious.

Take Mick, the keeper I work with. Mick and I flit every other day between the three Oxford locks: Iffley, Osney and Godstow. Here we open and close the gates to let the boats through. We mow the lawns and weed the flower beds. We raise and lower the weirs, check the levels, answer questions from passing Japanese tourists and make and drink a lot of tea.

Mick's been on the locks for decades. He used to be a painter-decorator, but he likes the job security. And he knows the river. He can tell what type of boat is making its way upstream from half a mile away. He knows by sight what will fit into the lock and what won't. He knows how to deal with bolshie tourists and narrowboats full of estate agents out on a pissed-up stag weekend. He knows precisely how much to raise and lower the weirs depending on the amount of rain that's been reported upstream. And he can tell you stories.

Stories about an old keeper who had been a POW in the Far East, and refused thereafter to let boats with Japanese engines through his locks. Stories about fights – literal fights – between old-school lockies and new-style managers. Stories about a skiff full of student rowers sucked to their deaths down the Stoney Sluice one raging midwinter dusk.

And he knows the characters. He's one of them, and so are the other keepers, who enjoy slagging off the management together on the phone, or in the pub after they close up. There is no shortage of characters here. There's the assistant keeper up at King's lock, who for the rest of the year lives as a water-gypsy, driving his two industrial narrowboats up and down the river, flogging coal and heating oil. He sleeps on a mattress on the floor of one of his boats, has never had a 'proper' job before, and had trouble getting paid for this one because he's never had a bank account either. I didn't think people like this existed any more but they do, for now, and not a mile away from my tidy, semi-normal life.

There are the middle-aged couples who spend all summer cruising up and down in their twee, over-painted narrowboats, in shorts too small for them, smoking pipes and smiling as their punchable little dogs yap at us from the roof. There are the hippies who live on the canal in their listing, unlicensed wrecks (known to the lock-keepers as 'scrote boats'), the locals who come crayfishing on the banks, the dodgy geezers from Rose Hill who affably try to flog us knocked-off garden tools or lumps of hash whenever they pass by.

And there's Ferd. Ferd, with his greying handlebar moustache, his combat trousers, his beloved boat, his forceful opinions and his poetry collection, self-published and left in the lock office for us to read when it's raining. Ferd, who skips up and down between London and Oxford, resting where he can, the smell of tea and weed seeping through the open windows of *Under Milk Wood*. Ferd belongs to the Thames. He calls it 'my river', or even 'my beloved river'. He has spent much of his life on it, and says he plans to stay as long as he can. But he is worried.

'They're fucking it up,' he says to me one day, loudly, as he leans on the doorframe of the lock office rolling a cigarette. 'These management wankers. It's all risk assessments now. Fucking health and safety, and leisure boaters and executive housing up the banks. This is a living river, a working river. They'll get rid of the lock-keepers, you wait. They've done it on the canals already. Sacked the keepers, flogged their houses to yuppies, sold the boatyards to sharks. I was up on a canal in the midlands last year, middle of the night it was, I was shipping a load of stuff to a company up there. I've got a deadline, so I'm going all night. I'm letting myself through this lock and this posh woman comes out of the lock cottage she's bought and dolled up, and starts complaining about the noise. I say, look, love, this is a *canal*. You think it's all peace and quiet and boats full of bourgeois friends of yours? Some of us have to *work*. Work the canals, and work the rivers, that's what keeps them alive.'

Ferd lights up, looking disgusted. He dominates the tiny hut just by opening his mouth. I feel for the posh woman.

'It's all going,' he continues, when he's taken his first drag. 'I've watched it happen. Working boats driven out, all the characters going, all the people who understood the river. They want tourists now. Weekend cruisers, postcards, yuppie flats, that's where the money is. Turn it into a dead ditch for "leisure pursuits". And my beloved river; my beloved Thames – they'll kill it. They'll drive us off, and they'll kill it.' He takes another drag and looks at me, intensely.

'Wankers,' he says.

England's navigable waterways have always been about much more than water. They have been, through accident or design, channels down which a different type of life was carried. People who didn't, or don't, quite fit into stationary life on the land could find a home on the water, and perhaps find work too. Bargemen, boat-builders, water-gypsies, lock-keepers, chandlers… for those whose constitution demanded a different rhythm and a different way of being than that offered by the mainstream, the waterways could provide.

But the waterways, like everywhere else, have also been a source of profit. 'All fish-weirs shall be removed from the Thames, the Medway, and throughout the whole of England,' reads Article 33 of Magna Carta. Eight hundred years ago, landowners and millers were already cashing in on people's desire to navigate the waters, putting up weirs and charging people to pass them. Nothing much changes.

Then there are the canals. The great age of canal building was launched with the construction of the Bridgewater Canal, which began in 1759. The Duke of Bridgewater needed a reliable method of transporting the coal from his mines at Worsley to the markets of Manchester. Roads were expensive and unreliable, so Bridgewater employed engineer James Brindley to design a canal.

The Bridgewater Canal was completed in 1776, and its success (the price of coal fell in Manchester, and Bridgewater became even richer), sparked half a century of 'canal mania' among other land-owners, merchants and industrialists, who knew a good thing when they saw one. By the 1840s, the canal system was at the height of its power, with almost 4500 miles of navigable waterway and 2700 locks. Thousands of working narrowboats traversed the country, fuelling the rise of industry before they were fatally weakened by the railways and finally killed off by the motorways.

In nature and in purpose, the canals have always been different to the rivers. But they are not as distinguishable as they once were. The motorways of their time, they are now, like most rivers, primarily focused on something called 'leisure' – a concept that barely existed when they were created.

But the canals, like the rivers, are more than that. They are a retreat too. A hideaway, an alternative reality. They are some of the last places where those who live differently can afford to exist. They provide 'affordable housing' in an environment far removed from the pressures of mainstream society. You have to fetch your own coal and empty your own toilet, but your home moves and when you open your blinds in the morning you'll see what you have chosen to see, be it the brickwork of an old bridge or a reed bed in the early day's mist.

England's navigable waterways have become, by accident rather than design, some of the last corridors of colour, character and distinctiveness in a landscape of increasingly bland conformity.

But for how long?

Castlemill Boatyard, Oxford
January 2005

It's a freezing morning. The canal is edged with ice and the tow-path grass is rimed silvery-white in the early sun. In the Victorian suburb of Jericho, in north Oxford, a boatyard is filling up with people; around fifty of them, rubbing their hands and stamping their feet against the cold. Around them stand boats in various states of semi-repair. Slate-grey barges, peeling black hulls, piles of scrap and all the detritus of a working boat repair operation. A traditionally painted narrowboat called *Gemini* sits up on skids. The air smells of frost and coal smoke, and small groups of boat-dwellers sit on the prows of their vessels, sipping from mugs of tea.

This is Castlemill Boatyard, and it is special. It is special because of its history: the first wharf on the canal in north Oxford, it has been here since at least 1842 and was one of the drivers of the prosperity and employment of the Victorian city. It is special, too, because of its current situation. From having been one of Oxford's first canal wharves, it is now one of its last – the only publicly accessible boatyard remaining in the city. As such, it is a lifeline for the community of 200 people who live permanently on boats in the city. Boat painting and servicing, craning, welding, emergency repairs – Castlemill provides the kinds of things you need within reach if your boat is also your home. The nearest alternatives are a day or two's cruise away up or downstream – not a lot of use if you've sprung a leak or your engine has conked out.

Finally, Castlemill is special because of what it contributes to the sense of place that makes Jericho what it is. It's a small, unkempt, lively place, where boaters wander in and out, dogs run free and boat-builder Steve Goodlad runs a popular small business. For the land-lubbers of Jericho, Castlemill provides a link with history; a last surviving connection between land and water in this place where land and water were once symbiotic. Jericho and the canal grew up together, provided for each other. Even now, the connection remains.

I've always loved the Oxford Canal. In the fifteen years I've known it, it's had a glamorously down-at-heel character. It's a place of ram-shackle factories, teetering, palatial Victorian houses – all dark-red brick and long thin gardens – old arched bridges and dozens of scruffy residential narrowboats, lined up bow to stern along the banks, their mooring ropes tangled together, their chimneys belching the sweet smell of coal smoke into the cold air. It has a nature, a character, a personality of its own.

Or it did have. That character is rapidly being erased, in the name of those two trusty old soldiers, profit and progress. Jericho has been moving 'upmarket' for years, and the canal has become a cash-generating development corridor. Great walls of homogenous brickwork are rising where industry or greenery once stood. Where once was a long strip of 'waste' ground, an old factory or a green space there is now a building site, on which high, tall new flats have risen in less than a year, like sunflowers on a prairie. Acre upon acre of 'luxury townhouses' and 'exclusive apartments' are raking in money for estate agents and developers.

It is in this context that Castlemill Boatyard has become, by default, the last redoubt of living colour on this stretch of water. But now Castlemill is under threat too. This small slice of land, ignored or overlooked for years, suddenly finds itself the focus of some serious attention. Not so long ago it would have been considered a dive. Today it is prime real estate; the last remnant of small-scale, neighbourhood industry in a neighbourhood now defined by its spiralling house prices. In an area where a pokey two-up, two-down terrace goes for over £300,000, the acre and a half that is the boatyard is suddenly a prize worth having.

With a heavy inevitability, then, Castlemill finds itself fighting for its existence against its own landowner, which wants to shut down Steve's business, level the yard and replace it with forty-six new 'apartments', a waterside restaurant and a public 'piazza', which will look as bland and placeless as that description suggests.

The development plans are almost universally unpopular: the city council, local MPs, the Jericho Community Association and the city's boating community have all come out against them. Planning permission has already been rejected twice by the council, on the grounds of visual impact, the loss of boatyard facilities and the lack of affordable housing included in the plans. In two months, the developers' appeal against these rejections comes up before a planning inspector. If he rules in its favour, Steve and the boaties are doomed.

Even before any decision is taken, though, Steve has been given notice to close up his yard, get out, and leave the boaters to it. His notice period expires today. We're here to support him, because nobody here wants him to go.

The idea seems to be to hold some sort of demonstration, but nobody seems quite sure what sort. Photographers with tripods wander about looking for angles. The square, Italianate campanile of St Barnabas's church, which will be obscured from view if the flats come, looms over the new developments that are creeping up from up- and downstream, and on the opposite bank.

'Horrible, isn't it?' says a woman in a red bobble hat, echoing my thoughts. 'I cycled down the canal to get here. It's all silver Porsches and flats that look like offices and offices that look like flats. And now they want this as well.'

Eventually a photographer from the local paper takes charge, climbing up on the bow of a dry-docked narrowboat and commanding us to stand in a group and look defiant for the cameras. We try our best. Squeezing in next to me, to get in shot, is a small, chunky bloke in a baseball cap and black puffa jacket. He looks out of place amongst the boaties, with their unkempt beards and knitted hats and cracked mugs of instant coffee.

'Heard about this on the radio this morning,' he tells me. 'So I jumped in the car and came down. Never done anything like this before. Missus said, "You don't want to do that." I said I do. We've been sitting around talking about it at work and it makes me furious. They're gonna destroy this place. It's happening all over, isn't it? If you've got the money you can just trample all over anyone.'

Perhaps half of the people here today live on boats. For them, this boatyard is not just a sliver of local colour; it is an essential service. Yet it's not simply colour to the rest of us either. This is why so many people are here this morning: they are passionate about what could be lost. They feel that something that matters is about to be taken from them, without their permission, by people from elsewhere who know nothing about it. They feel that price has trumped value, again. They want to be allowed to scream about it.

Oxford Town Hall
Two months later

Steve Goodlad sits with his back to me, facing the planning inspector. The fifty people in the room have been waiting for this moment for two days. From where I'm sitting, in the public gallery, I can feel the tension in the air.

Steve wears a green jumper and jeans. His interrogator, one of the country's leading property barristers, wears a pinstripe suit.

'So,' says the barrister, for probably the third time, 'the angle-grinder.'

'Yes,' says Steve. 'What about the angle grinder?' The barrister smiles.

'We seem to have established,' says the barrister, 'that the angle-grinder was the source of the problem. It is, is it not, an extremely noisy instrument to be using in a residential area on weekdays?'

'It's not an instrument,' says Steve. 'It's a piece of industrial plant. And because it's noisy, we came to an agreement with the community that the angle-grinder would only be used on weekday mornings. It's an example of how seriously we take our role as part of the local community.' The barrister looks pointedly at the planning inspector, who is taking notes and doesn't notice.

'Of course,' he says, 'you only came to this agreement after receiving complaints from residents about noise, that is correct?'

'One complaint.'

'About the angle-grinder?'

'Yes,' says Steve, heavily. 'About the angle-grinder.'

It's two months after the gathering in the boatyard and, on a March morning in Oxford Town Hall, the planning inquiry into the development of Castlemill is in full swing. I'm sitting in the public gallery, looking over a council chamber which is all wood panels, florid plaster ceiling and dark paintings of ancient notables. The bearded planning inspector sits at the head of the room, on a pompous carved wooden chair. On one side of the room sit the boat people from the canal, beards trimmed, ponytails pulled back, scuffed leather jackets buttoned. On the other sit the legal team for Bellway Homes, the developer, headed by the tenacious barrister, who is not going to let up until he's got the answers he wants.

The arguments are many and tedious. The case turns on precise definitions of 'essential services' for boaters, arguments about what constitutes the 'heritage' of the canal system, interpretations of the council's Local Plan and the requirements of Local Agenda 21 legislation. It turns on the noisiness of Steve's angle-grinder, the residential character of the neighbourhood and the adequacy or otherwise of the alternative facilities that boaters have been offered elsewhere.

And beneath it all lies a nasty undertone, which is never stated but is loud and clear to those who choose to hear it. Look at these people, it runs. Just *look* at them. Would you want people like this living near you, with their beards and nose-rings and crappy old boats? Their shoes are dirty and they're probably on drugs. Do they even have jobs? Would you want them near your daughters? Wouldn't you rather run them out of town and have a nice, new restaurant instead? Of course you would. Who wouldn't? Come on, people. We're all in this together.

I'm thinking of leaving. It's lunchtime anyway. Well, midday, which is near enough for me. I'm not getting that much out of being here any more. I've seen what I need to see. And then the bus driver stands up.

The bus driver is Jenny Mann, a Jericho resident. She has no particular expertise in this area. She is not a boater, a boat-builder, an architect or a developer. She just happens to live near the yard, and just happens to value it. What she says about it is mesmerising and powerfully delivered.

'I can't talk for long, because I have to go to work,' she says, standing up in her uniform. 'I just want to emphasise that at the public meetings concerning this development that I've been to, local residents have come out unanimously in support of the boatyard... There is huge shock and anger among local residents at Bellway's plans... People feel it as a body blow struck at our community.'

The Bellway people look bored.

'I chose to live in Jericho,' continues Jenny, 'because of its character and the interesting and chequered history of this area, which makes it a unique and special place to live. The canal running down one side is an integral part of this. The working boatyard is a living connection with the area's history. It is a rare example of an industry which actually enhances its setting – the view of the church tower rising above a jumble of little two-storey houses and the boats drawn up on the wharfside in front are all essential parts of the Jericho canalside scene.'

The boaters are paying close attention.

'If we lose this,' concludes Jenny, 'and replace it with a four-storey wall of flats it would be a tragedy for this community: Jericho will lose its character and identity and become yet another bland little suburb. I truly think this would destroy the heart of this community.'

Jenny has voiced what everyone here to defend the boatyard was feeling but hadn't expressed – nervous, perhaps, of their lack of legal expertise, relevant qualifications or verifiable facts. This, says the atmosphere in the room, is what this is actually all about; what it has always been about. This, after everything, is what it all comes down to.

Central London
January 2006

One year on, and 60 miles away, Del Brenner stands on a footbridge and looks aghast.

'Look at it!' he says, shaking his head. 'Just *look* at it.'

Del is in his fifties, with sandy hair and thick glasses which make him look slightly over-eager. He wears a blue jumper and holds a white plastic carrier bag stuffed full of reports, books and pamphlets, which he is going to make sure I see.

Canals are central to Del Brenner's life. His magnified eyes shine when he talks about basins, narrowboats, lock gates or the history of coal freight. He knows everything there is to know about the water-ways of the capital, over which he has appointed himself unofficial but zealous guardian. Del is founder of the Regents Network, a coalition of waterways lovers campaigning to save London's formerly working waterways from the breakneck over-development of the early twenty-first century.

Behind us is Paddington Basin, the old junction of the Grand Union and the Regent's Canal. Hidden behind the train station the Basin was, until recently, a worn-out, run-down industrial site. For years it sat decaying, empty and unused. But, like Castlemill Boatyard only much more so, this old site became a gold mine. Prime real estate, in the heart of one of the most expensive cities in the world, Paddington Basin was hardly likely to stay unused for long.

Those who knew the basin a few years ago would not recognise it now. The redevelopment of this site, which is roughly the size of Soho, is costing £300 million, and is part of a wider £2 billion scheme to provide a ritzy new 'quarter for London'. The inevitable phallic glass tower blocks, home to banks and consultancies, gaze sternly and cleanly over the re-engineered basin, which is edged neatly with swish wooden walkways. Nobody is walking on them, though. We are the only people here.

A new shopping centre and hotel development is rising on one side, while along the other are moored the only boats to be seen here – stationary, engine-less 'business barges', rented out as pricey floating offices. Floating restaurants will be joining them soon. Everything here is hard-edged, neat, reflective, progressive. Everything is in its place. Del looks on the verge of cardiac arrest.

'Sterile!' he pronounces. 'Characterless! See that building over there?' He points to an old warehouse, whitewashed and fragile, dwarfed by the new offices. The last remnant of the old basin, it looks entirely out of place.

'It's a nice old thing,' says Del. 'Very ordinary. It's not glamorous, it's not glitzy, but so what? It's part of the heritage of the basin, and they want to knock it down.' He glowers.

'I have no problem with redeveloping this basin,' he says. 'It needed something. But it's about the *type* of development that goes here. This is utterly inappropriate. They call this "regeneration" of the canal. Can you see any regeneration of the canal going on? It doesn't look like a canal, it's not used as a canal. There's no freight, no boats. It costs a bomb to moor here, and why would you want to? They seem to define "regeneration" of a canal as "building all around the outside of it". It should mean regenerating the *use* of the waterways. It is a completely different thing.' He looks around him, and sighs.

'They've lost the plot completely,' he says.

'They' are the owner of this land – the same organisation, in fact, that owns Castlemill Boatyard. The same organisation that owns thousands of other canalside sites around the country, many of which it is 'redeveloping' in similar ways, sparking similar objections as it goes. From Brentford to Berkhamsted, Macclesfield to Loughborough, Leeds to the Lee Valley, anger is mounting about the over-commercialisation of England's canals, and the consequent loss of character. What makes the canals special – their unique and often hard to define mixture of place, history, character and utility – is being blanded out of existence in the name of money, with rising land prices as its spur. The developer of Paddington and Castlemill is the one most often blamed for it. Yet this is no rapacious private corporation. This is the publicly owned, publicly accountable body charged with protecting the heritage, the infrastructure and the users of the canals: British Waterways.

The declining canal network was nationalised in 1948, and in 1962 an Act of Parliament set up the British Waterways Board to manage a network that was only half the size it had been in its heyday. Underfunded, ignored and apparently useless, the future of the canals looked grim. The Board had a tough job on its hands.

It still does. Forty years on British Waterways (BW), as it prefers to be known these days, manages by far the largest network of navigable inland waterways in England. It is responsible for over 2000 miles of canal, 1500 locks, 3000 bridges, 54 tunnels, 400 aqueducts and 90 reservoirs. Its holdings include 3000 listed buildings, 42 scheduled ancient monuments, 5 world heritage sites, 8 historic battlefields, 600 miles of hedgerow and 1000 wildlife conservation sites.[1]

At the same time as having to maintain all this, BW is pulled in various directions by its curious remit and ownership structure. Accountable to the government and largely funded by the taxpayer, it is charged with promoting and conserving the living history of the canal system while at the same time increasing visitor numbers (one of BW's unchallengeable success stories – over 400 million people a year visit the canals[2]) and increasing the amount of freight on the water. It is expected to maintain the waterways in a navigable state and work with everyone from farmers to boat owners to local councils to dog-walkers.

No one would suggest that its job is a particularly easy one.

Crucially, because this is the early twenty-first century and we are all capitalists now, it is also required to 'seek opportunities for private sector partnerships' and 'maximise, as far as practicable, revenue from its activities by charging a market rate for its services'. BW, in other words, is expected to pay its way. It doesn't, and can't, expect substantial public funding to continue for ever. If it wants to survive, the rationale goes, it will have to operate like a commercial organisation, covering its costs, and steadily increasing its stream of private income.

Few people have a problem with BW using its assets well and applying commercial sense to its operations. If the results are a more efficient organisation, losing less money – perhaps even making some, which can then be ploughed back into the upkeep of the canals – well, that just sounds like common sense.

The principle, in other words, is fine. The problem is the practice. Almost everywhere you turn, you will find that those who know and love the canals are up in arms. They are up in arms because they accuse BW of putting its fundraising targets before its management of the network. They are up in arms because they believe that its obsession with breaking even has trumped its interest in the canals. They believe, in particular, that BW's current focus on property development as a cash cow is destroying the very essence of what it exists to maintain.

And there's no doubt that BW's commercial operations – particularly its property development arm – are getting deadly serious. A decade or two ago British Waterways, by all accounts, was a slightly amateurish, underfunded organisation staffed by canal lovers and engineers. Not any more. These days, BW is an increasingly slick, well-organised commercial machine. It is run by people who have no background in canals but plenty in business. It is not going to be pushed around any more. It is going to be a player.

The first thing a player does is value his assets. In BW's case, those assets are substantial – £450 million-worth of property and land, for starters. In 2002 it set up its own development company, Isis, to develop this 'portfolio' in alliance with private development firms all over the country. BW Marinas Ltd, another associated company created in 2004, has caused controversy among private marina operators along the canal network, some of whom say it has been using BW's monopoly power to squeeze them out of business. It runs ten marinas at present. There will undoubtedly be more.

But BW is undeterred by criticism. It has big ambitions. Its Waterside Pubs Partnership aims to run a chain of fifty waterside pubs by 2009. Watergrid, launched in 2002, is a public-private partnership that provides 'bespoke water services and wastewater treatment facilities' and proudly boasts of supplying half of Bristol's drinking water from the canal system. The 'Business Barges' are rolling out across the network, having been tried and tested in Paddington Basin. All of this, according to BW, leads to 'customer satisfaction' and 'resource efficiency' – all within a framework of 'corporate social responsibility' and 'social inclusion', of course.[3]

It is the property developments, though, that remain both most lucrative and most controversial. The scrap over tiny Castlemill Boatyard is just one small example of the controversy they can cause – and the money they can make. In 2005, BW brought in over £26 million a year from its 'property assets'. By 2008, it plans to have bumped this up to over £30 million.[4]

Its means of achieving this goal include 'regeneration' in London's City Road Basin (shops, restaurants, a 28-storey tower block, 9000 square feet of office space); Wood Wharf in Docklands (more of the same, in the largest single development BW has ever undertaken); Brentford (a new 'vibrant community' of 900 homes, bus station, health club and business units); Manchester (a 'striking 21-storey building' next to the canal, containing 200 apartments); Leeds (Clarence Dock to become a 'revenue-generating leisure space') and Gloucester (a 50 per cent stake in a new factory-outlet centre, shops, houses and business units).[5]

It's not hard to see why some people find this litany worrying. Particularly if, like Steve Goodlad, they are losing their livelihood as a result of it. Particularly if, like the Jericho Community Association, they are seeing the character of their neighbourhood forcibly reworked because of it. Particularly if, like the network's thousands of residential boaters, they have just been hit with a hefty increase in boat licence and mooring fees, fuelling suspicions that BW is deliberately pricing the long-term and occasionally awkward residential boaters off the canals.[6]

Listen to boaters' representatives and long-time canal experts, and you'll hear some sharp criticism of BW, from all angles. Simon Robbins of the National Association of Boat Owners, for example. 'British Waterways are both landlord and tenant,' he says. 'They own a lot of canalside land and they're developing it fast. But if the developer is also the body which is supposed to police development, the conflict of interest is clear. In a nutshell, there's your problem.'

Or listen to Andy Jackson, long-time boater and founder of the newspaper *Towpath Talk*, whose assessment is blunter. 'Years ago,' he says, 'BW would have about thirty people working on the canal bank and two in the office. These days it's two on the bank and thirty in the office. British Waterways are run by property developers rather than lock-keepers, and it shows.'

Or, if you really want to know the mind of a true canal lover, who has no time for British Waterways, and can tell you exactly why – listen to Del Brenner.

Del and I are sitting in a floating café in Little Venice, a ten-minute walk from Paddington Basin. Redbrick, trees, lines of gaily painted boats, just a hint of tweeness – this is yet another version of canal life. Over a herbal tea, Del is asking me the question that I bet he asks everyone who comes to talk to him.

'Who owns the canals?' he demands. He looks at me, owl-like.

'Er,' I say, 'British Waterways, I suppose.'

I have made an elementary error. Del looks both pleased and horrified.

'No!' he insists. 'No! They don't! *You* do! *I* do! They're a *public asset.* British Waterways exists to maintain them, on our behalf.

They're a *public treasure*, not a handy little resource for asset-strippers. That's why this whole situation is so disgraceful!' I sip my coffee, chastened.

'The waterways are being squeezed dry by BW,' says Del. 'This is a public body – guardians of some of our most precious waterways. If they can act this way, what can we expect from private developers or landowners? They could be setting a positive example, but they're doing exactly the opposite. We don't oppose property development, but it needs to be done in a particular way that suits the waterways. So many of these developments are huge glass buildings that have no relationship to the canal or what the canals are for. Some of them are lovely buildings, but they're in the wrong place. Developments need to suit the nature of the canal and the long-term future of the canal. They need a bit of vision. BW doesn't do vision.'

Del sips his tea.

'We agree with BW being businesslike, and using their assets wisely,' he says. 'But what do they do with the money? How come, with a multi-million-pound scheme like Paddington, they still can't find the money to make some of their locks operate properly, or dredge the canals? Take a look at some of their projects – Wood Wharf, for example, or City Road Basin. We can't find out, because they won't tell us, exactly how much is being spent on these, but we've estimated it's costing them a couple of million just in consultation fees.'

Behind me, a cappuccino machine kicks into life. Del is drowned out for ten seconds.

'Think about this,' he is saying as it clunks into silence. 'BW are going full-pelt into property development, but they have no real expertise in that area. You can make a lot of money in property – it's a high-return business. But it's high return because it's high risk, and the money they're risking playing the property market is *ours* – public money, that should be used to maintain and restore the canals. They could get rich, maybe, with some of these schemes. But they could also lose their shirt, which is also our shirt.'

'Meanwhile,' he goes on, 'if you talk to any serious boaters they will tell you that parts of the network are so badly maintained that they can hardly use it. BW are also mandated by the government to promote the canals as a means of transporting business freight – a good, sustainable solution when the roads are congested and we're all worried about climate change. Well, I can tell you that some freight barges can't even use some of the canals around here because BW haven't dredged them properly. All their energy is going into this frantic rush for property money. But it's a *gamble*. The whole thing is a *gamble*, with *public money*. British Waterways exist to run the canals, not to speculate on the property market. If they want to develop some of the land – fine. But let property developers do it. Sell it or rent it to them, if it really is redundant land. But when BW gets into property itself, which is what is happening, in a big way, then it's a step too far.'

Del's eyes light up when he talks about canals. His body is animated, his passions are high and his enthusiasm is catching. 'Aren't they brilliant?' he asks, rhetorically. 'Everybody loves canals! Talk to anyone about canals and they've got some story to tell. And look what they're doing to these beautiful canals – the people who should be protecting them! I live in Camden. Camden lock cottage is now a Starbucks. A *Starbucks*! I *ask* you!'

Poor Del. He loves the canals, but they're breaking his heart.

Macclesfield Canal, Cheshire
December 2005

From Little Venice, follow the Grand Union canal north. Follow it out of the Great Wen and move on up country, into the midlands. You'll pass through Uxbridge, Hemel Hemsptead and Milton Keynes. As you near Northampton, you'll pass through the 3000-yard Blisworth tunnel, once the longest in Britain. You'll want to put your lights on.

After you've passed Daventry, take a left onto the Oxford Canal, which will wend its way up through Rugby and on to Coventry. There, take a slow right onto the Coventry Canal, past Nuneateon and up the great staircase of eleven locks at Atherstone. Chug your way through Tamworth and on until you reach another junction, where you join the Trent and Mersey Canal. This will take you through Stone, and Stoke, until you come to the small right turn of the Macclesfield Canal.

Take it, and follow the Macclesfield north. You'll see that its nineteenth-century arched brick bridges are numbered with little oval steel plates, painted in black and white. Follow the canal and keep your eye on those numbers. Just past Bridge 26, you'll come across a moored, black and red narrowboat with 'Arabia' painted on its side. On that narrowboat, you will find Simon Greer. After you've come all this way, he'll probably offer you a cup of tea.

Simon Greer buys, sells and reconditions traditional narrowboats. He too loves canals, so much so that he's lived on one, in various boats, since 1973. Over the last quarter of a century he reckons that he and his wife Mary have travelled 95 per cent of England's canal network. It's given him a canal's-edge view of the development of the network, the changes it has seen and the way that the inland waterways have progressed over time. Like Del Brenner, Simon is an enthusiast who can be hard to stop once he gets going. And like Del, he has, to put it politely, doubts about the way the canals are changing – and the way they're being managed.

It's New Year's Eve at Bridge 26 and Simon's coal-burning stove is going like the clappers. Outside *Arabia* the rain is pattering onto the roof and the tow-path. The trees are bare, the water is brown. It is comprehensively winter.

Inside, I'm sitting in a large armchair with a cup of tea. *Arabia* is not quite finished – Simon's been fitting her out. Panels are missing and wiring is exposed but everything works, most importantly the kettle.

'Twenty years ago,' says Simon, with a kind of defiant nostalgia in his voice, 'the canals tended to be a refuge for people with humble means, largely working class. It was a real community – relaxed, self-reliant, mostly overlooked by mainstream society. Over the last fifteen years they've introduced enough laws and regulations to carpet the tow-path with! I remember when British Waterways used to be run out of a shoebox by engineers in Watford. Now they're run by PR men, accountants and marketing Johnnies. They've got land values rather than boatie values, and it shows. These days it's all finger-wagging and gentrification and executive bonuses.'

He harrumphs into his tea. Greer has a sandy beard, a fleece and a pair of glasses hanging on a string around his neck. It's a curious thing, but I recognise him, though I've never met him before. Or rather I recognise in him a type of boatie character – the curious mix of lamentation and resistance that comes pouring forth from so many canal lovers when you get them onto the current state of the network.

Which is perhaps curious, for in many ways the canals are in a better state than they have been for a long time. The massive increase in visitor numbers that BW has brought about has been accompanied by some genuine practical improvements. Many tow-paths are more accessible than they once were. Lock gates are cleaner and newly painted. Restoration is in progress in many parts of the network, and there is, in general, more order, cleanliness and accessibility for the general public on the canal network as a whole than there has probably ever been.

This turns out, according to Simon, to be part of the problem.

'Boaties, in the old days,' he says, 'didn't believe anything belonged to them. It was a kind of linear village, if you like. You could buy a boat for a few thousand quid, and you could come and live on the canal, and you could find something unique here. I used to be in the business world, and I came here for a change. I found this amazing little parallel universe. We'd do everything ourselves, help each other, keep the paths clean, you know…'

Through the windows, the last sun of the year shines weak and low through the bare hedges that edge the tow-path. From where I'm sitting, the path is at eye level. A man and a dog pass by. I watch them, unobserved.

'The problem with BW is that they're destroying all of this,' says Simon. 'They're policing the waterways. They deny it, but they have an agenda to tidy the place up and get rid of anyone who's a bit scruffy, a bit odd. They want a certain type of wealthy, sensible, part-time boater who pay their fees and behave themselves. People with ninety-K boats who see conformity as the name of the game. They put signs up everywhere, charge for everything, they see us as an embarrassment. They'll spend millions on a new head office and fleets of vans, bring in colour consultants to change their logo every ten minutes, and then they say they're short of money so they need to introduce mooring fees. They're turning the canals into a theme park. They're ruining the whole reason to be here.'

This sounds to me, I say, like nostalgia. Like a lament for a lost way of life. Simon frowns.

'It's a good way of putting it,' he says. 'It is a lament. But it's not just nostalgia. Things genuinely used to be better, in my view. There used to be this sense of belonging to the canals – that they were ours. I remember the beautiful gardens they used to have at every lock cottage, maintained by the lock-keepers. They sacked them all and sold the houses off – an entire culture gone, at a stroke. We'd maintain the network ourselves back then, help each other out. Everyone had skills. Now they won't let us touch anything. Health and Safety, or some other nonsense. I said to BW recently – I will cut the hedges and maintain the tow-path for a mile on either side of my boat. I'll do it for free if you'll just bloody leave me alone!'

'Just bloody leave me alone!' It strikes me that this would be quite a good rallying cry for the gathering mass of canal lovers who have bones to pick with British Waterways. Simon would certainly agree.

'I think they just have their priorities wrong,' he says. 'Too much spending on flash new projects, too much focus on asset-stripping and property, and not enough on the little things that need doing. I can show you batteries that have been sitting in hedges for three years. I can show you undredged channels and crumbling tow-paths, just down the way. I'm not coming at this from some Trotskyist angle. I know how to run a business, and it's clear they're not running it properly. And you know what? I came to the canals to get away from that boardroom mentality; that cut and thrust, fast-moving world, that's got no time for real people. I came to here to escape it, and now the suits at BW are applying it to the canals!' He looks exasperated.

'The canals,' he says, 'were the last bit of England that hadn't been monkeyed about with. They were a secret, special place, when I first knew them. And now...'

It's possible, of course, that Simon Greer is just a grumpy old sod. It's possible that Del Brenner is an obsessive and that the Castlemill boaties just need to get jobs and haircuts. I suspect that BW's management certainly thinks so. But if this is true, there are an awful lot of grumpy old obsessives around, and many of them are both well-informed and determined to stand up to whatever BW can throw at them.

In the weeks and months after meeting Simon and Del, I speak to and visit others across the country who are fighting the closure of boatyards, the gentrification of canalside land and the loss of key facilities. The arguments I hear are always the same. I discover a network of canal fiends up and down England, coming together to save what they all seem to see as 'secret special places' from...

From what? That's the interesting question. Yes, they'll tell me about budget cuts and mismanagement, bonus schemes and misdirected spending. They'll complain about overpaid executives and the lack of dredging. But what they're really complaining about is exactly what Simon Greer managed to pin down – the smothering of a unique culture by something harder, sharper and more careless. For many, the canals were, and remain, that secret, special place – nonconformist, unpredictable, slow, steady, communal in a curiously English way.

They weren't efficient, profitable, clean or tidy. They didn't, perhaps, even make rational sense. Their continuing existence is a curious historical anomaly. And they represent one of the last bulwarks against the seepage of business culture into the landscapes and mindscapes of England. Now they, too, are being penetrated.

Watford, Hertfordshire
January 2006

The man supposedly responsible for this is slight, grey-haired, shirt-sleeved and, it seems, overworked. He's delayed his meeting with me by ten minutes so he can snatch a sandwich at his desk. Robin Evans, Chief Executive of British Waterways, works out of BW's corporate HQ, which is hidden away in the residential backstreets of Watford. 'Willow Grange' is a big redbrick building with a carp pond at its centre – the only stretch of water in an area in which neither canals nor willows are in evidence.

The thing about Robin Evans is that he can be quite persuasive. He seems to be passionate about waterways, and as a former head of the Landmark Trust and Historic Royal Palaces – both heritage charities – he is not quite the corporate shark that some people would like to believe. When he talks, he sounds fair and thoughtful. He says the canals are 'tremendous' and 'wonderful'. He talks about the 'difficult decisions that have to be made every day' about managing them and suggests, politely, that his critics would have to make the same ones he does.

He also takes a firm line when faced with criticism, and the line has numbers attached. BW's annual report, which is laid out before us on his desk, picks them out starkly enough. British Waterways costs £180 million to run, just over £70 million of which comes from the Treasury. In addition, it has a vast maintenance backlog, a hangover from the 1970s and 1980s when it was woefully underfunded by government. In the last year, it made a pre-tax loss of almost £8 million.[7] The gap to be made up, says Evans, is a big one, and he has to make it up somehow.

Is he making it up, though, I ask, by over-commercialising the network? He must know that people accuse BW of 'Disneyfying' the canals.

'They may do,' he says, with the air of a man who has heard this line a hundred times before, 'but that's very easy because they don't have the liability, the responsibility or the accountability of managing them. The canals cost £150 million a year to run. You can't get away from that. And people want to use them. Three hundred million people visit a year... they do that because they're safe, they're attractive and they're useful. We have places where you have a waterside pub, where you can go and get a cup of coffee in a café, where there are marinas...

'If you pickled them in aspic – if you didn't put all the water points in, you didn't put electricity in, you didn't have cafés or pubs alongside them, it wouldn't be three hundred million visits, and they'd cost £200 million to run. It's a balance. It's a judgement. We make it almost every day.'

Evans is clear, right through our conversation, what a canal is for, in his view – leisure. He is also clear that maintaining a living heritage – or 'used heritage' as he prefers to call it – requires compromises; but that, in his view, they are well worth making.

'If there's one thing I'm passionate about,' he says, 'I think it is that heritage is best preserved by having a viable use. The fewer bits we have which lie unused the better. I sometimes compare the canals to old stately homes. Fewer and fewer people can afford to have them as residential homes – fine, so let's have them as hotels. Yes, you've got to have *en suite* bathrooms, yes the plumbing's a bit intrusive, yes you've got to have lifts – but far better that than have them with holes in the roofs. They remain alive, they still have a use. Same with the canals. Yes, there are compromises. We've had to do things that are different. That's a difficult judgement, but you make it and you move on.'

What happens though, I ask, if the compromises go too far? If you decide, for example, to focus on property and land development to such a degree that you alienate a lot of canal users, and start to destroy the character of the network?

'Well, we're not turning ourselves into a property company,' he insists, 'but that is a part of earning income to be what we are, which is a navigation authority managing a 200-year-old heritage site. And as for canalside developments – I'd say, better us than someone else. Look at what we've done, and look at 100 ghastly schemes where people have built houses and put fences up against the canal. Look at where they build factories and they put up huge 16-foot barbed wire constructions. Then look at our mixed-use development. You may romantically prefer to have kept the rather charming open space or the boatyard or whatever was there, but the reality is that in metropolitan areas, 70 per cent of our housing's got to be built on urban brownfield sites. If we as a public organisation had all these sites languishing, they'd be taken off us… If we don't do it, someone else will.'

The other key point, he says, is that BW is aiming to be as financially self-sufficient as possible. Government funding can never be guaranteed, so the more it can bring in itself, the better.

'Look at our sources of income at present,' he says. '£75 million from the government, £25 million from property. But we don't see in the long term that the government is going to be a generous and reliable funder. Just look at history. We have £300 million-worth of arrears of maintenance because government didn't fund us in the seventies and eighties. Surely, if the people who are responsible for safeguarding and securing canals for the future have their own resource, then what can be more secure? It will be years, decades, if ever, before we can totally remove ourselves from public purse funding. But the less and less we're reliant on it, the less we're vulnerable to the fluctuations. £75 million is a vast amount of our net expense on the waterways – so if they hiccup, it's a big impact. If we can cut that by half and that hiccups, the impact is halved. So it must be a good thing to become less reliant on government.'

Robin Evans means what he says. He can make a convincing case. He talks at great length about Paddington Basin – what a wonderful project it is, how he wishes there were more like it. He defends BW's actions at Castlemill Boatyard. They didn't do much wrong at all, he tells me – all the problems were mere technicalities. He suggests that the long-time boaters are nostalgics who will be unhappy whatever he does. He presents a strong business case. I can imagine him doing the same to the Treasury, or a select committee, and winning them over.

So why, I ask him, are so many people still unconvinced? What does he think – and what can he do – about the changes in the character of the canal network, as a result of BW's actions? The disappearance of colour, character, community – all the things that spring from BW's zealous, corporate approach? Does he ever reflect on the fact that he is responsible for the disappearance of places that can never be replicated again, and their replacement with places that could be anywhere?

'I think what's interesting to do,' he says, 'is to say, OK... if around the country we left those places alone – Loughborough, Brentford, Jericho and other such places – if we left these under-utilised places alone, what would happen? There would be a huge outcry about the ineffectiveness and the poor management of the waterways assets. These things are worth two or three million pounds and we're currently getting two or three hundred pounds from them, from boatyard rent or whatever. What would the public think about that use of public assets? It's the same outcry as the national health estate now, the ministry of defence estate – buildings empty, under-utilised, what a waste of money... and it's your money! Why should you just allow five or fifteen people to benefit from £3 million worth of assets when you should really be doing something better with that?'

When pushed, Evans accepts that the character of the canals is changing as a result of BW's plans, and that some of the 'old, romantic associations' are being lost. 'But that's not a waterways issue,' he says. 'That is everywhere – you can level that accusation at so much of the country today, and I think society has to accept it moves on... a lot has changed and been lost as a result, but generally I think it's been for the better... It's very difficult to stand still. This is changing the character, yes. Should we be really worried about that? I don't think so.'

Blaming society: the last refuge of those who can't, or won't, take responsibility for their actions. And yet Evans has a point. Not everything on the waterways is in BW's control. Even on the canal system for which it is responsible, much of the destruction of the real, the vital and the particular is not down to BW. Commercial developers ruin the canal banks every day. Most canalside land is private and nothing to do with Evans's organisation.

Yet this is not quite the point. BW's critics are angry precisely because the organisation so often apes the worst of the private sector rather than setting a different example. After all, if it is simply going to compete on the open market with property developers, wharf owners and pub chains, then why spend any public money on it at all? Why not privatise it? This, say some critics, is the long-term agenda – something which BW is preparing for by stealth.

Whether or not this is true, the wider criticisms of BW still apply. Its focus on 'leisure' above all else, for example, infuriates many. It is one of Del Brenner's particular bugbears that BW fails to encourage more freight on the canals. In fact, BW is closing and building on many of the canalside wharves which would be necessary for this to happen – wharves like Castlemill. When challenged on this, it repeats its mantra about 'leisure' being the primary purpose of the canals.

The reason is clear enough. 'Leisure' – and property development – brings in quicker bucks, and perhaps more of them. But the underlying issues are more complex. 'Leisure' appeals to the tidy, well-off middle classes. It means cleanliness and order and none of the noise, smells and messiness of freight operations. Yet freight on the canals would, in Ferd the boatman's words, make them 'live'. They would earn their living again. Leisure, by contrast, turns them into watery museums; theme parks for wealthy weekenders. There is a class element to the choice that has been made; almost an existential one. This is twenty-first-century England, and we are all middle class now: 'leisure' is what we do. Apart from call centres and property investment, it is pretty much all we do. BW is part of that world. Perhaps it no longer knows how to be anything else.

But it may not have its own way for ever. And perhaps that world is starting, slowly, to change. While I was writing this chapter, a new organisation called Save Our Waterways launched itself into the public eye. A coalition of people who believe that 'our canals and rivers are part of our national heritage, not a political football',[8] they were inspired by the government's sheepish announcement that, because of DEFRA's mishandling of its finances, funding to BW was to be cut by up to £7 million in 2006, with more cuts likely to follow in coming years.[9] Robin Evans's fear had come true, and BW was to be squeezed. Save Our Waterways held a series of demonstrations up and down the canal network to call for the cuts to be reversed.

Then, one morning, shortly after Save Our Waterways had emerged from the undergrowth by the canal banks, I received an email from Del Brenner. It was short and sweet: 'Paul – government enquiry into British Waterways. This might be just what we needed.' Attached was a press release from the Environment, Food and Rural Affairs Committee of the House of Commons (not the government, but an influential voice), announcing that they were setting up an inquiry into BW's work – including, tellingly, into 'recent developments in the stewardship work and commercial activities of British Waterways, including its property portfolio'[10]

So perhaps something is changing. Perhaps the wildest commercial ambitions of BW will be reined in, and perhaps some of the last redoubts of living colour on England's canals will survive. But it's worth mentioning, while we're here, that British Waterways has become something of a whipping boy for a wider phenomenon. For while it is responsible for a lot, it is not responsible for everything. And some of the problems it is blamed for are much harder to sort out than maybe anyone would like to think.

British Waterways has become, it seems to me, a symbol. It is a symbol of the 'modernisation' of waterways all over England; of the tidying-up of river banks and of the march of the great armies of executive housing that disfigure them. Of the clearances that push the old guard from their patched-up boats and replace them with the part-time wealthy, with their shiny paintwork and roses and castles. Of the changing times that have fractured the old linear communities of the canal banks, and replaced them with a new, more venal 'leisure' age where everything is measured, paid for and monitored, and freedom and spontaneity have come to seem as rare as otters or water voles – though all, in living memory, used to be so common they were barely noticed.

Not all of this is the fault of British Waterways, though some of it is. It can be fairly convicted of encouraging the process, and of profiting from it; of playing the game enthusiastically, sometimes viciously, and perhaps a little too well. Yet it, too, has to ride a larger and more powerful tide.

It is an organisation, formerly operating a quiet, slightly backward but well-meaning public service, which is now mandated, by a business-obsessed government, and a property-hungry society, to behave like corporate raiders. Because nobody really cares, in the end, about a few boaters. Nobody cares about these last rebels, holding the lines against the armies of the bland and the commercial. We are interested in money, shopping and the housing ladder, and British Waterways is colluding in the process of us getting it. That, apparently, is democracy.

All of this means that, yes, Robin Evans is to blame; so is the organisation he runs, and so is the government. But so are you, and so am I. Who's buying into this model of consumer mega-development, anyway? Who are all the people buying the executive flats built on boatyards and renting the glass offices overhanging the demolished basins? Who's sitting back, complacent, as their landscape is ripped apart in the name of progress? Who's challenging the profiteers, or thinking about different ways forward?

British Waterways didn't create this tide; it just exploited it. That doesn't make it blameless, but it does mean that, for the roots of the damage it is wreaking, we have to look further afield. At ourselves, perhaps, and at the values of the society we have created.

The Gloucestershire Cotswolds
January 2006

It's a perfect winter day: cold, sharp, frosty, blue. The high, thin sun is golden on the bare trees, and the woods are hung with delicate, ancient ferns. The path I am walking winds through the woods, following the course of a great, overgrown ditch. The ditch is filled with decades of mud. In many places, its banks have collapsed in on it, and in others it is studded with pools of half-frozen water. Winter sedge and woodbine sprout from it, and curl into the leaf mould on the woodland ground.

This is what remains of the Thames and Severn Canal. Opened in 1786, to connect the two great rivers via the Cotswolds, it was one of the most remarkable engineering feats of its time. A 241-feet rise in its level required a total of twenty-eight locks, and the largest and longest canal tunnel of its time – the Sapperton Tunnel, still the third-longest in the country. Always hard to maintain, due to problems with leakage and maintenance, the canal was plagued with upsets, and was abandoned in stages, finally ending its life in 1933.

Now I'm walking half of its length, from its beginnings in Chalford, near Stroud, to the great, dark, faintly sinister opening of the Sapperton Tunnel, high up in the hills. I'm walking it because I want to see what happens when British Waterways doesn't restore a canal; when no one does. When it just rots away, back into the earth it was dug from. I want to know how it feels, what it looks like and if it matters.

It's the old locks which are the most remarkable feature of this dying industrial relic. I pass dozens of them as I walk, hidden in secluded valleys, shaded by old woods or stranded in frosty, cow-strung fields. They are 12 feet deep, perhaps: deep channels of crumbling brickwork with young alders and birch trees growing in them. The gate pins rust under grass and fern; giant square holes in the stone where gateposts once hung are filled with the sound of trickling, subterranean water. Stone walls are collapsed and mossy. The water and the woods have gone back to their own ways. It's a melancholy, beautiful scene.

So what do I think about it, and what do I feel? Well, first off, it's clear that an abandoned canal is still a canal; still a *place*, with an atmosphere altogether different from any other. It's also clear that some part of me rather likes its creeping death. When I ask myself if I prefer this or Paddington Basin, the question hardly seems worth answering. I find myself hoping that British Waterways don't get anywhere near it; feeling that somehow this way is the more dignified.

Secondly, it's clear that there's a degree of romance and wistfulness in my reaction. Perhaps some *schadenfreude* too: some grim satisfaction in how quickly Man's works can dissolve. Yet there was no wistfulness or romance here in its beginnings. This was a business plan, pure and simple. Canals were the motorways of their age, constructed for no other purpose than to get goods to market quicker. The reasoning behind them was the same as that which makes the CBI call for more motorways and new airport runways. Which should be strange. There should be something paradoxical – even ahistorical – about the beauty of an abandoned industrial relic. Yet there isn't, quite.

Because it's just a place now, with a feeling of its own, that will not quite be replicated anywhere else. However it got here, it is unique and real. Its decay and the evidence of its former utility are all one. I learn, later, that plans to reopen this canal are well under way, wanting only money and time. One day soon, it will probably be rescued, and boats will pass through these locks again. I welcome that. It has to be a good thing. And yet when it happens I know that something will be lost, too.

For this place is quiet, unassuming, unvisited and rare. It is, in a way, that 'secret, special place'; the kind of place you would discover as a child and hold tight to, as your own. Unregulated, unplanned, with no information boards or well-maintained paths or car parks or brown heritage signs, it is the kind of place where you and your imagination can, for a while, be free.

Simon Greer's words now ring in my ears: 'Just bloody leave me alone.' It's a pointless sentiment, in the end, and yet a noble and an ancient one, too. I know it won't get us anywhere, and yet there is something almost radical in its despair; in its angry recognition that change is coming, whether we like it or not – and that its impact and its direction are not up to us, never was. It appeals to me. Leaving things alone these days is a sign of failure. Control, utility, is all, and progress means having fewer and fewer places to hide. But for now, at least, you could hide here.

JUSTICE FOR TONY AND BROADWAY MARKET
OCCUPATION BY THE LOCAL COMMUNITY AGAINST CORRUPT DEVELOPERS WE WANT OUR CAFE NOT YUPPIE FLATS!

4

An Accursed Altar of Mammon

Wherever something is wrong, something is too big.
Leopold Kohr, *The Breakdown of Nations*, 1957

Bury St Edmunds, Suffolk
20 November 2005: St Edmund's Day

I'm constantly naïve about these things. From the medievalist prose that lured me here, I suppose I was expecting some vibrant, characterful little market town, all timber-fronted butchers' shops and town criers. From what I've seen so far, Bury St Edmunds is pretty much like a lot of other English towns of its size: utterly, instantly recognisable, from the 24-hour Tesco shed on the outskirts to the pedestrianised central shopping streets with their black bollards, wooden benches, clean cobbles and branches of Boots and Currys. The only really distinctive landmark I've seen is the enormous Silver Spoon sugar-beet processing factory on the ring road, which dominates the landscape for miles around, belching white, sugary smoke straight up into the Anglian skies.

It's been a stunning winter day; waves of freezing fog falling and lifting to reveal black rooks in white trees, the hoar frost making even the bottle-strewn verges of the A-roads look magical. Driving here, I came down over a line of hills to see the vast sweep of the eastern flatlands laid out before me. Dominating the sightlines, way off in the distance but startlingly visible, were two huge white warehouses; cubist monuments in a defiantly asymmetrical landscape.

Twenty minutes later I drove past them: massive, windowless, utterly incongruous, not even bothering to pretend to belong to the place that supported them, they bore a proud maker's mark:

Welcome to Asda.
Part of the Wal-Mart Family.

It's the word 'family' that I like.

In Bury, now, it's early evening. The tall shadow of St Edmundsbury Cathedral looms high and black above the medieval square in which we wait. By the statue of the town's founder, St Edmund, stands a middle-aged man in chain mail and jeans. He wears a plastic knight's helmet. His name is Alan Murdey, and he is currently being interviewed by a man from the local paper, the *Bury Free Press*. Alan doesn't like the *Bury Free Press*.

'The ritual that we are about to perform,' says Alan, as the reporter scribbles in shorthand, 'has not been conducted in the British Isles for over thirty years.'

'And what might the results of it be?' asks the reporter.

'Death, insanity, destruction of property and venereal disease,' says Alan, with an entirely straight face.

'And this is allowed in Christianity, is it?' asks the reporter doubtfully.

'You haven't read your Book of Common Prayer recently,' says Alan.

'No,' says the reporter. 'Not really.'

'If you did so,' says Alan, 'you would discover a prayer known as Commination. A denouncing of God's anger and judgement against sinners. This is what we will be using to evoke the spirit of Saint Edmund against those who threaten to desecrate this town. It is entirely consistent with Christian ethics. Saint Edmund's curse has been active many times before. In the eleventh century it worked on King Svein Forkbeard.'

'King who... sorry?'

'Svein Forkbeard.' Alan spells it, slowly.

'And who is the curse aimed at tonight?' asks the reporter. Alan looks at him, evenly.

'Debenhams,' he intones.

Ten minutes later. A crowd of about twenty-five people has gathered around Alan, who is still waiting by the statue. The sound of choral evensong drifts through the lighted, stained-glass windows of the cathedral. It is still bitterly cold. Stamping my feet, rubbing my gloved hands together, I get talking to a small, well-wrapped old lady who has 'motored from Walsingham' to be here tonight.

'What else can you do?' she asks, rhetorically. 'Bloody MPs don't listen, the councillors are all corrupt. We end up going back 800 years and putting a curse on the buggers! Do you believe in it, by the way? Do you think it might work? With any luck, someone on the board of Debenhams will drop dead. That'll make them take notice!' She laughs so hard that she has to clutch my elbow for support.

At precisely 7.30 p.m., a silent procession emerges from behind the cathedral. Six knights dressed like Alan, and five monks, who have clearly rented their habits for the duration, walk slowly towards us. Some carry banners. Four carry what looks like a coffin; a kind of makeshift shrine, draped in blue silk. A plastic crown sits on top of it. The procession reaches us and we part, silently, to make way for it. Alan joins it and it makes its way, slowly, away from the cathedral green and onto the streets of the town.

For the next fifteen minutes, this curious procession winds its slow way through the streets of Bury. It is followed by supporters with lanterns and flaming torches and, absurdly, a police van, occupied by bored-looking cops who would probably rather be at home

91

in front of the telly. We pass chain pubs and branches of Pizza Hut, from which people give us very strange looks indeed behind the plate glass. Characters in souped-up Audis with vast exhaust pipes rev their engines ostentatiously and leer into their wing mirrors. Others lean out of second-floor windows and shout 'What's going on?' as we pass. None of the knights or monks answer. They are focused on their holy ritual.

Past the shopping streets, on the other side of town, we approach a grey, grim, deserted car park. The leading monk, who carries a large wooden cross (unlike the lamps and torches this, thankfully, is not burning), turns into it, and we all follow.

The car park is the focus of tonight's activity. This was once the old Cattle Market of Bury St Edmunds. The market's old buildings now stand empty, and its car park is used for visitors to the town centre. But not for long.

St Edmundsbury Borough Council has plans for this place. The council believes that Bury is in trouble. It is losing ground as a 'major retail centre'. The council has conducted research to prove it. The research shows that the local population will rise by over seven thousand people in the next few years. In the same timeframe, projected future spending by this expanding base of local 'consumers' – especially on 'fashion and household goods' – is projected to zoom up by over 20 per cent.

Bury is under-prepared for this sizzling new demand. It needs to be dragged into the twenty-first century, and fast. In the words of the research which the council commissioned from a firm of retail consultants to support its case, 'there is no "do nothing" option' – 'If Bury St Edmunds does not meet shoppers' needs by expanding its shopping facilities... it will lose business to its major competitors.'[1]

Losing business to major competitors is, of course, one of our contemporary deadly sins, and the solution for it has long been carved on tablets of stone. The solution is more shops: not rickety, uncompetitive, backward-looking independent, local shops, of course, but smashing, shiny new chain outlets, of the sort in which 'fashion and household goods' can be bought, and their purchases totted up to the success of the local economy.

Which is where the Cattle Market comes in. The council, working closely with a developer called Centros Miller, has big plans for this windswept stretch of asphalt. By the end of 2008 it is scheduled to be a 'vibrant new quarter' of the town. Highlights of the £80 million scheme will include 35 new retail outlets (with H&M, Waterstone's, River Island, HMV, Top Man, Next and Accessorize among the exciting line-up) with 68 'apartments' above them, 850 parking spaces, a new public square and – at the heart of the whole development – a very large new branch of Debenhams.[2]

The knights, monks and supporters here tonight do not like this idea. They do not like it at all. As their costume and behaviour suggests, they see Bury as a medieval town, in character and spirit. They say they don't object to change – though I have my doubts – but they do object to this. They think that Bury St Edmunds is on the verge of losing its unique character to overweening commerce, becoming just another 'clone town', addicted to shopping.

They have tried to make this point to the council through more conventional methods over the past few years, but the council is not very interested. Hence tonight's activity. The people I am standing around with in the car park call themselves the Knights of St Edmund. They say they have a holy duty to preserve the memory of the town's founder, St Edmund the martyr. They say that Bury's future is too important to be left to councillors and developers. They say they have tried everything else, but that the reticence of the council, Centros Miller and Debenhams has left them with no choice but to unleash the most powerful weapon in their armoury.

So the Knights of St Edmund have come to the Cattle Market tonight to lay a curse on their enemies. One which, they claim, has religious justification. One which will work.

Their torches flaming, the knights and spectators fall silent. A gibbous moon is suddenly covered by what I presume is smoke from the sugar factory. The leading knight lays down his cross, takes a few sheets of paper out of his pocket and steps forward. The ceremony has begun.

'St Edmund, holy martyr, dread Lord and most Christian sovereign,' intones the knight. 'We, the people of your town, liberty and kingdom implore and beseech you, in this the hour of our need. Once again the heathens seek to raise an accursed altar of Mammon in your lands, in order to desecrate your hallowed town with false gods and idols! In order to trample your right and liberties! In order to enslave and impoverish your people! In order to tempt those who love temptation, sin and worldly things!'

As I listen, I turn over the events of this afternoon in my head. I had met Alan Murdey in a local pub to talk about the Knights, the curse and the changing face of Bury. I didn't know quite what to expect. What I got was a respectable middle-aged man – a local, Bury-born lawyer – who took his Christianity and his civic duty very seriously indeed. A man who prayed for the souls of his enemies and believed that 'the Christian heritage' of his town – and, I suspect, his country – was under threat.

The formation of the Knights, Alan explained (or, rather, the re-formation: the original Knights of St Edmund guarded the Abbey after the Norman Conquest) was a 'spontaneous development from people concerned about the future of Bury St Edmunds. There is a huge amount of local opposition to this development. The council are not fulfilling their duties, and Centros Miller and Debenhams are taking advantage of our town. This is a spiritual town. Although it's been badly mauled by commercial development and the expansion of big business, it still remains, just, a town on a human scale. It has links with Cromwell and the *Mayflower* pilgrims. Dickens and Betjeman praised this town. Defoe stayed here. The very essence of culture in England is rooted in places like Bury St Edmunds.'

I suppose I had been assuming that the curse was a joke: an attention-seeking, media-aware, post-modern gag. It seemed not. Alan actually thought it would work. He talked me through the convoluted religious justification for it, and explained why it was acceptable to rain it down upon the heads of the executives of Debenhams and Centros Miller. I asked him how he would feel if the CEO of Debenhams died of a heart attack tomorrow.

'That would be God's judgement,' he replied solemnly. 'They have been warned. What they are about to do will blight the lives of thousands of people in this town.'

He leaned towards me, as if about to impart a great secret.

'Bury St Edmunds,' he said, 'was laid out on a sacred geometry. Did you know that?'

I indicated that I didn't.

'Yes,' he went on. 'The Abbey represents Heaven. The grid pattern of the main streets and the medieval market-place represents man's domain. Where does this leave the last remaining section of the town? The section that is now the Cattle Market site? In medieval cosmology, what remains?'

I knew the answer, but for some reason I didn't want to tell him. So he told me.

'Hell!' he said. 'And that's where they're building Debenhams!'

Back at the Cattle Market, the knight has reached the part of the ceremony which is supposed to trigger the curse. He raises his eyes to the moon and bellows two words.

'Debenhams PLC!'

He enunciates it slowly. Contrasting so sharply with the faux ancient language of the rest of the ceremony, this raises a stifled giggle from a couple of spectators. The rest of the Knights are unfazed.

'Anathema! Anathema! Anathema!' they shout, in reply.

'The Miller Group!' intones the knight.

'Anathema! Anathema! Anathema!'

'Centros Miller!'

'Anathema! Anathema! Anathema!'

'We declare those who despoil St Edmund's town will themselves be despoiled!'

And it is done. The curse hangs in the air. The knights turn around, slowly, and begin to make their way back to the cathedral. Something odd hangs above us. The whole evening has teetered painfully on the edge of absurdity, and yet there is something uneasy going on too. Some feeling in the winter air. Something slightly... strange.

When I get back home, I develop the photos I have taken of the ceremony. Almost every one of them is shrouded in a weird, ghostly, white mist which I can't explain. In some of them, the mist seems to twist itself into strange, shadowy forms. They almost look like...

No. That would be stupid.

Hackney, East London
January 2006

'How do I *feel*?' Tony Platia shrugs his shoulders in a very Sicilian way. 'How d'you *think* I feel? I tell you, I'm sick of talkin' about it. Look at what they done to my place. Thirty-one years of my life I put into this and they leave me with nothin' to show for it.' He touches my elbow and gestures at the street outside, unseen beyond the impromptu barricades that shore up what's left of Francesca's Café.

'This used to be a lovely community,' he says intensely. 'When I come here it was old East End, real rag trade. Now it's all money. It's all being killed, all the ordinary people pushed out. They don't care whose lives they ruin, these people. They don't fuckin' care. You look around you – see what they're doin'. It's fuckin' obvious, innit? They

take from the poor and they give to the rich. Look around you.'
Another elbow touch, another shrug, a bleak look.

'Breaks my heart,' he says.

Tony Platia is a sharply dressed, sharply spoken Sicilian. Thirty-one
years ago he opened Francesca's Café here in Broadway Market,
Hackney. It was a traditional London Italian caff: cappuccinos, pasta,
loyal customers and Tony, behind the counter, every day, making a
living.

It's just gone 7 a.m. on a freezing, dark January morning, but
Francesca's no longer serves breakfasts or early morning coffee.
Targeted by developers, it is under threat of eviction, to be replaced
by luxury flats and a new theatre. The bailiffs could be here at any
moment. This could be Tony's last stand.

Three decades ago, much of Hackney was run down, shabby,
boarded up. Today the artists, media types and city workers who have
been flooding into nearby Hoxton and Shoreditch have discovered
Broadway Market. These days the streets are lined with over-large,
showy baby buggies, silver BMWs and Italian scooters. Every
Saturday, Broadway Market is home to up-market stalls where you
can buy loaves of artisanal bread for £2.75, or stock up on porcini
mushrooms and alpaca scarves. Hackney is officially happening.

In theory, this influx of new people and new money ought to
mean more trade for local businesses like Tony's. It ought to mean
'regeneration'. Everybody, so the theory goes, should be a winner. But
it hasn't quite worked out that way. Instead, an unholy alliance of
hawk-eyed property developers and a rapacious local council has
launched a land grab which is ripping the heart out of the neighbourhood and impoverishing its local people.

Years of corruption and incompetence have left Hackney council
in debt – a staggering £72 million of it, as auditors discovered in
2001. Mandated by the government to sort it out, and quickly, one
of the council's solutions was to sell off its commercial properties;

properties like Tony's café and dozens of other independent businesses in Broadway Market. When Tony heard this he prepared to make
an offer for Francesca's himself; the council had assured leaseholders
that, if they could meet the guide price for the properties, they would
have first refusal on them.

But Tony had competition. A Kent-based millionaire property
developer named Roger Wratten, who had recently snapped up the
properties on either side of Tony's place, had his eye on Francesca's.
An unidentified 'someone' informed him that Tony was trying to buy
it and, from that point on, all Tony's attempts to do so were thwarted
– paperwork was lost, phone calls went unreturned. For three years,
Tony struggled for the simple right to buy his own business. But in
February 2003 it was sold, at auction, to Roger Wratten.

Cock-up? Coincidence? Wratten and the council say so – but Tony
and his supporters say otherwise. They see a conspiracy of council and
developers, aimed at clearing out the small, less-profitable local businesses, and replacing them with new, up-market developments that
will bring in a lot more cash. Developments like the one that Roger
Wratten wants to build on the site of Francesca's and the adjoining
properties – a combination of luxury flats and a new theatre, in which
his theatre-director wife can bring Shakespeare to the masses.

There is certainly something convenient about the speed and
apparent ease with which whole blocks of properties in Broadway
Market and the surrounding area are being sold to wealthy developers, none of whom are from the local area – and many of whom
bought them at knock-down prices, often lower than the leaseholders
were prepared to pay for them.

A company registered at a PO Box in Nassau bought a whole row
of shops for less than their leaseholders would have paid. Another
registered in Dubai did the same. A Russian property company now
owns nine properties in Broadway Market; it bought them for
£250,000, though they had an estimated value of almost £5 million.
Roger Wratten's Kent-based business owns several more.

Start to look at this from a distance and it looks uncomfortably like the neighbourhood is being socially engineered: cleansed of undesirables; made comfortable for people in designer shirts who don't like getting their shoes dirty and who get suspicious if a cup of coffee costs less than two quid.

In financial terms, this certainly makes sense; property prices in east London are shooting up, as the cappuccino colonisation continues. Now, too, there is the added impetus of the 2012 Olympic Games, which are to take place less than a mile from Broadway Market, and which are adding fuel to the fire of breakneck and often careless 'regeneration'.

Francesca's, then, is the latest victim of a process of rocketing gentrification across the old East End. Unfortunately for the developers and the council, Tony is not prepared to roll over. Tony is going to do down fighting, and he wants everyone to know it.

He is not alone. A substantial proportion of the local community – recently arrived yuppies included, as it happens – wants Tony and his café to remain. A petition has gathered thousands of signatures. What began as a local campaign to save Francesca's and other properties along Broadway Market threatened with the same fate has spiralled into something of a movement, in which Tony and the other threatened local businesses have become a symbol of resistance to the changes going on across the area. Articles about Tony's stand have popped up everywhere from the *Guardian* to *Der Spiegel*.

Not that any of this has really helped. The eviction orders are still extant, and the bailiffs are still primed. This morning, with rumours flying of imminent eviction, Francesca's is shuttered, shored and occupied. Inside, the café is a dark swirl of conversation, rumour, anger and cigarette smoke. There are no windows: they were broken by petrol-bombers, then boarded up. A man sits in the corner tapping away on a shabby laptop. Two ratty gas fires provide what warmth there is, and two bare bulbs what light.

Around one of the fires, in the centre of the front room, huddles a multicultural tableau that would gladden the heart of any Hoxton liberal. Here's Tony, his black cashmere coat still buttoned, his shoes still shiny, talking and swearing and generally acting like he's on the set of an early Coppola. Here's Elijah, a great black bear of a man, an artist who says that Tony and Francesca's saved his life when things were at their bleakest. Here's Arthur, a thin, harassed East Ender, the mastermind behind this campaign, smoking and sweating off a dose of the flu. And here's Betty, seventy-six years old, a former mayor of Hackney who's here to show her dislike of the current regime and her support for the locals.

The conversation is a mixture of lamentation and anger, but what strikes me most is the real, unforced, community spirit. You hear a lot about 'community' these days, often from people who don't quite know what it means but wish they did, and feel they are missing something. Here it seems to be a fact of life.

Elijah buttonholes me whenever he can, telling me how 'my man Tony got me through it', how he's standing by the Sicilian now that he's in need. Betty talks of the importance of fighting back. 'I'm sick of being pushed around,' she says. 'You're never too old to stand up for yourself.' She says how nice it is to live in a mixed community, and to see all the 'coloured people' side by side with old East Enders like her, and the phrase, which would cause a sharp intake of breath at a Notting Hill dinner party, raises not an eyebrow from Elijah, who's as coloured as they come and perhaps thinks that deeds matter more than words.

And Arthur, drinking tea and smoking cigarettes to fend off the freezing chill outside, mildly explains the politics that have put poor, bemused, pissed-off Tony at the front line of a development war.

'I can understand the council's position,' says Arthur. 'If they give in on Tony's they will lose millions, the developer who bought it will be furious and it will set a precedent. The council like to say things are out of their hands. The developer claims he's putting something back into the local community. But we've shown him what community really is.'

Elijah interrupts. 'He doesn't care about the community!' he says, scornfully, of the developer. 'He's a corporate guy. People would come to Tony with their problems, and he'd always have a solution, y' know? He was like a community leader. He helped me through the hardest time of my life. This is nothing to do with community – it's all about money. They didn't reckon on us standing up to them, that's all. We don't like bullies.'

'And they are bullies,' says Arthur. 'They think they can turf people out of their homes and their businesses. The council talks about "regeneration" and "best value". They use all the right words. But they've been caught out, and they're in a real fix.' He stubs his cigarette out in an overflowing ashtray.

'The trouble with us is that we won't go quietly,' he says. 'They don't like that.'

Bury and Broadway have very little in common, and yet the enemy they face is a common one. It's one they share with most communities in what was once, a very long time ago, sneeringly referred to as this 'nation of shopkeepers'. If ever that description were true it is far from it now, for one of the characteristics of the last two decades has been a virtual holocaust of small, independent and local retailers.

If you would see its monument, look around you. Wherever you are, there'll be the kind of evidence you can see, touch, experience for yourself. Boarded-up shops. Rows of chain stores. Queues of cars outside the edge-of-town mall. And if that's not enough for you, there are always the statistics.

The UK has lost nearly 30,000 independent food, beverage and tobacco retailers over the past decade.[3] 8,600 independent grocery stores closed between 2000 and 2005 (nationally, that's a 25 per cent decline in just five years) and 3,700 post offices between 1999 and 2004 (a 21 per cent decline, with much more to come soon).

A stunning 13,000 independent newsagents closed in just nine years between 1995 and 2004. Fifty specialist shops (butchers, bakers, candlestick makers, etc.) closed every *week* between 1997 and 2002.[4]

A quarter of all the country's bank branches disappeared in the ten years between 1990 and 2000.[5] The number of second-hand bookshops halved from 1200 to 600 in the three years between 2002 and 2005.[6] Meanwhile, the number of out-of-town shopping areas increased four-fold between 1986 and 1997,[7] and large town centre chain 'malls' have proliferated in the last half-decade.

It's hard to read such numbers without experiencing a surge of both surprise and anger. Surprise at what is being permanently lost and at the speed of its loss. Anger that it is allowed to happen There are two, interlinked reasons why it does happen, and why nobody in authority is willing to stop it. The first, and most obvious, is the enormous and growing power of big national and global chain stores, from Tesco to Next, Asda to Top Shop, Starbucks to The Gap. The second is enthusiastic government encouragement of their activities.

The mega-stores that now dominate England – which in many cases were single shops or small local chains just a few decades ago – are now multinational behemoths, able to influence and shape the policies and actions of governments, global regulatory bodies like the World Trade Organization and – very easily, in comparison – local councils like that of Bury and Hackney.

The power and influence of these ubiquitous chain retailers has grown apace in a very short time. Four decades ago, Wal-Mart was a small clutch of grocery stores in Arkansas and Kansas. Today it has 6,500 stores worldwide (a new one opens somewhere in the world every three days), including over three hundred ASDA outlets in the UK. Tesco has grown from one tiny shop in 1919 to control a third of the country's entire grocery market. Starbucks only turned up here ten years ago, but it already has almost five hundred outlets, and London has more of them than New York. (Its well-attested policy of 'clustering' its stores close together, the more effectively to wipe out local competition, may have helped.) There are plenty of other equally large and powerful, if less attention-seeking, examples.

But the mega-retailers have not grown this big and powerful by accident. They have been assisted by government, both by accident and by design. Over the last two decades, governments of both major parties, taking their lead from the United States on this as on so many other things, have positively begged the global chains to work their magic over here. To encourage them, they have reworked planning, regulatory and other laws, to help the big and hinder the small.

This is the terrible irony of the situation. The rise of the mega-stores, and the consequent hollowing out of local economies all over the country, has been done in the name of 'competitiveness'. The common riposte to criticism of supermarket power is that supermarkets are only powerful because people shop in them, and that people only shop in them because they provide a better (which usually means cheaper) service than their local competitors. It would be dishonest to deny that there is a real measure of truth in this. But it would be dishonest, too, to pretend that the mega-stores and the independents are competing on anything like the 'level playing field' of which we hear so much. In reality, the system is weighted heavily against the little guys.

This bias can be found at the highest level. Internationally, for example, the World Trade Organization, which sets the rules for international trade, bans national and local government in the UK from giving any preference to goods produced in this country, or the producers of them. At Continental level, the rules of the European Union prevent local authorities from applying 'territorial discrimination' (i.e., favouring the local) in their purchasing policies.[8] Local authorities are also powerless to promote or protect independent businesses.

Then there is the currently buoyant property market, which has pushed many small shops, pubs and other independent retailers over the edge, and in which the government stubbornly refuses to intervene. Rising land and property prices mean rising rents for those who don't own their properties, and rising rents can be the end of them. A superstore or a global chain has no problem meeting rapid and large rent rises, but for a small local shop it can be a death knell.

Where I live, in Oxford, the local papers are currently full of stories with headlines like 'Store Wars', about an alliance of local shopkeepers trying to save their businesses from huge rent rises, some of them over 50 per cent. Record shops, jewellery-makers, clothes shops, cafés, grocers and newsagents have been suddenly burdened with bills, sometimes in the tens of thousands, courtesy of both private landlords and the city council. Similar examples can be found all over the country, especially in the south-east where the property market is booming insanely, putting the ownership of both homes and shops out of the reach of all but the wealthy.

This is bolstered by the fact that the retail market is highly concentrated, with a relatively small number of landlords owning properties in many locations, and typically insisting on lease agreements which include 'upward only' clauses – giving them the right to raise their rents, but immunity from having to lower than.[9]

Then there are the superstores, which have hollowed out high streets, killed off hundreds of small farms and carved a huge gash through the culture of small specialist shops, all with the blessing of the authorities. Having encouraged supermarkets to build out-of-town developments for over a decade – gutting hundreds of town centres in the process – the government finally made it harder for them to do this in the 1990s. Undeterred, the supermarkets decided to break back into the town centres, with their 'Metro', 'Express' and 'Local' stores, aiming quite deliberately, with the use of predatory pricing, below-cost selling and all the usual tricks, to destroy what local shops remained.[10]

And again, government did nothing. It did nothing because, although the supermarkets were approaching a monopoly of the grocery market in their out-of-town stores, town centres had been classified as an entirely separate market. This meant that the big supermarkets, having laid waste to the nation's high streets, now had every right to set up camp in the ruins and rake in the proceeds. Needing no encouragement, they are doing so with gusto, as local authorities look on, powerless to stop them.

These are just a few examples – there are many more – of the skewed framework within which local, independent shops operate in England. In effect, the game is weighted against them from the start. They are fighting giants with their hands tied behind their backs, while the referee insists that all the rules are being upheld. A combination of corporate power and corporate government has allowed our small and independent retailers to be destroyed, at an unprecedented rate.

This matters because small, local, independently run shops are a key part of the fabric of our urban landscapes. Whether a high street is a patchwork of independent businesses or a dreary mess of corporate pottage has an impact on the kind of country we live in. It makes a difference to the character of neighbourhoods, the quality of jobs, the diversity and quality of products. It makes a difference to the kind of country we end up living in.

For a long time, people who said this sort of thing were patted metaphorically on the head and smiled at indulgently. In the last few years, though, some kind of tipping point seems to have been reached. All over the place, these days, you can hear rumbling. Sometimes it manifests itself in café occupations or torchlit curses, but more often it can be detected in a growing undercurrent of discontent on the letters pages of local papers, in the community centre or in the local council chambers.

It seems that people do not like the individuality and character of their towns being taken away. They do not like seeing independent traders go to the wall, replaced by yet another corporate coffee shop or sandwich bar selling chargrilled paninis. And perhaps they don't like admitting, either, that their shopping habits might have something to do with the change.

In 2004, the think tank the New Economics Foundation (NEF) issued a report claiming that the rapid collapse of independent retailers, and the onward march of the chains, was creating 'clone towns'.[11] The phrase caught something in the public imagination. Travelling through England I've heard it used many times, unprompted, from people all over the country. It was as if people had been aware of the problem for years, but hadn't known whether, or how, to mention it. Now it was suddenly everywhere. The media was full of it. The homogenisation of the high street, the death of local character and independence and everything that came with it were suddenly acceptable topics of conversation.

On the surface this was a debate about the state of the shops on the main streets of our towns. But it was also, quite obviously, about other things. It was about identity and reality; about belonging and corporate power and local control and who is in charge; about a sense of place and what constitutes it. It was about the direction in which we are travelling, whether we have got it right, and why so many people feel so clearly uncomfortable about seeing their landscapes bled white in the name of economic growth.

A year later, in 2005, impetus was added to what seemed to be becoming a growing campaign against clone towns when NEF released the results of a survey it had carried out of 130 towns across the nation.[12] Based on the proportion of local, national or global stores on each high streets, NEF divided the towns into three groups: 'clone towns' (individuality and independence of shops largely replaced by corporate chains); 'home towns' (high street which is dominated by local retailers, and is thus unique, recognisable and locally distinctive) and 'border towns', which teeter on the brink between the two.

Overall, stated the report, 41 per cent of surveyed towns (including Bury St Edmunds) were clone towns, and a further 26 per cent (including Oxford) were border towns. 34 per cent remained 'home towns', but unless action was taken nationally and locally, it was clear which direction things would continue to move. Something, in other words, needed to change.

I'm sitting in a Little Chef outside Bedford. It's a sunny day, struggling into spring, and I'm making my way in a rented car towards the Norfolk coast. I've been stuck behind a Tesco lorry for half an hour, trundling along at forty. The irony is not lost on me.

I'm gulping tea from a big white mug, looking out of the window at the grime-smeared lorries in the car park and thinking how great Little Chefs are. They've hardly changed at all since I was ten, when a gammon steak seemed hopelessly exotic and the prospect of a free lolly on the way out was worth eating up every last overcooked bean for. These days, their menus are a bit more jazzy – vegetarian sausages and chargrilled mushroom salad sit like impostors amid the black puddings and fried bread – but it's a mostly cosmetic tipping of the fat chef's hat towards contemporary England. Everything else remains the same, right down to the ashtrays.[13]

The landscape outside, beyond the lorries, is a palimpsest. The roads are still edged with ancient trees and tall, twisting hedgerows – not managed now, but hacked into splinters every few months by a man from the council with a tractor. The lanes still wind and creep over the hills, their brows crowned with inns or farmhouses.

But slapped on top of them, across them, beside them, among them, are the bypasses, the roundabouts, the neat lines of trees, the halogen street lights, the reflective road signs, and the huge white storage warehouses; hubs of an ever-expanding global economy, where those Tesco trucks pick up their loads. The old, pre-industrial landscape is still here. It is the solid base on which a more fragile present has been carelessly laid. I wonder which will last longest. I finish my tea.

Sheringham, Norfolk
March 2006

This is the second time that Ronald Wright has shown me his collection of nails. Ron, it seems, is proud of his nails.

'Look at this range,' he says. He indicates the back wall, which is lined with dozens of trays of nails, in every size, shape and quantity imaginable. He looks at me through his large, square, gold-rimmed glasses.

'You won't find this in B&Q,' he says. 'You won't find this range, and you won't find them sold individually either. No. In there it's all little plastic packets, and you get what you're given. Here, we give the customer what they want – one nail or one hundred. We've got them all, and we know what we're talking about. You don't see this anymore, do you? Well, you still see it here.'

We're in the back room of Ron's ironmonger's shop, which takes pride of place, by virtue of its longevity, in the thriving high street of Sheringham on the north Norfolk coast. Seventy-five-year-old Ron has worked here for sixty years, as his father and grandfather did before him, and as his two sons do now. Blythe and Wright, founded in 1897, is truly a family firm.

Out front it's a busy Saturday afternoon. The sun is shining, and the shop is full of men buying paintbrushes, wheelbarrows, drill bits and dowelling. Staff sweep past, talking about laminate and MDF, cutting keys, opening and closing drawers. Ron tells me to pour myself a cuppa from the huge brown teapot that sits on top of a filing cabinet. Small, white-haired and immaculately dressed in shirt and tie, brown shoes and a blue Blythe and Wright overcoat, Ron is proud of what he has built up. It makes a good living for himself and his family, and it is part of the town's social fabric. It stands for something.

'We're one of the last ironmongers in England,' he says. 'One of the last real ones.'

'Ironmongers' seems a bit of a misnomer to me. Blythe and Wright seems to sell everything – or everything that a hardware enthusiast, DIY-er or gardener could possibly want. Personal service, says Ron, is their speciality. It could be said to be Sheringham's speciality too. For this small town, huddled on the flat, East Anglian coast, is one of the last in England without a giant supermarket. As a result, it has a thriving mass of individual, independent local shops, and retains the sense of place, dignity, independence of labour and individuality of outlook that has been cloned out of most other towns in England.

Naturally, then, it seems the ideal place for a vast new Tesco.

Tesco. The name that sends a shudder down the spines of small shopkeepers and independent businesspeople from Truro to Carlisle has for the past few years been haunting the dreams of the people of Sheringham. The nation's fastest-growing and most successful super-store has already captured over 30 per cent of the grocery market[14] and is almost twice as big as its nearest rival, Sainsbury's. One in every three pounds spent on groceries in England is spent in Tesco,[15] and the company is expanding rapidly abroad: it now has branches in China, Korea, Poland, Hungary, Thailand, Slovakia, Turkey, Taiwan, and, most recently and ambitiously, the USA.

But this, apparently, is not enough. No corner of the market must be allowed to go untapped, for this would be a tragic waste of growth potential. Almost a decade ago, the company identified Sheringham, with its rich local economy and lack of other large competitors, as prime territory. For seven years it engaged in secret negotiations with town, district and county councils, to ensure that it got exactly what it wanted. In cahoots with local councillors, the company redrew the map of Sheringham to accommodate its plans. Only after it had got what it wanted from the council did the company apply for planning permission. And only after that did the people of Sheringham find out what was about to hit them.

When they did find out, there was consternation. To the horror of local shopkeepers, many local residents and plenty of the tourists who flock to this little seaside town every summer, it was revealed that part of the historic town centre was to be demolished for the benefit of the country's biggest grocery chain. Sheringham's fire station and community centre, an old people's home and a row of historic Norfolk flint cottages were to make way for a town centre superstore serving 38,000 people – in a town whose population numbers less than eight thousand. The intention was clear: Tesco planned to hoover up the grocery trade not just in Sheringham itself but in the whole of north Norfolk.

What this would mean for the rich diversity of Sheringham's high street is clear to those whose living depends on it. People like Ronald Wright, who can talk for hours about the good old days, when 'towns looked after themselves', before the mega-stores arrived. 'Ah,' he'll say, with regret in his voice as he leans on the filing cabinet out back, clutching a tea mug with 'Ron' printed on it in big red letters, 'but they don't really care about people like us, do they? Not the big boys. We can all go the wall and they won't even notice. They're not here for the people of this town. They're here for themselves.'

Ron can talk for hours about his town, too, and he will. It's worth listening to, because his words convey a sense of another time and place, when retailing was not just about turnover, share prices and year-end profits, but was part of the fabric of a town.

'Sheringham may be a small town, but it's a special one,' he says. 'Did you know that we're the only town of six or seven thousand people in England that doesn't straddle a main road? Sheringham wasn't developed, you see. It evolved. We're a bit unique, and being unique, we don't want it spoilt by Tesco.' He steps back a couple of paces to allow one of his two sons past with a bit of plywood.

'It's old family firms like this that built England,' he says. 'They forget that.'

*

Maybe Mike Crowe's shop built England too. If so, it must have built one of its odder bits. A few doors down from Blythe and Wright, Crowe's of Sheringham is a chaos of random items. It has a musty smell which I remember from some unidentified part of my childhood. Cluttered, cold and utterly fascinating, Crowe's sells everything you never knew you wanted. Brass pokers and pans hang from the ceiling. A rack of swords sits above the counter, over a handwritten sign that tells you that you can't have one unless you're over eighteen. Glass cases are stuffed with plaster ducks, old kettles, brooches, lamps, bells, old photos and bedpans. Little rooms off the back have their floors strewn with baskets full of golf balls, old cassette-players, bags of marbles, coal-scuttles, old postcards and signs that say things like 'Hands off the barmaid'.

Mike Crowe has piercing blue eyes and a face reddened by the sea wind. He was born in Sheringham over sixty years ago, and has run this shop for thirty of them. He is also chairman of Sheringham Regeneration, a local group dedicated to improving quality of life in the town. The ironic thing, he says, is that the people of Sheringham would actually like a new food shop. They can see a need for one – but not this one.

'I think the problem with these big stores is that they're not really interested in the individual, or in anything different,' he says, leaning on the scuffed wooden shop counter, underneath the swords and in front of the shop's only heater. 'If Tesco came to Sheringham and said to us "What do you want?" I think the town would be almost unanimous. Ask anyone, and we'll all say that the town needs a medium-sized food store. We've got tiny food shops here and nothing more. But Tesco won't supply a medium-sized food store because it doesn't fit in with what they do. There's no profits there. They want a big food store, with all the extras.'

We're interrupted by a woman who has been mooching around in the buckets and cabinets for the last five minutes.

'Do you sell fire grates?' she says to Mike.

'No,' he says, slowly. 'Try next door.'

'I already have.'

'Sorry,' says Mike, and smiles. He turns back to me.

'The problem,' he says, 'and it's not just with Tesco, is that the big boys will always do what is good for them. I suppose that's a problem with society as a whole. It's that classic thing, isn't it – the big guy trampling all over the little man.'

The shop is filling up with people now, browsing, wandering, poking about. I wonder how Mike deters shoplifters. How would he know if someone had nicked a golf ball?

'If you walk down Sheringam's streets,' Mike is saying, 'you can still see all the individual shops. Shops run by people who own the business. And there used to be more. Just down the high street, by the town clock, there was a most magnificent gent's outfitters. It'd been there a hundred-and-something years. The Hunt family had run it for years. They decided that they'd finish last year. Peter was getting on and his son didn't want to take on the business, so they offered it for sale. No one wanted it, so in walks Betfred – you know, the chain of bookies. And what does he do, he rips out all the beautiful facia and the Italian marble and sticks his plastic blue and gold frontage in.' He sighs.

'I can tell you,' he continues, very much warmed to his theme, 'that a lot of the holidaymakers who come here will say that they come here because of all the little shops, and the character they give to the place. People in this town have a very strong sense of place and identity. Some of them, to be honest, take it to the extreme, and say that what we have is what we want and they don't want any form of progress at all. But the real question for me is who *controls* the progress. It's about what we are, and what we want to be. An individual town, or just like everywhere else? An individual life, or a life controlled by someone else?'

Sheringham is certainly picturesque. Its buildings are mostly brick and Norfolk flint, its roads are narrow and the town is bound at one end by the arm of the sea wall, sweeping low between the sea and the shore. I have some time on my hands. Time to wander and take in the ambience of the town. Time, too, to conduct my own deeply unscientific clone town survey.

I get out my notebook and pen and walk the three main shopping streets, counting the numbers of shops and businesses that are independent and the number that are chains. As I do so, two things become apparent. First, the sheer variety of shops. This place has over forty different types of shop, ranging from jewellers to cobblers via pet shops, hairdressers, bookshops and chemists. Secondly, the local far outweighs the national or global. By my reckoning, Sheringham is home to ninety-five independent local shops, cafés, pubs and restaurants. Chains, either national or global, have just eighteen outlets, and six of these are banks.

When the New Economics Foundation surveyed the nation's town centres for the *Clone Town* report, it used a simple methodology to calculate whether somewhere was a clone, a home or a border town. You note down all the shops on the high street, up to a maximum of fifty, excluding things like banks, post offices, doctors' surgeries and job centres. Each type of shop gets five points. Each independent shop gets an additional fifty points. Each chain store gets another five points. You add up this total, then divide it by the total number of shops you surveyed.

This will give you a figure somewhere between one and sixty, and it's this figure that determines where you are on the clone scale. Between one and twenty-five and you're a clone town. Between twenty-five and thirty-five and you're a border town. Between thirty-five and sixty and you're a home town. I haven't quite followed all the rules here: I looked at way over fifty shops, in three streets rather than one, but the basic methodology is the same.

Do the maths for Sheringham, and the score you come up with is 46.9. Drop this into the 130 listed in NEF's final report, and it comes out a remarkable second – pipped at the post, just, by Hebden Bridge in Yorkshire, with 48.6.[16] Assuming I have done my sums correctly, this makes Sheringham one of the least cloned, and most individual, towns in the whole of England.

It's quite a result. If you want to know the reason for it, just ask Reg Grimes. Reg will tell you in no uncertain terms that the lack of a superstore and this thriving local economy go hand in hand – and that he intends to keep it that way.

People like Ron and Mike will tell you that Reg is a one-man crusade against the destruction of Sheringham by Tesco, or any other monster retailer that dares to try and get its grubby hands on his town. Reg is chairman of the Sheringham Preservation Society, but he is also the founder of the intricately named SCAMROD – the Sheringham Campaign Against Major Retail Overdevelopment – which has spearheaded the town's resistance to Tesco. It takes a while to find Reg. He seems to be in demand. Eventually I locate him in the town's old boatshed, which is in the midst of being converted into a gallery to display shell art. Reg has big, grey bushy eyebrows, tinted glasses and a grainy Norfolk accent. He sits on a paint-stained wooden chair surrounded by empty glass display cases and spirit levels, and fills me in on the details of Sheringham's fight.

'Their policy,' he says of Tesco, 'is to take as much trade from the rest of the town as they possibly can. Wherever they've set up store, they've come out with the same old rubbish every time: "This will encourage more people into the town." Utter rubbish. People go there with their cars, there's a two-hour restriction on their car parks, people go in, buy their food, get in their car and go home. You look at what happened down the road in Stalham, when Tesco opened a year or two ago. Used to be a thriving little place. Walk down the high streets now and it's a ghost town. Tesco have forty-four stores in Norfolk already. Look at a map of the county and you'll see this is the last "catchment" of potential customers that they haven't got. The actual population here is tiny – maybe four thousand households. They want 38,000 customers. What they're looking at is bringing in people from surrounding areas, in their cars. They want to fill their map in.'

As Reg and SCAMROD began looking at the Tesco plan, they began to uncover more and more things that made them uncomfortable. They discovered that the council, which had just spent £2.5 million of public money refurbishing a block of council flats, now proposed to allow Tesco to demolish them to make way for its new store. They discovered that towns of similar size all over Norfolk and elsewhere had seen a rapid collapse in their local business base after Tesco arrived. They discovered that the flint cottages to be demolished were to be replaced by new flats on the town's allotments, with an access road across common land.

They discovered, too, that the district council, charged with representing the interests of its people, believed that it had no chance of doing so. 'They are too big and powerful for us,' said the leader of the council at the time. 'If we try and deny them they will appeal and we cannot afford to fight a planning appeal and lose. If they got costs it would bankrupt us.'[17]

And so, apparently believing that they had no choice, the council's planning committee voted to approve Tesco's application in 2004. But they hadn't banked on SCAMROD. Reg and the gang swung into action, organising a petition, filing objections at every possible point, and working to convince councillors, the local media and the town as a whole that Tesco would be a disaster for Sheringham. Their battle made the national press.

While Tesco jumped through hoops and battled increasingly vociferous local opinion, government planning guidance on superstores changed, and doubts grew among local authorities about the wisdom of their decision to give Tesco the go-ahead. Eventually the district council caved in and commissioned an independent report on the Tesco proposal. The report's conclusion was unequivocal: the Tesco plan was bad for Sheringham – the least justified of the four major supermarket applications currently under consideration in the surrounding district. It recommended that such big stores should stick to bigger towns.

The report buoyed up SCAMROD and forced a rethink in the district council. Despite frantic lobbying, the tide seemed to have turned against Tesco. In 2005, the council's planning committee, which had approved the superstore application two years before, rejected it by twenty votes to nil. Reg, Ron, Mike and hundreds of other local people celebrated openly. After years of work, they had won: David had taken down Goliath.

And then it all went wrong.

Less than six months later, to the total astonishment of everyone, the same councillors met again and voted, again, on the same application. This time, they voted to allow the superstore to go ahead. When asked why, they refused to explain.

Eventually, the truth came out. The councillors, when they voted to turn down Tesco's application, had voted at the same time to explore the possibility of selling a smaller plot of council land to a smaller company – Budgens was mentioned – for a smaller supermarket: the sort of shop that Mike, Reg, Ron and the rest say they want. Then they discovered a legal document they had not been aware of. It turned out that, in 2003, a previous council had signed a secret deal with Tesco, banning it, and its successors, from allowing any rival supermarket to operate on its land if Tesco's offer was turned down. The deal included a confidentiality clause, which banned councillors from actually telling their constituents about any of it.[18]

To this day, North Norfolk District Council will not talk about this. And even without such a deal, they have made it clear that they could not afford the cost of any appeal by Tesco against the rejection of its application, which could cost anything up to £1 million in court.

And so it seems that Tesco will be coming to Sheringham after all. Despite the unanimous objections of the council, despite the majority opinion of local people, despite the popular campaign against it, the company's map of north Norfolk will finally be filled in, and there will be nothing anyone can do about it. That, it seems, is free and fair competition. That, it seems, is democracy.

Westminster, London
March 2006

I'm sitting in the lobby of the Palace of Westminster, on a green leather bench, fiddling with my tape-recorder and marvelling at Pugin's fantastically overblown gold Gothic ceiling. To my right is the House of Lords and to my left the House of Commons. It seems a reasonable place to ask some questions about democracy.

After five minutes of waiting my name is announced over a loud-speaker and I approach the reception desk, whose attendants wear tailcoats and white bow-ties. Standing next to the desk is Jim Dowd MP: silver-haired, self-contained, scribbling something in a pocket diary. He looks up as I approach him and shakes my hand, briskly. 'Sorry I'm late,' he says.

Together we head down a panelled corridor, in search of refreshments. 'Tea? Coffee?' says Jim. 'Beer…?' We're passing a door marked 'Strangers' Bar'.

'Beer,' I say.

It's a small bar, dominated by a view of the Thames, and by men in suits with redder faces than might be expected from elected representatives at 2.15 on a weekday afternoon. Jim orders a lager and buys me a subsidised bitter. We find a small table. Jim sits down and looks up at a TV screen, which has the words 'Identity Cards Bill. Motions to disagree and amendments in lieu' emblazoned on it.

'I may have to leave in fifteen minutes,' he says. 'There's going to be a vote. But let's talk.'

Jim Dowd is a bluff, Labour bloke. If I were looking for an appropriate cliché to describe him, I would probably alight on 'no nonsense'. He is MP for Lewisham West, but this is not why I'm here. I'm here because Jim is also chairman of the All-Party Parliamentary Small Shops Group, a group of MPs concerned about precisely the kind of thing that is happening in Bury, Hackney and Sheringham. The group has just issued a report, entitled *High Street Britain: 2015*, which contains dire warnings of further decline in local shops, and consequently in local character, if something is not done soon.

The report is the result of months of work, during which the group heard evidence from a diverse array of witnesses, from the Association of Convenience Stores to Friends of the Earth, Sainsbury's to Which?, and the Institute of Directors to the Town and Country Planning Association. It is peppered with examples of big stores, especially supermarkets, using their power adversely, and in some cases illegally, to drive small shops out of business. It speculates that small shops across the country could be about to reach a 'tipping point' beyond which they are no longer able to function, and the already steep decline in their numbers becomes precipitous and final.

By 2015 the situation, according to the report, could look almost apocalyptic. Do nothing now and a virtual wipeout of small retailers will lead to a consolidation of the power of the big supermarkets and mega-stores. They will control so much of the market that the low prices they offer today, precisely in order to destroy smaller competition, will no longer be necessary. Much of the current network of wholesalers, suppliers, farmers and others who supply or rely on small shops will be gone or going fast. Elderly people, those without cars and those with little mobility or flexibility will suffer most as the little guys close and the big guys keep growing.

There will be a 'reduction in the overall employment levels' – big stores provide far fewer jobs overall than small ones – and the quality of employment will be worse. There will be 'reduced self-employment opportunities' especially in poor and minority communities.

'The vast array of skills demonstrated by specialist retailers will be lost.' 'Local economies will be severely damaged across the country.' 'The retail sector will be less innovative.' 'Access to affordable, healthy food will deteriorate.' 'Regular social contact will be lost for certain members of the community, thereby entrenching social exclusion.' 'The environment will suffer, in terms of increased food and air miles.'

This grim roll-call paints a vivid picture of the wider role of small shops in people's lives. Read it, and it becomes obvious that this is not just about fair competition or the price of bread. It's about a web of relationships between people and places, which is being rent by the careless power of big business:

> The biggest losers however, will be the consumers. Restricted choice of store brands, restricted choice of available products, restricted choice of shopping locations, higher prices and reduced customer service are all strong possibilities in 2015. Although some consumers today may be benefiting from a competitive market this is entirely unsustainable and cannot continue.
>
> People will not just be disadvantaged in their role as consumers but also as members of communities. The erosion of small shops is viewed as the erosion of the 'social glue' that binds communities together, entrenching social exclusion in the UK.[19]

In the bar, lager in hand, glancing up at the TV screen every couple of minutes, Jim Dowd explains why his team produced the report, and what he thinks it means.

'Supermarkets,' he says, 'have become a commercial black hole – nothing can survive around them. Big stores are getting so much bigger so much faster that the advantage that some of them have over small traders and their suppliers is just completely disproportionate. We're not calling for supermarkets to be banned, or abolished. That would be ridiculous. But, you know, you hear a lot about the benefits of competition, how it keeps prices down and all the rest of it – and much of it is true. But the big multiples have been allowed to slant the so-called playing field in their own favour.'

This is certainly true. In any case, I suggest, that tired old playing field metaphor is pretty much worthless anyway. What are the chances of the eleven-man after-work footie team from your local boozer coming off best against Chelsea, however flat the pitch is?

'That's true,' says Jim, 'and, of course, the big guys have a vested interest in trying to depress their market share figures. They get very twitchy when you say, you know, Tesco has got 30 per cent of the market. They go off and rejig the figures and say, "No, no, no, look it's only 18 per cent." But the level of public concern about the state of things – even among people who shop at the big supermarkets or the multiples – is very high now. This report took us two months longer, in the end, because of the sheer volume of evidence that we received. I think that in itself is indication of a widespread concern that so many people have.' He drains his pint, looks at his glass and then the TV and asks me if I want another one.

'Why not?' I say. I'm subsidising it, after all. It seems only sensible to get my money's worth. Jim returns to the table and sets the glasses down just as a clanging sound rings out across the river. It reminds me of school.

'Division bell,' says Jim. 'I've got to go and vote. I'll be back in five minutes. Don't go away.'

I don't go away. Fifteen minutes later, Jim's back. His pint is waiting. Whether it's the beer or the vote, he seems noticeably more relaxed. As he continues talking about superstore power it's clear he's feeling more relaxed too – and that whatever his public role as committee chair and representative of the people, he's got some personal views on the big stores which are perhaps not too far away from my own. He wants to see them reined in – but he's not sure that either government or people, whatever they might say or think they think, actually want that to happen.

'There's a degree of inertia in government, and there's also a degree of caution,' he says. 'These are very big and very powerful organisations, and even though they only account for a relatively small number of outlets, they have a financial and political clout out of all proportion. And they are very successful businesses – and the government likes successful businesses. They're hard to tackle. There's an example in the report of a Tesco store that was put up in Stockport. It was 20 per cent bigger than planning permission granted them. To which they said, "Oh, OK, we'll just put in retrospective planning permission for the extra 20 per cent." Which they got. That sort of thing is quite common. Tesco aren't the only ones who do this sort of thing, they're just the most aggressive – they've openly said that they will take any local authority which tackles them to court – but all the big chains are very hard to take on.'

Meanwhile, says Jim, whatever they might say, most people can't quite make their minds up either.

'There is a degree of public... well, schizophrenia is probably too strong a word,' he says, doubtfully. 'But you do surveys that ask "Do you appreciate your local shops? Are they important to your community?" and you get figures of 80 per cent plus. Then when you ask "Do you use them?" the figures plummet. No business can survive on goodwill. Part of it is a reflection on twenty-first-century life – it's convenience. When I was at school, most of us only had one parent working, the father. Which meant the mother had time to shop in all the little local shops. Things have changed hugely now.'

Two hours on and we're still in the bar, chewing over the issues. By this time there are four empty pint glasses on the table. This is what I call representation. And Jim's opening up – talking about how supermarkets condition people's behaviour, throwing out examples of their bullying, criticising the market fundamentalism of the government. He talks, too, about how high streets are dying out – not just through the dominance of superstores but through spiralling rents, the growth of car culture and the increasing prevalence of online shopping.

The obvious question to ask him is what can be done about it. Here, the report, and Jim, have a lot of suggestions. The question is whether any of them will ever make it past the suggestions stage.

'You'll hear from their defenders that the big stores' primary responsibility is to their shareholders,' he says. 'But that is not the only interest. There is a broader public interest and a broader degree of accountability. You'll also hear that "This is just the way the market works", people will vote with their feet, you can't put a cap on market share – all the rest of it. Well, the fact is that you can – you can do virtually whatever you like providing there's a majority in Parliament for it. The issue is, what effect is it going to have? Will it have the desired effect? Or will there be unintended consequences?'

Jim gives an intriguing example of how well-intentioned legislation can make things worse: the 1989 Beer Orders. Remember them? That sweeping legislation limited the number of pubs a brewer could own, in the interests of drinkers. The result was the rise of non-brewing PubCos, more concentration of ownership – and a bigger threat to pubs. It's worth remembering. Legislation to tame the big guys might look like a good idea, but when you're that big and that powerful, you'll get around it if you can.

So what can we do? What does Jim think the future's going to be like? Is that 2015 vision going to come true? Behind the rhetoric and the politics, what does the real future look like?

Jim does a sort of sigh. He looks at the table top, which is pooled with glass-rings of beer.

'Let me tell you something that struck me at the launch of the report,' he says. 'We had various members of the group there. One was the MP for Inverness, and he said a few words. Then directly after him, we had the MP for St Ives, who represents Land's End, standing up to speak. In other words, we had representation virtually from Lands End to John O' Groat's. Nothing could better illustrate what a national issue this is. And my approach was – well, OK, if this really *is* going to be the future, if it's all going to be run by Tesco and a few other big players, and if it's going to be to the public benefit that it should be so, and if there's really no way of stopping it… well, then let's at least understand that, and approach it with our eyes open. The worst of all worlds would be to stumble into it without realising the full implications.'

He finishes his last pint.

'Then,' he says, 'only when irreparable damage has been done to irreplaceable community assets, will people realise the true value of them. That's what really concerns me.'

Where, then, does this leave us? Where does it leave Alan and Reg, Tony and Ron, Tesco and Debenhams? Where will we be in 2015? What sort of country are we going to end up with? What can we do to repulse the attack of the clones?

If it's policy solutions you're looking for, you're not short of them. Jim Dowd's report is a good place to start. Here you'll find all sorts of well thought-through recommendations: abolish upward-only rent reviews; establish a new retail regulator; implement a moratorium on further mergers and takeovers; change the tax system; empower local authorities to take stronger action on retail giants.[20] All or any of them would certainly help.

If you don't think that's tough enough, you could dip instead into the New Economics Foundation's recommendations in its *Clone Town Britain* report.[21] Here you can try using local planning powers to fight chain stores – and increasing those powers so that local authorities are allowed to set limits on the number of chains in their area (something they are presently banned from doing); give 'special and differential treatment' to local shops, on the grounds that they make a 'disproportionately positive contribution to the local economy'; bring in a mandatory code of conduct for supermarkets to replace the current, failing, voluntary one; limit the market share of leading supermarkets to 8 per cent and strengthen the hand of local communities via everything from community land trusts to local campaigns to preserve diversity and character.

Or, you could look further afield. A few years ago I visited the USA, where some excellent examples of local fightbacks were going on. In Colorado, California and Massachusetts, I met people who had successfully used local laws to force city-wide votes on limiting the number of chain stores and supermarkets; created new acts which gave local shops precisely the kind of hand-ups that NEF recommend; and set up local shopkeepers' alliances which had successfully repulsed the big boys.[22]

Meanwhile, the French have restrictions in place which prevent 'inappropriate use' of over half of Paris's 71,000 shops. This is part of a twenty-year plan to prevent the destruction of the city's heritage and character by clone stores and supermarkets. The name they use to describe this unwanted process should bring us up short: they call it 'la Londonisation.'[23]

But maybe that last example tells us something more intriguing. Policy suggestions are all very well, and undoubtedly very necessary, but isn't there a wider concern? Isn't there something about England that tolerates – no, embraces – the destruction of the small and local and the march of the vast and faceless? Something cultural; something in the national blood. We let it happen; we participate in it, even while we claim to dislike it.

As Jim Dowd pointed out, we don't have to do this. There's nothing magical or natural about 'the market' that requires us to. We can do things differently if we choose. We just have to make that choice. If we don't, then perhaps it's because we don't want to. Perhaps we are happy to blame the government and the chains – both of which deserve blame – and to leave ourselves conveniently out of the picture. There are, as we've seen, no shortage of solutions. They only become solutions, though, when we accept the existence of the problem; really accept it, in our deeds as well as our words. And they only start to work when, like a recovering alcoholic, we first acknowledge that problem, and then begin to walk towards the alternative – slowly, at first, but with determination.

When something is as delicate, as hard to define as the true role which independent shops play in our lives and our landscapes, it is easy to destroy it carelessly, and almost impossible to re-create it once it is gone. None of this is taken into account by the sort of people who make life or death decisions about them, or the people with enough power, financial or political or both, to wipe them out as a way of life. But all of it matters, every day, to many, many people.

I can remember this, dimly, myself. When I was young, my grand-parents owned a sweetshop in the Sussex village of Lingfield. Naturally this was absolutely the best thing that any child's grandpar-ents could be doing with their lives, especially when they let you pilfer from the sweet jars now and then, and occasionally pretend to serve customers.

I can probably remember the look, the layout, the smells and the atmosphere of this shop better than I can remember anything else from my childhood. It was a proper old sweetshop, with individual tubs of sweets spanning long shelves above the counter, and stacks of bottles of tooth-rotting, fluorescent fizzy pop next to the ice-cream freezer.

But what I can also remember was the customers. Not any of them individually (except the owner of the Chinese take-away next door and the fusty old man who ran the gents' outfitters over the road; for some reason, they stuck with me), but the way they used the place.

It didn't just sell sweets, you see: that was just my primary focus. It also sold crisps, cigarettes, maybe magazines. Enough to tempt adults in, and when they came in, they stayed. They talked, they gossiped. They shared stories, exchanged tips, offered and received help, extended invitations, did all the things that people do when they get together as equals. I was far more interested in the butterscotch and the barley sugars. But something else must have sunk in.

This is what makes local shops, cafés, pubs and other such gathering places the arbiters of place and community. Talk to any independent shop owner and they will tell you that they do a lot more than sell things to people. Chatting to customers. Keeping the elderly company. Giving credit where it's needed. Counselling people. Giving directions. Lending. Swapping. Being flexible, approachable, part of the community. Being human.

All of the things, in other words, that no corporate chain could ever do. Who stands chatting to the check-out workers in an out-of-town Tesco? Which B&Q outlet will give you a quid's credit on a bag of nails till next weekend? Which Virgin Megastore manager will lean on the counter and share his opinions about the latest releases by The Decemberists or Band of Horses? Which Starbucks employee will be there for Elijah when his days are darkest?

Use turnover, market share, expansion rates, shareholder value as your measurements – all of the things, in other words, that contribute to our childishly simple definition of 'economic growth' – and there's no doubt about it: things look great on our high streets. Bring on the chains, and let them raze all before them. Let us grow!

Use any of the more intangible measurements, though – judge these places on their ability to give us some of the things that make being human worthwhile, and make a place worth living in – and suddenly the picture looks very different. Perhaps it will always be hard to explain this to some people. But that just makes it all the more important.

5

Rural Rides

When the old farm-houses are down (and down they must
come in time) what a miserable thing the country shall be!
William Cobbett, *Rural Rides*, 1830

Upper Teesdale, County Durham
June 2006

There's a racing, battering wind roaring down the valley from
Cauldron Snout to Langdon Beck. Low grey clouds are carried by it.
It looks like rain. I don't care. I am exhilarated. I do up my boots,
strap on my pack and stride out through the hay meadows towards
the river.

I feel good. I feel smug. This is the way to do it. I could be sitting
at my desk Googling other people's research and passing it off as my
own, but instead I'm out here, roughed up and ready, doing it the
hard way; the real way. Walking the walk. I'm going to seek out the
fruits of this land's rough but real rural wisdom. I'm going to see the
farmer.

I'm on my way to Widdybank Farm, which sits on a bare Pennine
hillside a couple of miles up this bleak valley, where hawks circle and
the wild river Tees froths and foams across brown rock and brown
soil. I've been here before, a long time ago. When I was twelve, I

walked the Pennine Way with my father. It was a long, two-week trek across some of the toughest landscapes in England. Twenty-one years on, and it's interesting what stays with you. I still have a few memories of that fortnight which remain clear, almost fresh, even now. One of them is of Widdybank Farm.

It was a worn-down old place then; a classic Pennine hill-farm, with acres of sheep grazing the surrounding moors. The Pennine Way veers around Widdybank, but we detoured into the farmyard, pulled in by a hand-painted sign that advertised refreshments. I don't remember if the farmer was there, but I remember his wife, serving us drinks as I gleefully took the weight off my feet. I kept a diary on that walk, which I still have. It mostly seemed to concern itself with what I ate, allowing me to report two decades later that at Widdybank I had a cheese and onion sandwich, a glass of orange squash and a bowl of ice cream.

My writing was so focused on my stomach, in fact, that I failed completely to mention the puppies, which is odd because that's now what I remember best. About an hour before we got there, the sheep-dog had given birth. I remember being taken to see the newborns in the barn; their eyes still closed, their mother cautious, exhausted. I'd never seen newborn puppies before. It was great.

Maybe it was that which engraved Widdybank on some part of my mind. Maybe it was the name, which I still love: so distinctive, such a comical sound when spoken. Maybe it was the cheese and onion sandwich. Or maybe it was the place itself – so bleak yet so human, in the best and hardest sense. A mile from its nearest neighbour, itself a wild hill-farm, itself strung out on the marsh grass hills, tortured by the winds that howled down from the sinister uplands. I couldn't imagine living in a place like this. I thought it must be so exciting – so Other.

I don't quite know why I'm back. I just know that I want to find out more about farms; their place in the landscape and culture of England, their ongoing troubles, the life of the people who run them and what they make of the future. Widdybank, layered as it already is with personal meaning, seems a good place for me to start.

The meadows that lead up to the farm gates are empty but for me. There's yellow rattle and red clover in the grass, and curlews, lapwings and skylarks overhead. There is even, I notice when the river's rocky banks come into view, a lost, lone oystercatcher patrolling the shoreline.

It's 4.45 p.m. when I arrive in the farmyard. Stupid of me, really, to expect them still to be serving tea after two decades, but I was looking forward to it. But there's no farmer's wife here now. No farmer either. No tea, no puppies. What did I expect? I don't quite know – but not this.

There is nothing here at all. The barn is empty. The sheep pens are clogged with nettles. The farm's front door is closed and locked. It is also PVC; a door that could be in any suburb anywhere in the country. On the wall next to it is a small, oval plaque:

ENGLISH NATURE
Upper Teesdale National Nature Reserve
WIDDYBANK FARM
Reserve Base
Opened by Lord Barnard
12th June 1998

English Nature. Reserve Base. Lord Barnard. Widdybank is gone. It is no longer a farm. It's an office. Curious, nosy, dispirited, I peer through the windows. Desks. Mugs. Papers. A fan. On another outside wall is a big coloured signboard detailing all the 'nature' to be found in what is now a reserve: bird's eye primrose, northern marsh orchid, black grouse, redshank, mountain pansy.

In one window is a small plastic sign, propped up to lean on the glass where I can see it. Inside an aggressive red triangle are the words YOU ARE BEING WATCHED. I look around. I am. Up in one corner of the whitewashed former farmhouse is a CCTV camera.

I drop my rucksack to the ground, cross the ex-farmyard and lean on a metal gate. The wind is still rampaging down the valley. I look across at the fells and the clouds scudding low above them. I feel suddenly lonely. I wish I had brought somebody with me. There is silence, stillness – a lack of any reachable life. A curlew screams into the wind. Rain is coming. I am miserable.

Why? I'm supposed to be an environmentalist, and English Nature are supposed to be the good guys. They're here, according to the signboard, to study the effects of climate change on upland landscapes. It sounds like useful work. They are protecting rare ground-nesting birds. They are encouraging wildflowers, using 'traditional hay meadow management techniques'. They are planting native trees.

Presumably the old farmer couldn't make a living. He may be gone, but the valley – sorry, the Reserve – is in good hands. I am in favour of this sort of thing. I must be. So what's the problem?

Perhaps it's the artificiality of all this. 'Conservation' is always artificial – the very name implies stasis, something that nature abhors. This reserve base and the green signs that have been stuck up around the valley detailing what you can see and what it means – they are man-made intrusions into the landscape. They reduce its grandeur, its wildness. They tell you what to look for and at. They define what matters and what doesn't. They bring places like this one step closer to the urban world that I come to places like this to escape from.

But that's not the only reason. This landscape was man-made anyway – sheep farming is hardly natural. This valley has been man-made, or at least man-managed, for millennia. The difference is the way it is used. Hill-farming is ordinary folk making a hard living from a hard land. This is a government-funded bureaucracy doing good works for tourists and researchers. And while the works are good, something essential has been lost.

These people all go home at night. No one lives on or from this land any more. A whole land-based culture and knowledge grew up from these hill-farms; something entirely separate from the mindset that has now replaced it, a mindset instantly recognisable to anyone who works in an office or donates to a charity. New Widdybank is a distinctly urban intrusion, in philosophy if not in form.

So, out goes working the land – in comes 'conservation'. Out goes farming – in comes 'managing the environment'. Out goes any real, unsentimental, everyday link between people and place. In comes a government-mandated response to climate change. On the surface, it probably makes sense. Beneath, there's a sadness.

The South Hams, Devon
August 2006

To get to Ley Coombe Farm you make your way through a warren of ancient, winding, beautiful green lanes, walled up with high Devon hedges and overhung with trees. Grass grows up through the asphalt. The tree boles are huge and the sky barely visible between the canopied branches overhead. It's a hidden place. So well hidden, in fact, that I pass the farm's entrance twice before I finally see it.

Ley Coombe farmhouse is a square, grey stone building with yellow guttering, at the end of a branch-hung track. From inside a green-doored, slate-roofed barn comes the heavy shuffling and low grumbling of cows. Rooks cackle in the high branches of a group of impassive old trees behind the house. Three white doves sit on a worn stone trough, and two collies come bounding towards me, barking unconvincingly. This is an ancient place. Sometimes you can just feel it in the air and in the land.

Its owner now emerges from the cow shed and waves at me. An old man with fraying wisps of grey hair and a bow-legged walk, a thin coat covering a blue jumper with green elbow patches, a flat cap, hobnail boots. This is Philip Hoskins, who has farmed Ley Coombe's hundred acres all his life, as his parents did before him.

It's the end of the day. I'd been planning to meet Philip this morning, but he put me off because it was good weather and he wanted to get the hay in. Now he's running late, so I offer to take on the task of hefting bales from his tractor trailer into the barn, while he finishes feeding the cows. The collies get consistently and deliberately under my feet as I drag the bales down off the tractor and swing them though the old wooden doors onto the dusty floor. The rooks continue to swear at the approaching dusk.

Hay stacked, cows fed, Philip leads me into the farmhouse and into some other time. The wooden entrance hall is hung with stag antlers, hunting horns and raincoats. The whole house is whitewashed – no wallpaper here, no carpets. The walls are as thick as the great stones they were made from, the doors are white, wooden and heavy, the floors are flagstones. The sitting room contains large and solid sofas and armchairs. The kitchen is simple: the sink on blocks under the window, an old dresser, a thick, scarred table. There are cobwebs everywhere. Nothing twee, affected, 'rural'. An old house, from an old world.

Philip, in his faded slippers, takes his time making a pot of tea, then sits slowly down at the table with a bowl of stewed plums and some Madeira cake. He has a slow, thoughtful way of speaking; very Devon, a pleasure to listen to.

'I'm a traditional farmer,' he says. 'A small farmer. For a long time, people like me were very unfashionable. It has long been government policy to do away with us. They say we're not efficient, that we can't survive in this so-called global market. I think they don't understand why farms like this matter; what they give to the place. I think they have no idea, really.'

If you know Devon or Cornwall you'll have noticed the ancient fields with their old hedges or stone walls. You'll have noticed how small those fields are compared to, say, those of much of East Anglia or the central arable counties. You'll have noticed the tree-capped hills, the asymmetric pastures, the hollow green lanes, the deep, tangled spindle hedges, the mossy drystone walls, the solid old farmhouses; the combined beauty and utility of the landscape.

It's a landscape not quite matched by any other in England; a landscape that draws tourists in their tens of thousands. It's an ancient landscape, which has not changed in its particulars for thousands of years, and it has been created by farmers like Philip. Eighty per cent of west country farms, according to Philip, are under 180 acres in size. They have created the character and the culture of this region. Compare it to a Cambridgeshire prairie – those 'efficient', modern, market-competitive farms – then consider which you prefer and, perhaps, what efficiency means.

Philip Hoskins has been making the case for farms and farmers like this for years, convinced that their place and contribution has gone unappreciated for too long. In 1997 he got together with half a dozen others, all similarly frustrated by the lack of representation they received from big national farming bodies like the National Farmers' Union. Together, they set up the Small Farms Association (SFA) to represent their interests. Philip runs it still, from Ley Coombe, when he's not getting the hay in or feeding the cows.

'My parents were dairy farmers, just before the beginning of the last war,' says Philip, over the plums. 'We had the Milk Marketing Board then, and it was a good time to do it; a real step up on the ladder. I was dairy up until last year, but I'm just beef now. What's happening to dairy farmers was one of the reasons we started the SFA. It's just criminal, really. Small producers get paid less per litre than the big boys, and we're totally at the mercy of the supermarkets now. They sell milk at a loss. Who makes the loss? Us, not them. That's what's ruining the milk industry. They'll take ninety days to pay, and if they want to do a special promotion they'll say to the small producer, "Do you want to donate a couple of tons of produce for this? We're not paying you, though." All these promotions you see

– buy one, get one free – it's us producers taking the hit. And they have such clout you can't say no, unless you want to be de-listed. The supermarkets have made it clear that they don't want too many small producers anyway, because they don't like dealing with them.'

Talking to a farmer about supermarkets is guaranteed to raise the room temperature. They are one of the primary drivers of the decline in farming across England. But they're not the only one.

'It used to be said that a viable acreage for a farmer was 45 acres or more,' says Philip. 'These days, the NFU will say that if you haven't got 500 acres, forget it. The entire farming world has been colonised by agri-business over the last few decades. They treat farming like an industry – they even call it one. When the NFU started, fifty years ago, they represented the grass-roots farmers. Today they're dominated by agri-business. What happened was that as labourers disappeared from the farms, the smaller farmers couldn't get away to the meetings. The people who turned up were the big agri-businesses, the ones who had farm managers or could afford to hire contractors, and they pushed things in that direction. Now here we are. Government doesn't want us, the NFU doesn't want us.'

He scoops up the last of the plum juice with his spoon and turns his attention to the Madeira cake. I ask him why this all matters to him.

'I'm so passionate about this because I was seeing all these farmers like myself, producing good stuff, then going to market and seeing all these big guys with their cows blown out on chemicals pulling the wool over people's eyes.' He speaks slowly, evenly, whatever he's saying.

'People want good food,' he says, 'and we know how to produce it. It's just not right that we should go to the wall if we can do that. The big farmers want us out of the way, and so does the government. They say we can't compete with China, and they say we need to "diversify". You know, run a B&B, or get into horseyculture. But then you're taking away somebody else's living. Farmers can get grants now to convert their buildings for holiday cottages or whatever – so you end up undercutting people who are doing it already.' He offers me a biscuit to go with my cup of coffee, which I gladly accept.

'After everything,' he says, 'I'm a farmer. I'm good at it, and if people would pay me fairly I could make a decent living providing decent food for people who want it. You know, I've been farming for decades using hardly any chemicals, looking after my animals, looking after the land. For years they told me I was living in the past. Now people can't get enough of our stuff. Small farms are the future, you know. That's what I think. If they can survive the next ten years, they can make a comeback. Our whole way of life right now is built on oil, and once that changes, things will change. All we have to do now is make the government understand it.'

In 1999 the New Labour government, two years in office and still bubbling with that Blairite optimism about the future of our New Britain, which now seems both charmingly retro and fundamentally irritating, set up a body called the Countryside Agency. The Countryside Agency's grandiose mission was to 'conserve and enhance England's countryside, spread social and economic opportunity for the people who live there and help everyone, wherever they live and whatever their background, to enjoy the countryside and share in this priceless asset more'.[1] It set about this task with relish and enthusiasm. Then it realised what it was up against.

The countryside was in trouble. Rapid changes out in rural England were destroying rural communities and exterminating village shops, pubs and post offices at unprecedented rates. Car culture, supermarket power, property prices, land distribution, the global market, the internet, house-building, planning law, EU regulations, cultural and lifestyle shifts, demographic change… you could choose your favoured culprit. It was becoming tough for anyone who wasn't a wealthy retiree to live in the country at all.

And then there was farming.

The impact of the global economy, which the keen young Blairites were openly in awe of, was ripping farming apart. Commodity prices were falling, farm wages were consequently crashing and the concentration of power in the rapacious supermarket chains and multinational seed and pharmaceutical companies was, for many farmers, the last straw. As if this wasn't enough, farmers had to contend with first the BSE crisis of the 1990s, and then the foot-and-mouth outbreak of 2001. There had not been a worse time to be a farmer since the Second World War.

Undaunted, the Countryside Agency did what all bureaucracies do when they lose their way among the thorny thickets of reality. They commissioned a report. It was a report about the future of the countryside; one of those 'if current trends continue' pieces of semi-prediction. The idea of this report was to give the Agency an idea of what the countryside might look like in fifteen years' time, and consequently how we might prepare for the changes which the exciting new global economy would be bringing to rural England.

The report was published in 2003. It was called *The State of the Countryside 2020*, and it was a stupendously depressing piece of work. Though not an official government policy document, it gave a good indication of the sort of future that politicians were preparing for and expecting. Shot through with the dead vocabulary of the business school – 'main drivers of change', 'radical outsourcing', 'providers may not innovate sufficiently to meet new consumer demands' – it was, in essence, a prediction of the final and long-expected death of the English countryside in general, and English farming in particular.

The assumptions underlying the report were those of the urban political and business classes. The story of the age was 'greater connectedness between nations and the creation of a customised economy' (otherwise known as the spread of '"it must fit me" values'). In future, 'global capitalism will continue to head towards mass customisation' and we will all, as we are told so often with wearying predictability, have to compete to survive.

The countryside will be no exception. Its current problem is simple – it is nowhere near competitive enough. Things are going to need to change. By 2020 the countryside is likely to be rid of most of its pesky farmers, with their noisy animals, slow tractors and stinky 5 a.m. slurry spraying. Instead, the rolling green acres will become the haunt of 'choice managers' – whatever they are – who will be 'focused more on virtual networks than geographical communities'.

As the 'experience economy' intensifies, warns the report, 'the experiences the countryside will provide will determine how well it competes'. Or, to put it another way, 'the countryside's ability to offer a superior "whole-life" experience will be even more important than it is today, especially in attracting entrepreneurs'.

Farmers like Philip Hoskins, then, had better buck their ideas up, and sharpish. 'The present exodus from farming is likely to continue,' explains the report. 'Farming will survive, but many farms will go under.' Why? Because 'supermarkets and food processors will exert even greater control over producers' (note the tone of resignation: the idea of government stopping them from doing so is clearly inconceivable), and will 'increasingly switch to lower cost suppliers in Eastern Europe'. Farmers who can switch to specialised, niche products could be OK, as could those who transform their barns into B&Bs, or offices for all the new 'choice managers'. Overall, though, the vision is stark: 'By 2020, the idea that the countryside equals farming may be well and truly buried.'[2]

This report is worth remembering because it is an excellent reflection of how farming and rural life are viewed by the office-bound political and business classes who are deciding its future. The underlying assumptions of this report, and of this class, are so huge that they are, paradoxically, almost hard to see.

They assume that the business ethos of the city is applicable to the countryside. They assume that people are prepared to accept a countryside in which the barns are empty of cows but full of 'choice managers'. Above all, they assume one huge and untrue thing: that, in essence, the countryside is the same as the town. It is a green business park, with the same pace of life, experiential framework, morality and ethos as the town. It is the city with more trees, less pollution and a lot more free parking, and anyone sufficiently sentimental to imagine otherwise is just not being competitive enough.

On my bookshelves I have quite a few books about farming and the countryside, some of which I've had for years and have never got round to reading. Perhaps this has something to do with their titles. *The Killing of the Countryside, The Death of Rural England, The Decline of an English Village...* it's a grim genre. In fact, it seems impossible to find an optimistic book about the state of agriculture and rural life in England today. Perhaps this is not surprising.

Farming, as you cannot have failed to hear, is in crisis. 'Crisis' is a steeply devalued word these days, but it could be fairly applied to the state of contemporary English agriculture. The next time you hear some bore in a pub or an ultra-free market think tank (the intellectual level is often similar) chuntering on about how rich and lazy those subsidised farmers are, you may wish gently to remind him of the facts.

In the decade between 1995 and 2005 total income from farming in Britain fell by 60 per cent. The number of farm employees fell by almost a quarter, as 59,000 workers left the land.[3] Twenty-three per cent of English farms had a net farm income of *less than zero* in 2005; that's almost a quarter of all farmers not only failing to rake it in but actually making a loss. Almost two-thirds of them had a net income of less than £20,000 – considerably less than the national average salary[4] – and less than 13 per cent earned over £50,000.[5]

Some farms are worse hit than others. Upland hill-farms like Widdybank are especially badly affected, with some farmers earning less than the minimum wage. One study in 2004 showed hill-farmers in Derbyshire earning an average hourly wage of £2.50 for working a

58-hour week.[6] Dairy farms were badly hit too, as milk prices collapsed. Seven thousand dairy farms went out of business between 1994 and 2003 – a decline of over 40 per cent.[7]

It's often impossible to cope with. Officially, farmers are the occupational group with the fourth highest risk of suicide, and women married to farmers have a suicide rate more than 20 per cent higher than the national average. Even this is likely to be an underestimate though: the percentage of farm deaths whose causes are officially 'open' or 'undetermined' is unusually high, and it seems likely that many of these are 'unofficial' suicides too.[8] So much for the rural idyll.

The decline of farming, though, and the encroachment of the urban upon the rural, is not a new phenomenon. Here's William Cobbett, rural chronicler and angry agitator, complaining in 1830 about the new class of gentry colonising the countryside and scorning its rural ways:

> Go to plough! Good God! What, young gentlemen go to plough! They become clerks, or some skimmy-dish thing or other. They flee from dirty work as cunning horses do from the bridle. What misery is all this! What a mass of materials for producing that general and dreadful convulsion that must, first or last, come and blow this funding and jobbing and enslaving and starving system to atoms![9]

Certainly English farming, which in some ways had remained largely unchanged since the Iron Age, began to be turned upside down in the late eighteenth century, when the impacts of the industrial revolution, the age of empires and the first great wave of market globalisation began to sweep across the land. The patterns of change which continue to drive farms out of business today have been in place since Cobbett was writing: the trend towards mechanisation, intensification and specialisation, the expansion of world markets, the removal of trade barriers, the growth of large farms at the expense of small ones, and the disappearance of subsistence agriculture, replaced by the concept of farming as an 'industry' – the usurping of agri*culture* by agri-*business*.

It was the rapid and unprecedented acceleration of these trends in the latter half of the twentieth century, as 'industrial agriculture' became a widespread reality, that really did the damage. The destruction unleashed by artificial pesticides, fertilisers and insecticides, the rapid advance in sophistication of farm machinery, the rise and consolidation of supermarket chains and multinational seed companies, the political and economic impacts of globalisation and, in a new and highly damaging innovation, the production subsidies doled out by the EU's Common Agricultural Policy, unleashed a rural firestorm.

In the past five years, these converging trends have been exacerbated by the combined and unexpected body blows of BSE and foot-and-mouth. And so we find ourselves where we are: in a landscape in which farming is harder than ever before. A landscape in which, for the first time ever, it seems possible to genuinely imagine the effective end of English farming within our lifetimes.

The state of farming, and its future, matter because it is not simply about wages, commodity prices or even the fate of individual farmers. It is existential, metaphysical. If a real England is to be found anywhere, it is surely in its countryside – the landscape that has fuelled the national imagination for centuries.

From John Clare to John Constable, Gerrard Winstanley to Laurie Lee, Candleford to Akenfield, Vaughan Williams to *The Archers*: the idea of farming matters to the English as much as, probably more than, the reality. As long as red-faced Hodge is out there somewhere, living his 'real' country life, whistling to his dog while his jolly fat wife churns butter, all is right with the world. Something solid and unbroken continues. Whatever we do in the Sodom and Gomorrah of our cityscapes and traffic queues can later be undone in the distant rural landscapes of the mind.

Rightly or wrongly, this is the England of our mental and spiritual, as well as our physical, geography. Where would our national landscape, both internal and actual, be without the countryside? And where would that countryside be without its farms?

It may be that we will soon find out.

Nocton, Lincolnshire
June 2006

A grey morning mist hangs over this flat country as I park my car in a damp field among thousands of others. There are acres of cars here, and beyond them tents, marquees, flags, stalls, people, noise. I could be at Glastonbury, except that the cars are 4x4s, the clientele are dressed either in vests and jeans or tweed jackets and stodgy ties, and the main stage presents not Keane or The Killers but one of the biggest, yellowest combine harvesters I have ever seen.

This is Cereals 2006 – 'the UK's premier arable event'. It's a trade show for the agri-businesses which predominate in this part of the country, and some of the biggest machinery, chemical and agri-finance companies in the land are here to try and sell them their wares. Everything is sponsored by HSBC – 'the world's local bank'. It's as far away from the Upper Tees or the South Hams as it's possible to get while remaining in the same country.

Inside, vast, shiny, green John Deere tractors pose provocatively on pedestals. Sugar-beet companies have planted out their wares in temporary raised beds for us to examine and compare. Monsanto is giving away free wallets and pens. The air smells of roast pork and tobacco. Every stall informs me of a 'new crop opportunity', of 'high performance heavyweight crops', of the triumphant arrival of a new type of sprayer. Lining every row of stalls and tents there are signboards, clamouring for my attention:

DEFY BLACKGRASS. Strike hard, strike early!
Syngenta.

MERLO:
Come and see the new power in farming.

A clear sign of success – accept no imitations.
AMISTAR. The UK's foremost T3 strobilurin.

Defy. Strike. Power. Success. Farming here is hard, muscular, male –
the unsmiling penetration of the land. It is a campaign of conquest,
in which new weapons are developed by some of the biggest corporations in the world. Virtually everyone here is a man, and they all
mean business. Stalls are laid out and cases made. Faces are set and
serious. Gangs of blokes cluster around demonstrations of 'post-har-
vest technology'. These are the people the National Farmers' Union
calls 'serious arable farmers', and they're not here for fun.

I'm here to meet Peter Lundgren, a local farmer who possesses no
yellow combines or T3 strobilurin, and whose paltry hundred acres
would probably be laughed at by many of today's patrons. Peter is
also the director of FARM, a campaign group set up in 2002 to voice
the concerns of small and independent farmers, and bring them
together with others who were worried about the future of the countryside and of agriculture.

I meet Peter by the HSBC stall. He's slim and tall, serious and
well-presented, wearing a green tweed jacket ('trying to fit in' he
says). Together, we explore more of the festival. We pass stalls of
accountants, bankers and lawyers – or 'parasites' as Peter calls them,
in an echo of Cobbett. We pass more clean, green tractors, and Peter
tells me that today's machines, with their GPS tracking systems, can
be set to plough the ground in a pre-programmed pattern, with a
margin of error of only a centimetre or two. 'That's a lot more accu-
rate than a driver,' he says. I wonder how long it will be before the

driver – the last remnant of the old plough teams – is redundant too.

We come across a giant soil map of Britain. It's a remarkable, beautiful thing, which lays out in detail every soil type and variation by geographical area. Every few miles, a new colour begins. The country looks like a Jackson Pollock, chaotic in its natural diversity. The contrast with the one-size-fits-all crops, machines, sprays and technologies here is stark. I stand and think about it for probably too long.

Then I stumble across the biggest machine I have ever seen.

Well, perhaps not the biggest. But it seems like it at the time. The 400 horsepower Massey Ferguson Cerea combine harvester dwarfs all around it. It dwarfs the marquees and the banners, the 4x4s and the John Deere tractors. It is bigger than a house. A small house.

Grey and red and utterly enormous, the Cerea has an eight-bar cylinder with backing bars, a rotary separator, a 10,000-litre grain tank, a HiStream 100 Grain Management System, a separate re-thresher and an eight-walker system, which increases agitation of the straw mat by 33 per cent when compared with six-walker systems. I have no idea what any of this means. The rotary blade at the front of this elephantine piece of technology is as wide as the whole thing is high: long steel barrels hung with small, sinister, metal flails.

'It looks like an instrument of torture,' I say to Peter in wonder.

'It'll set you back about a quarter of a million,' he replies. 'The payments will be torture.'

At the side of the machine is a ladder, which leads up to its cockpit. I climb it. Inside, I settle myself into its comfortable leather seat, close the door and try to imagine myself operating it. I try to imagine my circumstance; who I am and how I feel. To my right is a GPS screen. To my left is a CD-player. The cab is air-conditioned, and I can hardly see the ground.

Peter Lundgren, like Philip Hoskins, farms 100 acres of land. There, though, the comparison ends. White Home Farm inhabits a reclaimed landscape, on which the mark of Man lies lighter. Low and flat, peaty and green, the enormous fields stretching away to the sky, its fertility is in inverse proportion to its character. The horizon is wide and unreachable. There's not a rise in sight.

It is a classic Lincolnshire fen farm, five or ten miles away from the site of Cereals 2006. Here Peter farms sugar-beet, wheat, linseed and Gloucester Old Spot pigs, which he butchers himself. Later, in his small, chaotic bungalow, which is subsiding slowly into the stunningly rich soil and is soon to be rebuilt, we will dine on their sausages and I'll understand why he bothers.

Before that though, next year's sausages need to be fed. Peter drives me from the farmhouse to the pig field in his rattling 1950s Land Rover. Lapwings call. Skylarks are everywhere. On either side of the track walls of yellow wheat rise, channelling us towards a line of trees on a distant horizon.

'My father was a dairy farmer down in Sussex,' says Peter as we drive. 'His farm failed though, so I consider myself a first-generation farmer. Personally, I just feel that farming is something I need to do. I have a dreadful time without it.' The Land Rover is jerking over clods of peaty loam. It's a great vehicle: Peter says it's as old as he is, but he looks to be in better condition.

'For most farmers,' says Peter, 'ultimately what's important to them is their place in the community, and for a number of them this very strong feeling that they inherited the land from past generations and their job is to tend it well and then pass it on to future generations. And actually that's possibly one of the problems as well, because it leads to a lot of extra pressure for them. For me, I bought this farm eight years ago, so I don't have that pressure, but I know many people who do. If they can't make it work there's an enormous feeling of failure.'

What I'd like to know, I ask Peter, is what makes you do what you do. It's the same question I asked Philip Hoskins, and for good reason. Those who stand up for farming are often represented as truculent, selfish jobs-for-the-boys relics. Perhaps some of them are. But more of them, probably most of them, put up a fight for other reasons. Non-economic reasons. Farming isn't just a job. It never has been.

'Farming is a primary industry, but it's more than that,' says Peter. 'Other primary industries – coal and steel and shipbuilding – have gone, and there's been a big impact on employment and on the communities that grew up around them. Farming has all that, but it has something else as well, because farming is what creates the country-side. It's a man-made countryside, everyone values it, and most of it has been created by farmers. That, for me, is where it's all gone so wrong. It's not important that a farmer like me stays on the land – I have no God-given right to farm. But what I think is wrong is when farmers being forced off the land has a direct impact on the environment and the communities that live in and depend on the country-side.'

It's this knock-on effect that is often missed when the decline of farming is considered. When a farm goes under, it's far from being an isolated problem. Fewer people working on the land means fewer people visiting the village pub, the shop, or any other local business-es. Workers leave not only the farm but the countryside, with an impact on the local community. Their places are often taken by wealthy urbanites, working in the city or town, which has the effect of pushing property prices up, making it hard for locals to stay in or return to the village. Mechanics, repairmen, vets, seed suppliers, wholesalers, abattoirs – a whole economic network is hit when farm-ing suffers.

'In some places,' says Peter, 'it has a bigger impact than in others. Some rural communities survive precisely because people move out from the towns and contribute to the community and it flourishes. Here we're in trouble because nobody wants to live in this village. It's not attractive housing stock, there's no school or shop, the pub has just closed... you can actually see it falling apart. What you rarely hear about in the farming discussion is the real poverty and deprivation you will find in some rural communities. It's just as real as anything you will find in an inner city, but it's much less talked about.'

Again, I ask Peter a question I asked Philip. How does he see the future of farming? It must be hard to be optimistic.

'There's a polarisation going on,' he says. 'I think we will end up with two distinct types of farm. One will be very big – they'll expand and amalgamate and they'll try and fit in with the global model. At the other end, we'll see smaller farmers survive. It's hard to say how many, but they'll be people prepared to make that sacrifice and effort for a way of life that they love. They'll survive by concentrating on local markets, finding products with a distinct identity to them, that sort of thing. The problem is with farmers in the middle. Those farmers who've done what's been asked of them – bought more acres or more cows, restructured – they're the ones who are most vulnerable. People with between 250 and 1500 acres. I really don't know if they've got a future.'

We're not far from the pig field now. Looking over to my left, across me, out of the passenger window, Peter points across the wheat field to where something moves in the grass. He stops the Land Rover.

'Hare,' he says. 'We get a lot of them here. No rabbits. Lots of hares.' He points it out as you might point out a bus stop or a 10p piece on the pavement. I've seen perhaps two or three hares before in my life. It crouches in the field, looking in our direction; alert, angular, ready. Hares were once considered magical. Eastre, the hare goddess, was pre-eminent in the fields of pre-Christian England. I can see why. The hare is as still as a tree in a windless field. It looks like it has been here for ever.

'Efficient farming,' sighs Peter, taking the handbrake off. 'That's been what we're all supposed to aspire to, and it's been defined as producing food at the lowest unit cost. We ought to define an efficient farming model as one which gives a farmer a decent income to provide good-quality food that people want, and enhance the environment and the landscape at the same time. I've heard economists say that we don't need to farm at all in this country – we can just import all our food from elsewhere. But it's not something most people would want, because most people don't want a society based on those values alone. Farming provides all sorts of benefits to society that no other industry does.'

Up ahead, now, perhaps twenty yards away, I can see half a dozen Gloucester Old Spots lumbering around behind the wire fence. They can see us coming, and they know what it means. Food. They're getting frantic.

'This model that farms have to get bigger to survive,' says Peter as he pulls up by the pig pens, 'it won't work. It won't stop until you've got one corporate farm farming the whole world. I think we've got a bust model, and we need to do something about it. There's a lot of talk about farmers in this country competing against farmers in Brazil and China. Actually, that's not who we're competing against. We're competing against the giant retailers like Tesco and the giant multinational grain companies like Cargill. It's just so entrenched that it's hard to know where to start. I think the only way you can change it is by changing public opinion.'

He turns off the engine. The pigs push against the wire and squeal.

'I'll tell you what scares the shit out of Tesco,' says Peter. 'It's not the farmers – they can squash us. It's not the government – they've bought them. It's the consumers. If they decide to go somewhere else, Tesco is stuffed, and they know it. That's where the power is. I wish more people would realise it.'

Barton, Cambridgeshire
June 2006

In a small, brick ex-council house at the end of an overgrown drive in the Cambridgeshire village of Barton lives a man who styles himself, somewhat contentiously it must be said, 'the last English peasant'. The house is easily identified by the stickers that are pasted on every available window. The one on the back window of the muddy 4x4 in the drive says 'Fight Prejudice, Fight the Ban'. The one on the front door of the house says 'English Spoken Here' – that's English pounds, ounces and other such real weights and measures, banned by Barmy Brussels Bureaucrats. The one on the porch window says, 'Keep Your Bullshit in Westminster – We'll Keep Ours in the Countryside.' All of them are big on primary colours and exclamation marks.

The man who answers the door is small, solid and gnome-like. He wears trainers, tracksuit trousers and an old sweatshirt. He does look like a peasant. His long sideburns, prominent single wonky front tooth, swept-forward greying hair and red nose would probably have been recognised by Cobbett. Actually, come to think of it, he looks a bit *like* Cobbett.

'Welcome,' he says, in a Cambridgeshire burr. 'Come in. You found us, then?'

This is Robin Page: farmer, conservationist, writer, *Daily Telegraph* columnist, controversialist and self-appointed representative of the last of England's rural people. Page is the sort of person who divides opinions. Undoubtedly he cultivates his image as a red-faced, bow-legged English Hodge: scourge of Brussels-mandated nonsense, defender of simple country values, representative of ordinary folk in their battle against the Metrovincial elite. The fact that he cultivates it, though, doesn't mean there's nothing to it.

I have come to see Robin Page for two reasons. First, because it seems to me that, whatever you think of his views, they are representative of a very significant section of English rural opinion, and probably non-rural opinion too. It's an angry, proud, rooted, frustrated opinion which feels, rightly or wrongly, that it is being overlooked. It is rarely heard in the liberal media or on the airwaves and rarely represented in Parliament, and when it is voiced – in the *Mail*, the *Telegraph*, the red-top tabloids or on phone-in radio shows – it can often sound bitter, paranoid, antediluvian: a function of how little it feels it is heard.

Robin Page has published almost thirty books. Among titles like *The Benefits Racket, Down among the Dossers, The Hunting Gene, Vocal Yokel,* and *Animal Cures: the Country Way* is his 1974 semi-auto-biography *The Decline of an English Village,* a detailed, amusing and often moving account of traditional village life in Barton, where he was born and has always lived, and its disappearance. Page's life has coincided exactly with the post-war rise of industrial agriculture in England, and as such the story he tells of his village is also the wider story of the countryside. In the book's new edition, issued thirty years after its first publication, he sums up the countryside's problems as he sees them:

> In thirty years, the trickle from the land has become a torrent with hundreds of thousands of farmers and farm workers joining the exodus, and as I write there is a farming suicide every six days... I am told by those who want to improve me, and direct me, that my standard of living has increased in the last thirty years – I have the benefit of new roads, runways, street lights, wheelie bins, health centres, houses and cars, as well as access to more gadgets and electronic wonders than apples on a tree. But ironically, as my 'standard of living' has increased so the quality of my life has dramatically decreased because of noise pollution, light pollution, air pollution, traffic jams, no policemen, the disappearance of the family doctor, litter, agitation, regulation, speeding lorries, junk food, supermarkets, dumbed-down television, political correctness, mindless development, materialism out of control, and the number of career politicians who clearly have never done a proper day's work in their lives.[10]

It's a comprehensive *J'Accuse.* Regardless, though, of whether you agree with his views on foxhunting (for), the European Union (against), 'didecoys' (against) or the Labour Party (best not to get him started), Page is interesting because he doesn't just talk about things, he does them. Specifically, he does saving the farmed country-side from the scourge of industrial agriculture. He's been doing it for decades now, and the rest of the country has finally caught up with him. This is the second reason I'm here. It's called the Countryside Restoration Trust.

The English farming landscape in 1940 would have been largely recognisable to someone who knew it in 1840 or 1740. Much of it today is unrecognisable to those who knew it in 1940. The rise and rise of intensive agriculture since the end of the Second World War has remoulded it in ways that can never be undone. Its impact on small and family farmers has been extremely damaging, but its impact on wildlife and the wider environment has been devastating.

The extent and impact of the destruction of the English country-side by industrial agriculture has been widely documented, but you can never point out too many times just how much damage was done, and you can never fail to be astonished by what happened, and the fact that it was allowed to. Everyone in England should know about it, in the hope that their knowing means it can never happen again.

Hedges were filled in, downlands destroyed, water meadows and marshes drained and ancient monuments ploughed into history to create more land for crops that no one needed. Farmers were paid to do this through the European Union's Common Agricultural Policy, which raped England's countryside and charged its people £10 billion of their own money every year for the privilege.[11]

The results were pitiful. Since the end of the Second World War we have lost – no, not lost, destroyed – 95 per cent of our wildflower meadows, 50 per cent of our chalk grasslands, half of our ancient lowland woodlands, half of our wetlands, 94 per cent of our lowland raised bog and 186,000 miles of ancient hedgerow.[12] Some of these landscapes and landscape features should have been as precious to us, and as well protected, as any great works of art. They were certainly as unique, as beautiful and as impossible to reproduce.

Then there was the wildlife. Once-typical farmland birds crashed in numbers and their populations have only recently begun to stabilise. The skylark, corn bunting and grey partridge declined by 58 per cent, 80 per cent and 82 per cent respectively in the last three decades of the twentieth century.[13] Over 70 per cent of butterfly and 54 per cent of bird species declined in the last two decades of the century. Almost 30 per cent of native plants declined in numbers between the 1960s and the year 2000.[14] Familiar names for familiar things – corncockle, shepherd's needle, crowcups, the chequered skipper and marbled white butterflies – became rare, extinct, or in need of state protection.

Agriculture in England was transformed from the creator of the countryside to its destroyer. This was not the inevitable and gradual process of historical change. What was lost was not replaced by things of equal or similar value. This was a rural Year-Zero; a deliberate, systematic and heartbreaking clearance of character, meaning and life from a landscape which had built it up, layer by layer, over millennia. It was an act of national vandalism. Countryside historian Oliver Rackham sadly summarised its effects in his classic book *The History of the Countryside* in 1986:

> I cannot analyze the historic landscape without noticing how much of almost every aspect of it has been lost since 1945... Almost every rural change since 1945 has extended what is already commonplace at the expense of what is wonderful or rare or has meaning.[15]

These days the powers that be claim to have seen the error of their ways. Today, farmers are paid to be 'stewards' of the land they were once paid to raze. Subsidies now are paid not for every ton of wheat or gallon of milk, but for managing hedgerows, maintaining stone walls and developing wildlife-friendly 'buffer strips' around arable field edges. Much of the destruction that has been meted out to the English countryside by intensive agriculture in the last sixty years can never be reversed but at least, finally, the destruction has been acknowledged, and is being, in some small way, compensated for.

But Robin Page is not much impressed with this belated nod towards the rural environment. He has dedicated his life to restoring wildlife, colour and character to English farming, and trying to show other farmers that doing so is compatible with making a living, and he's not about to thank those who have destroyed so much for finally ceasing to do so.

We sit at his kitchen table, drinking wincingly strong tea. Robin's house is small, lived-in and packed full of *stuff*. The back garden is overgrown and hung with bird feeders. A lopey young lurcher gets under my feet. A three-pronged wooden fork leans on the wall in the upstairs hall. Tabletops overflow with leaflets about farming and conservation. Robin is in the middle of writing three different books, he tells me, all of which are destined to be late for the publisher. Books aside, it all strikes me as an English archetype: a red-faced peasant living down a lane, railing at Them Up There in Europe and the government, the cities and the offices – feeling persecuted. There have been Robin Pages around for centuries. They just haven't had columns in the *Daily Telegraph.*

'The wildlife all disappeared,' Robin tells me. He's dealing not in generalities now, but in specifics: what he saw here in Barton. What he has lived through, and with.

'The reason was a loss of habitat,' he goes on, 'and also that people were chucking chemicals about without realising what they did. You had sparrowhawks, barn owls, otters – they all went. You had the wildflowers vanish. We had this huge transformation. And it struck me one day – I was down in the field in the middle of summer, and I thought something wasn't right, and I couldn't work out what it was. And then it dawned on me that I couldn't hear a skylark. We'd always heard them, everywhere. They'd gone.'

These experiences spurred him to act. Together with a group of like-minded farmers and conservationists, Page began to talk about setting up what would become The Countryside Restoration Trust (CRT) in the late 1980s.

'We kind of set it up in desperation,' he remembers. 'The conservation establishment only wanted to protect selected areas – reserves and the like. We thought it should all be protected. We could see the swallow, the cuckoo, all the birds still going, and the hedgerows, the wet meadows, the water meadows – all of it. In the 1970s our wonderful natural brook was turned into a drainage channel. Eighteen inches deep, regulation width, straightened out. It had dragonflies, water lilies, fish, yellow irises – they stuffed it all, and then they would come and mow the banks every year to make sure it couldn't come back.'

The brook became a kind of litmus test of what could be done. 'We argued and argued and argued and we finally got them to stop mowing the bank,' he remembers. 'Eventually they allowed us to vary the depth. And the otters came back. The people who looked at their spraints discovered that their greatest activity was in our part of the brook where we had stopped the mowing and turned it back into something close to natural. Then some land by the brook came up for sale. We bought it and used it to launch the CRT in 1993.'

There's pleasure in Robin's voice when he remembers how they proved everyone wrong. He likes proving everyone wrong.

'We were told this would never work,' he says. 'Now we've raised about £3 million, we've got property worth getting on for £10 million, we've got over a thousand acres, four farms, 5000 members, and the farm here has expanded from 40 acres to about 450. And the wildlife has quite literally flooded back. We've got brown hares in such large numbers that when I hear people talking about the brown hare being rare, it seems a joke. They're back to the same numbers as when I was a boy. Barn owls have come back. Otters are in the brook. We've got the highest density of skylarks in East Anglia. We've got grey partridge, which is claimed to be rare.' He is enthused just talking about it.

'Want to see?' he says.

We drive through Barton in Robin's 4x4, a bright red 'Bollocks to Blair' badge rattling about on the dashboard, on our way to Lark Rise Farm. As we drive, Robin tells me how he used to know everyone in the village, but that its size has doubled during his lifetime and now he only knows about 10 per cent of its inhabitants. He's not happy about it. 'If I'm wearing wellies and I've got a bit of straw on me, some of them look at me like a piece of shit,' he says. He tells me about an estate agent he met who was a looking for a farmhouse for a wealthy client of his from London. The buyer had stipulated not only that the farmhouse should no longer be part of a working farm but that there should be no working farms in the village at all. 'Because he didn't want to get his bloody BMW dirty,' says Robin. 'Not uncommon. They come to the country and they want it to be like the town.'

After a few minutes we pull up on a grass verge at the side of a road. Robin leads me down a bank and through a strung-together five-bar gate to a restored hay meadow. Long, tall, gently waving grasses are woven with patterns of multi-coloured wildflowers.

'This was the first hay meadow that we planted,' says Robin, leading me through it slowly. 'This had been arable for years. If you walked through it now, you would think it was ancient hay meadow. We have a grass meadow expert who records all the species, and I think we have about forty-five to fifty in this field.' He bends over and fingers a small yellow flower.

'This is yellow rattle,' he says. 'It hasn't been found growing wild in Cambridgeshire for years. Lovely flower, though not everyone thinks so. I have a cousin who farms up in the Pennines. He came down here and he just couldn't believe that we'd planted yellow rattle. He'd spent twenty years trying to get rid of it. Traditionally this plant's also called hay rattle, because it tells you when to bring the hay in. You let it seed and when you can hear the seeds rattle inside, it's time to harvest. The birds have come back because of all this. It's all very good for yellowhammers, and we get reed buntings here too. It's good for butterflies, it's good for cows. So it makes me feel good too.'

Our next stop is the brook. We plunge down a nettley bank under a road bridge to look for otter spraints. We find fresh footprints. Then it's on to another field, where Robin shows me replanted hedges, grass edges and woodland. A hare lollops away through the wheat. We are perhaps a few hundred yards away from the M11 – constructed in the late 1970s, in what Page calls a 'disaster' for the village, bringing with it light, air and noise pollution, driving away the badgers and the larks. Yet even here, the birdsong is cacophonous.

Then we move on to a field of rape, to look for rare marbled white butterflies which have started breeding on the banks of the old Oxford to Cambridge railway line. We have no luck, but we see two young fox cubs fighting noisily in the rape. When they see us, they bound away like excitable puppies. Then it's on to a final meadow – even more stunning than the first, dotted and dashed with huge red poppies. We're looking for bee orchids, but it looks like it's too early in the year.

It is genuinely hard for someone of my generation to imagine that much of the English countryside was like this just fifty years ago. I almost wish I hadn't seen it. If you don't know what you've lost, it doesn't hurt. But I am glad I wasn't around to see the loss of places like this on a national scale. It would have been hard to take. As a nation, our mental image of rural England is still composed of places like this. Hay meadows, gambolling lambs, poppy fields, spinneys. A curious, almost childish country landscape: part Beatrix Potter, part *Rupert Bear*. We don't know, or don't want to know, how broken it really is. I trail my hand through the flowers and get them spotted with cuckoo spit.

An hour or so later, and Robin and his wife have taken me for lunch in the village pub, where Robin is both animated and frustrated. Animated because when he talks about his work to restore the farming environment, there is a passion in his voice. Frustrated because when he talks about the 'establishment''s response to it, he can barely contain himself.

'We've got everything that the government claims it wants back in the countryside,' he says, 'but because I'm politically incorrect and hate them, they won't come and look and see what we're doing. We've invited every Agriculture Minister they've ever had, and they won't set foot.' Despite that, though, he thinks that he's got the model right, and he knows that people elsewhere are taking a lead from it.

One of the things that has changed since he launched the CRT in 1993, though, is the acceleration of that farming crisis – to the point where, as he puts it, 'the farmer and the farm worker are now as endangered as the skylarks and the hares'. He now finds himself fighting on two fronts: to save the wildlife and the remaining people who make a living from the land.

'Our farmer at Lark Rise lives and work in the village, which is very important,' he says. 'If you go and see Hope Farm, which is the RSPB farm, the farmhouse is empty. It's an office. All their farming is done by contractors.' I think back to the shell of Widdybank. It was obviously not an isolated case. Robin has a beef with the RSPB, and major wildlife charities like them. 'If the RSPB wants to influence farmers,' he says, 'I can't see why they say "We're farming for skylarks" and not "We're farming for farmers and skylarks". We should be looking to keep people on the land – to keep all the skills going and all the old accumulated knowledge and to contribute to the local community and supply local food to local people during the appropriate season. As we've become urbanised and as we've become dominated by the supermarkets that's a very difficult message to get over.'

He is clearly warming to his subject.

'There are villages now within seven or eight miles of here with no resident farmer,' he says. 'I would think that in the village school here there is only one child attending whose family is linked to farming. Incomers abound. One classic is that the old squire's house is now being tarted up by a *Sunday Times* Rich List developer. He's put a wall round the house so that you can't see the house or the garden. He even knocked the rooks' nests out of the trees. They were noisy and scruffy, you see: not the done thing. I got the police onto him and they gave him a warning because it was against the Wildlife and Countryside Act. The rooks immediately rebuilt. I hope they shit on his car.'

He bears a lot of grudges, does Robin. His anger is sardonic, humorous, often scattergun, but real. It's time to ask him the question I asked Philip Hoskins and Peter Lundgren. Why? Why does it matter? What moves you?

'I do it because I'm a great believer in our wonderful government,' he says, sarcastically. 'I really do believe that we're in multicultural Britain, and the culture I'm part of is one of the most neglected minorities, and that is rural culture. I want to keep that alive. And I do think there is this link with the natural world and nature which we have lost. I think that people actually want to be in proper touch with it, because that is where their roots are, and that is where our physical and spiritual roots are locked, going back 10,000 years. I do think staying in touch with what I'm looking out of the window at is actually staying in touch with reality.'

This is Robin Page's reality. It's a reality in which farming, the countryside and people are intrinsically linked. To pull away any of these parts is to destroy the whole.

'There can't be a rural culture without farming,' he says, decisively. 'There would be culture, but it wouldn't be a rural culture. It would be a suburban and an urban culture. I call it urban colonialism. We are having urban values imposed on us, which I don't like at all. When white people go up to black people and impose their views on them, that is said to be not wanted and culturally and racially objectionable, and then you tell me that you're doing me a favour by doing that to me. It's a version of ethnic cleansing, is what it is. I think it's a disgrace.'

Politically incorrect indeed. It's this sort of talk that ensures government ministers won't visit Robin Page, and that mean he ends up alienating people he might otherwise convince. 'Ethnic cleansing' is not a term that should be thrown around lightly. And it's a shame, because he has a point: one echoed by everyone else I have spoken to who has genuine links with the land, and is heartbroken by the way those links are being razed, those roots torn up, that land made safe for those who do not understand or care much about it.

Because there is no doubt that what Robin Page calls 'urban colonialism' is a reality. Read any colour supplement, or any TV schedule, and feast on the many glowing, approving stories of idiot yuppies pouring into the countryside, splashing out 900 grand on an old cottage with a perfect view (it's all about the investment potential, you understand) while the rural economy collapses around them, and it's hard not to share Robin Page's contempt for them and everything they represent.

Yet even those urban colonisers are searching for something. Even they have a feeling for what rural England means to them. Many of them carry it thoughtlessly, selfishly, destructively. Many of them deserve that contempt. But many others go looking for what Robin, Peter, Philip and others describe so well, and feel so deeply about – that rural life, separate from the urban and the urbane. Those other values. People will always want to move from the city to the countryside. What they need to take with them is an awareness of the reality as well as the naïvety of the idyll. Without it, they come as destroyers.

But there is no doubt either that the old farming ways are virtually gone now, and will probably never return. There is no doubt that the countryside as a living, working environment is dying; that most people in England today have never worked the land, don't understand it, see it as little more than a view from the window of a holiday cottage. It's not their fault: brought up in a town or city, how are you supposed to know anything else?

Probably the mass exodus from the land was unavoidable, even if the way it happened was often outrageous. Probably we will never go back, unless we are forced to by events outside our control: climate change, economic collapse, war. But the loss caused by the exodus is real. It is a material and spiritual reality, which can be all-consuming for those who understand what is being lost – really understand it, in their guts and in their hearts as well as in their heads.

I don't, and I don't pretend to. I have lived in the countryside, even worked on farms, but I've never been part of the land; never been of it, rather than simply on it. I come from a family with an urban history: a family of bus drivers, businessmen, policemen, shopkeepers. There's no living memory, with us, of the soil. But even dipping into this loss, skirting around its edges to gain some small taste of what it must be like, I can feel its heartbreaking power. I can forgive Robin Page his anger, and his refusal to mince words, because I think I can begin to understand what is behind them.

6

Trouble in Paradise

Buying and Selling is an Art, whereby people endeavour to
cheat one another of the Land.

> Gerrard Winstanley, *A New-yeers Gift for the
> Parliament and Armie*, 1650

Chinatown, London
May 2006

It's the warmest day of the year so far, and I'm sitting on the steps of
the Feng Shui pagoda fiddling with my mobile phone and hoping I've
got the right day. Behind me is a large, long redbrick building; an ugly
thing with an underground car park beneath it and a line of boarded-
up shop fronts on its lower level. The shop fronts all have notices
stuck on them announcing their closure. Each notice bears a word. A
logo, actually. It says 'Rosewheel'.

My phone rings.

'Hello,' says a voice. 'Is that Paul?'

'Yes,' I say. 'Is that Jabez?'

As I speak, I see a Chinese man approaching me from about ten
yards away. He's talking into a mobile phone and is looking at me.

'I think I can see you,' says Jabez Lam.

'I think I can see you too,' I say. We sort of look at each other until he gets to me, which takes rather longer than is comfortable.

Jabez puts his phone away, approaches me and shakes my hand. He is thin and rangy, with a blue shirt tucked into his jeans, a tweed jacket over them, white trainers beneath. He has greying hair and a genuine smile. He points to the redbrick building behind me.

'This is the one,' he says. 'Let me show you.'

This building is called Sandringham Court, and it's the reason that I'm here. Jabez walks me around the building, showing me the ex-shops, the surrounding streets and the public colonnades. He gives me potted histories of the people who used to own the shops. There was the Golden Gate Chinese Grocers – very popular, he says. There was the Garden Restaurant – popular too, presumably, as it had pretty stiff competition from the dozens of other Chinese restaurants here. There was Chinatown's only fresh fish shop, its only Chinese jewellery shop and its only Chinese kitchen utensil shop. They were all run by independent traders, all of whom have now been evicted from the building by the company whose logo is on those signs: Rosewheel.

Sandringham Court lies at one end of Chinatown, separating it from the busy Charing Cross Road. Built in 1985, it was taken over by Rosewheel when its previous – Chinese – owners went bust. Rosewheel is not Chinese. It has no connections with Chinatown, and has no previous involvement with this place or its people. The residents of Chinatown had never heard of it until the shopkeepers in Sandringham Court received their eviction notices in spring 2005.

None of them wanted to move, but they had little choice. Rosewheel had plans. Sandringham Court was to be demolished and replaced by a spanking new Chinese-themed shopping mall known as the 'Chinatown Gateway'. The shopkeepers were told they were welcome to apply for floor space in the new mall when it was built. Unfortunately, their rents would be at least double what they were before.

The company, having closed down a clutch of genuine Chinese businesses, then took upon itself the role of saviour of Chinatown.

The Chinatown Gateway, said the company's founder, Robert Bourne, would be '110 per cent Chinese-focused'.[1] Rosewheel would arrest the 'decline of Chinatown' with an 'exciting retail development' – 'a showcase for the cultural heritage and economic power of China', which would attract 'new customers and opportunities'. It would feature '100 shops, restaurants and concessions in an innovative setting'. It would be good news for Chinatown and its Chinese people.

On its website, the company proudly displayed a list of all of the benefits which the Chinatown Gateway would bring to the benighted locals:

Regenerating London Chinatown to build a home for a new generation of Chinese brands and traders

Opening up new opportunities for the next generation

Supplementing today's Chinese businesses with new brands and traditional crafts

Embracing the rich cultural heritage of an historic community

Working for a brand new Chinese retail experience for customers

Honouring traditional Chinese festivals and celebrations in style

Empowering today's traders in a well-managed and internationally promoted retail centre

Encompassing the energy of Chinese culture

Leveraging the energy and power of China's new economy[2]

But this is not just another story about a huge corporate shopping mall being built against the wishes of local people. Rosewheel, it seems, has bigger ambitions than that. It does not just want the building; it wants part of the street too. Rosewheel wants to enclose what is currently public space in Chinatown within its private domain.

Much of the local Chinese community is furious about Rosewheel's evictions, and its self-appointed role as the saviour of Chinatown. But what has probably angered them most is what Rosewheel wants to do to the pagoda I have been sitting on. The pagoda is not just a pretty piece of street furniture. Its positioning affects the Feng Shui, and thus the fate, of Chinatown itself. But Rosewheel, once it has demolished Sandringham Court, intends to annex the pagoda as part of the Chinatown Gateway.

The company wants to enclose part of the street upon which the pagoda sits, demolish it and rebuild it as the centrepiece of its new mall. It is also rumoured, according to Jabez, to want to fence in what is currently a publicly accessible colonnade on Charing Cross Road, and possibly also enclose the entirety of the adjacent Newport Court, transforming it from a public road to a private covered walkway.

The fear is that the public streets of Chinatown are to be privatised. The pagoda, which stands in the way of this plan, has become a symbol of what is happening to Chinatown. Jabez Lam calls it a 'cultural metaphor', and he is fearful for the future of both the metaphor and what it represents.

He's not the only one who worries. Jabez Lam is the founder of the Save Chinatown Campaign, a group of locals who got together to object precisely because neither Rosewheel nor Westminster City Council, which owns the lease on Sandringham Court, bothered to consult the local Chinese community properly before any of this happened.

'It's not just going on in Chinatown, of course,' says Jabez, as we walk around the building. 'It's all over the country. The high streets, the loss of character: it is increasingly common. Whether it's in London, or in the country, whether it's an ethnic or a village community, independent people are being driven out, and character also. In this case, it is about a minority community that has made an investment of fifty years. Money, time, blood and sweat have been put in to build this place.'

This, he says, is what makes people here really furious; that their hard work is being not only overlooked, but piggybacked on – and that the future of Chinatown may no longer be theirs to decide.

'It's the work that the Chinese communities did that has made this place desirable now, and that's why the property developers want to come,' he says. 'That's the historical context of this area. It is the Chinese community's history in London. More than 70 per cent of Chinese businesses here are rented. Think what will happen if developments like this start to push those rents up. Think what will happen to the small businesses who have built this area. This would be end of Chinatown as we know it.'

This is the real worry, then. It's not just about this building, or even its ex-shopkeepers, it's about the future of this whole place. A place imbued with meaning.

'In Camberwell, recently,' says Jabez 'the council were evicting black businesses from their shops, and there was an outcry. They had an enquiry into it, it was headed by Lord Herman Ouseley, who used to run the Commission for Racial Equality, and his report concluded that what they were doing was the equivalent of ethnic cleansing. So I ask you, what is this? The same thing is happening here. Small Chinese business owners are being pushed out by the council and a rich developer.'

Ethnic cleansing. Here we are again. First I hear it in the fields of Cambridgeshire, now on the streets of Chinatown. First Robin Page, now Jabez Lam; in different contexts, yet with the same passion behind them. What is going on?

Trying to get an answer from Rosewheel doesn't get me very far. I can't even find it. Its previous website, which in any case contained no contact details, has been replaced with a message declaring that it is 'currently being updated'. I check with Companies House, but it has no telephone, fax or email for the company, just a postal address. I discover that Rosewheel was incorporated in 2003, just before it bought the 200-year lease on this building. It appears to have no other projects up and running, and no stated previous history. Its accounts are overdue.

I call Westminster City Council five times. Eventually I am told that no one there can give me any contact details for the company, despite having leased it a huge building in central London. Digging deeper, I discover that Rosewheel's founder, a man called Robert Bourne, is a multi-millionaire property developer, well known for his closeness to the government. He once threw a surprise birthday party for Peter Mandelson[3] and has made several five-figure donations to the Labour Party.[4] He is a man with fingers in many pies: as well as being a director of more than fifty other companies, he was also involved in a failed bid to buy the Millennium Dome and turn it into 'London's silicon valley.'[5] In 2005, he popped up at number 938 on the *Sunday Times* Rich List.[6] He's not a man, though, who seems to want to shout about it in public. All my efforts to talk to someone from Rosewheel are in vain.

Jabez wants to show me something. He walks me around the corner from Sandringham Court, over to Gerrard Street. There he directs my attention to a dingy little staircase leading upwards from street level. To one side of it is a red plaque with gold Chinese lettering on it.

'This used to be a brothel,' he says, with a slight smile. 'Now it is a family club. Most of the people in Chinatown came from Hong Kong and the New Territories, where there are five major surnames.' He names them all, but there's no way I can write them down. 'When they got to London,' he continues, 'they formed their own clubs. Five clubs for the five surnames. This is one of them. This is what I'm talking about. All of this took decades to build up, but it could be uprooted in a day. This is why the buildings are not the point. All of this is the point – this is what makes Chinatown, not the golden dragons. This is what can't be replaced.'

In one obvious sense there's nothing especially English about Chinatown. Yet it has become a fixed part of the London landscape, a definitive feature of England's capital city, and is treasured by people far beyond the Chinese community that has built it. Those who did build it, however, have a fierce commitment and attachment to it. I find myself thinking that we could learn a lot of lessons from them about appreciating the place you live in, fighting for it, and understanding its unique character. If more people in England had the sort of commitment to their place that London's Chinese community does to theirs, the country might look very different.

But what is this talk of ethnic cleansing? Why the extreme language, from so many different directions? The answer, I think, is that people who regard themselves as minorities feel that they are being pushed out of the picture. Not only as individuals and as communities, but as cultures. Cultures that took time and effort to build up and are now shoved carelessly aside by the power of money. The anger and the grief are understandable, and the language is necessarily intemperate. What would you say, or do, if you thought that everything you loved and understood was being lost? The complexities of rural life or the complexities of life in Chinatown: suddenly, what seemed fixed and unassailable is tiny and fragile. Suddenly you find yourself fighting for the very existence of what you always took for granted.

The irony is that more and more people seem to feel themselves part of a minority. Some of them, like London's Chinese community, or other ethnic minority communities, genuinely are. England's traditional farmers are too. Yet your average white-skinned, mainstream English person often feels beleaguered too.

Read the *Mail*, the *Express*, the *Sun* – the papers that are read by the largest numbers of English people. Take in the fury about crazy Health and Safety rulings, anti-English discrimination in public services, schools or local authorities, compensation culture destroying traditional pursuits. Before your liberal knee starts jerking too hard and you comfortably dismiss it as the raving of far-right crazies, ask yourself what might be at its root, and why. Ask yourself why a very large proportion of English people, who are plainly not foaming far-right xenophobes, should feel beleaguered in their own land. Isn't it just ridiculous?

Perhaps it's not as ridiculous as it sounds, because it seems to me that it's a minority, in fact, that is doing the damage. This minority consists of the chain stores, the developers, the agri-businesses, the big landowners. The destruction of culture, community and landscape that has been chronicled in this book keeps coming back to the same people – or the same type of people. And they are minorities – rich, powerful, influential ones – who can get things done.

They can close down a hundred pubs, build on acres of green fields, destroy entire industries, raze meaning from the landscape and call it investment. We are in the grip of the tyranny of this minority: not a minority defined by its race or religion, but by its power and wealth. They run the show, and their lack of accountability makes all those who don't share their bounties feel discriminated against. Call me a Marxist if you like – you'd be wrong, as it happens – but that, based on what I have seen, is the way it works in modern England.

We've seen plenty of examples of this already. What's happening in Chinatown, in one sense, is simply an extension of what is happening in Bury St Edmunds, in Castlemill Boatyard and in Broadway Market. Yet it is much more than this too. It is something, actually, considerably more sinister. However much you might disagree with Tony's cafe being bought out from under him, or with local boozers being snapped up by rapacious PubCos, these, at least, were all market transactions. They were private properties changing hands – in controversial circumstances, and with negative results, but they were private nonetheless. What's happening in Chinatown is an assault on public space. It is an attempt by developers to extend their power so that it impacts not merely on small shopkeepers and independent business people, but on the places where we all gather to do our own thing and to be free. It is an act of enclosure. And it is not the only one.

Urban public space is at the heart of city and town life, in England as in every other country. It is the essence of public freedom: a gathering space, a discussion point, a place to rally, to protest, to sit and contemplate, to smoke or talk or watch the stars. No matter what happens in the shops and cafés, the offices and houses, the very existence of genuine public space means there is always somewhere to go to express yourself or simply to escape.

Yet this, too, is now under assault. From urban parks to pedestrian streets, public squares to market-places, we are seeing a fencing-in, a buying-up and a closing-down of our public spaces. Often it is done with little consultation or publicity. In towns and cities all over England, what was once urban public space is now, suddenly, private. It is effectively owned by corporations, which set the standards of behaviour. It's been many centuries now since the gentry discovered that enclosure was an immensely profitable activity. We should probably not be too surprised that this lesson has not been forgotten by today's equivalents.

The standards that this new gentry set are the standards that are most congenial to their aim – and their aim is getting you to buy things. So there will be no begging. There will be no being homeless, in fact. There will be no wearing hoodies. There will be no busking, and often there will be no sitting either, except in designated areas. You will eat and drink where you are told to eat and drink. You will not skateboard or cycle or behave 'inappropriately'. And as for political demonstrations – don't even think about it.

None of this is an exaggeration. It would be nice if it were, but over the last few decades we have created an atmosphere in this country that makes this kind of thing a perfectly logical extension of our politics and our social attitudes. If everything else can be privatised, why not the streets? A government which is prepared to push through an Act of Parliament to criminalise one man's embarrassing demonstration outside the Palace of Westminster against an unpopular war is unlikely to worry too much about the corporate enclosure of our urban public spaces. And a nation which has docilely allowed itself to be transformed in just a few decades from one of citizens to one of consumers is unlikely to be interested in doing much about it.

For a cash-strapped local authority, handing over control of public streets can seem like a boon. Private companies provide security guards to police them, keep them tidy, and enforce the rules. It saves money and time, and few people seem to complain about it, perhaps because they have no idea it is happening. But the consequences are potentially dire. Our public spaces are on the way to becoming sterile, top-down, controlled consumption zones.

Urban public space, throughout history, has been a source of danger to those in authority. It is public spaces where people gather to discuss seditious topics. Demonstrations start there, and revolutions too. To all but the most enlightened public authority, then, they are expensive and they are trouble. Political logic leads to a clear conclusion – sell them off, if you can. Efficiency and control will be your reward.

The battle that Jabez Lam is fighting may be much bigger than he knows. The good news for him, though, is that he may have allies that he doesn't even know about.

Liverpool
April 2006

The place is a mass of cranes and concrete. Men in hard hats move behind the high, green fences topped with barbed wire and studded at intervals with explanatory notice-boards. You need to get up above street level before you can see what's really going on. Once you do, you'll bear witness to a vast hole in this city: a hole soon to be filled with something entirely new and incomparable. Paradise is coming to Liverpool.

Old, empty, collapsing buildings around the edge of the hole are hung with giant sky-blue banners. The banners read: 'Requisitioned for the Paradise Project'. The creators of Paradise are proud, and they want people to know it.

'By what right?' asks Don. 'That's the key question. And who's asking it?'

Donald Lee and I are in central Liverpool, walking the boundaries of the biggest retail development in Europe – the Paradise Project. The walk takes forty minutes, which gives some idea of its size. Again, what's happening here is a familiar story: a vast shopping centre being carved out of a city; a shopping centre that will be filled to bursting point with chain stores, chain restaurants, chain cafés and chain cinemas. But again, this is different. Paradise, as might be expected, is not a normal place.

Liverpool is not short of corporate shopping space already. The retail centre of the sixth-largest city in England is a grey wilderness of underpasses and branches of H&M. Wander into this concrete maze after the shops close and it is almost suicidally depressing. Liverpool is hardly alone in this – it's simply a typical example of the kind of hideous concrete mess created in the 1960s by planners and architects who thought that they, too, were creating paradise.

The Paradise Project will be this generation's equivalent of these previous urban mega-developments. Since its central concrete wilderness was built, Liverpool's 'retail competitiveness' has declined. During the 1990s the growth of massive out-of-town retail parks nearby have sucked shoppers away. The Trafford Centre near Manchester has been a key culprit, and there is no way Liverpool is going to lose out to Manchester. Paradise will re-establish Liverpool as a 'premier retail destination'.

Architecturally, the Paradise Project will certainly be an improvement on what went before: something which the City Council, and the developer it is working with, is trumpeting from the roof-tops. What they are less keen to trumpet is that Paradise requires the first privatisation of a city centre anywhere in England.

Liverpool City Council has sanctioned the corporate enclosure of the 42-acre city-centre site, which encompasses thirty-four streets and a public park. The development company Grosvenor, owned by the Duke of Westminster, the country's third-richest man, has been given a 250-year lease on this area. Within it Grosvenor, with the enthusiastic blessing of the Council, is putting into practice the kind of massive, consumer-focused re-engineering of the landscape previously only seen in private malls like Bluewater.

Bluewater, in fact, is the best comparison to what is going to happen here – with the crucial difference that these are, or were, public streets. At the centre of the development, on Paradise Street, will be a 280,000 square foot John Lewis department store and 'a host of major high street names' comprising 1.6 million square feet of new shopping space. Nearby Hanover Street will be a 'lifestyle-focused district with an eclectic atmosphere', while Peter's Lane will be a 'designer-led area' with 'a range of shops that will attract fashion-conscious consumers'. South John Street will be the 'family orientated district'. Then there is Chavasse Park. Previously a publicly accessible green space, the park is now a giant hole in the ground. This hole will be filled with a 2000-space car park with a new landscaped park put back on top of it.[7]

This is not a development which will allow the area's own character to evolve over time. Its character has been predetermined beforehand by architects, marketing specialists and planners. No room is left for the exercise of the human imagination, for personal creativity, for responsiveness to people and locality. This is not about any of those things. It is about money, and in that sense it has already been a great success.

This is the way the deal works. The City Council gets an expensive, flashy renovation of a currently run-down area, costing almost a billion pounds, for which it has to pay virtually nothing. In return, however, it must give up – in other words, the public must give up – their rights to it. In Chavasse Park, South John Street, Paradise Street or anywhere else on the site, the rules you will follow will be the rules set down by Grosvenor. The uniformed officers on the streets will not be the police, they will be private security guards, and they will be enforcing those rules.

These are the streets of one of our major cities. But they no longer belong to its people.

Don Lee is from the Open Spaces Society, a venerable campaign group founded in 1865 to protect common land and public rights of way from encroachment. He is of pensionable age, with frizzy grey hair, hooded eyes and a dry sense of humour. He wears purple track-suit trousers and a blue anorak. And he is not happy. His lack of happiness is the reason he's here today talking to me, rather than savouring his carriage clock or sitting in his garden. Don is a born campaigner, and there is still plenty for him to do.

'In Des Moines, in Iowa,' he tells me conspiratorially as we stand looking over the cranes and rubble, 'there is a private network of tunnels. Underground tunnels and walkways. You can only access them with a password, and only people who can afford to pay for it get a password. It's absolutely true. It's the ultimate privatisation of public space. What is happening in Liverpool is a step towards this kind of thing. You think that sounds extreme? Come back in ten years, and see where we are.'

The thing that bothers Don, apart from the details of the Paradise Project itself, is that virtually no one else in Liverpool seems to care. Perhaps no one in Liverpool: Don is from Manchester, and is here in a rare show of north-western solidarity. If the Scousers can't be bothered to do anything about the privatisation of half of their city centre, he says, then maybe they'll get what they deserve.

About the only other significant opposition to the Paradise Project, in fact, comes from the place where we're headed now, having finished our walk around the site, to pick up a spot of lunch – Quiggins. Quiggins is a three-storey shopping centre, but not the kind which Grosvenor or the Council likes to promote. A Liverpool institution, Quiggins is a chaos of clothes shops for teenage Goths, nooks and crannies which house antique- and second-hand furniture shops, racks of second-hand clothes for a fiver and shelves of second-hand books for 50p. It's a warren of stairs, dusty corners and intriguing happenings. It's a centre of alternative culture; culture that doesn't have to be paid for or officially sanctioned. It's also about to be demolished, to make way for Paradise.

Quiggins' founders, brothers John and Peter Tierney, are gutted by what is about to happen to them. They set up the centre eighteen years ago, they say, as a conscious attempt to keep alternative culture alive in an increasingly corporate city centre. They kept rents deliberately low, and provided a space for creative talent to flourish. The City Council says it will find Quiggins another home, but the brothers are not satisfied. 'We have a disadvantage,' they write bitterly on their website: 'we are indigenous to Liverpool, not outsiders. This City Council only trusts outside companies. Quiggins is committed to Liverpool's cultural industry and has been since its formation... It houses 45 local businesses, employing 250 local people, all helping to recycle within our local economy.'[8]

It doesn't matter much what the brothers say, though. Quiggins has already had a compulsory purchase order issued against it, and by the time you read this, the place, like public rights of way in the centre of Liverpool, will be no more than a memory.

In the noisy, wholefood cafe on Quiggins' third floor, Don and I sit down with pizzas and salad to talk. Don has a lot to talk about. He has spent months at a time poring over the details of the Paradise Project – details that have either not been put into the public domain or, if they have, have been slipped in so quietly that no one has noticed.

'It took me a long time, and a lot of correspondence with the developers and the council, before they finally admitted what was happening with this project,' Don tells me. 'There was a very low-key public announcement – you had to know where to look to find it –

that they were removing the rights of way from thirty-three streets in the city centre, in what was going to be the Paradise Project. It took a lot of to-ing and fro-ing, but I finally got them to admit to me that they were replacing these rights of way with something called "public realm agreements".'

He looks at me with raised eyebrows and sips mysteriously from his glass of water.

'Well, I'd never heard of these things,' he goes on, 'so I kept pressing them, and it turned out that these "public realm agreements" would give the public very limited access to the streets, on Grosvenor's terms. They're based on similar agreements in the US, where privatisation of this sort is quite common. The access would begin half an hour before the shops opened and it would end half an hour after they closed. During that period they would allow you in. Outside it, they would not, and it would be their people who would police it. Remember, these are *streets* – this is not some private shopping centre. Yet now you will have no right to use them unless you're shopping. Things aren't good. While the public are winning new rights of access in the countryside, they're having these rights taken away in towns and cities.' He looks unhappy.

'Things aren't right,' he says. 'It can be depressing sometimes. Especially that so few people in Liverpool seem to be protesting about it. Maybe people just expect it these days. They've rebuilt the Cavern Club, you know; the place where the Beatles used to play. They've built a replica of it. I see all these Japanese tourists trooping around it and I often wonder if they know it's not the real thing.'

'It's not always easy to tell any more,' I say.

'You've got that right,' says Don.

After I meet Don, I go to Liverpool's impressive Victorian Municipal Buildings to see the City Council, in the form of Councillor Peter Mullen. Mullen is responsible for maintenance and repair in the city centre, and is an enthusiast for the Paradise Project. He's an affable

Scouser who takes pride in his city and thinks that the project will improve it. He waxes lyrical about the money it will bring in, how people will learn to love it, and how it will allow Liverpool to compete for shoppers with Manchester and Chester.

What Grosvenor is doing, he tells me, unprompted, is emphatically not privatisation of the streets; it's more a kind of clean-up. 'Grosvenor will employ its own security people and they will patrol the streets, but that will be in addition to the police,' he says. 'They will take responsibility for maintenance and repair, and I'm quite pleased that that's the case... For the pedestrian going into the district, the shopper going into the shops, you really won't notice the difference. It's not as if the security guards are going to stop and search people.'

It's telling that Mullen felt he had to bring all this up before I even asked him: there's some real sensitivity within the Council about this issue. When you press him, though, you find that he's not quite sure what powers Grosvenor is actually going to have, or how exactly it will exercise them. Will the abolition of public rights of way prevent public access? I ask him. 'I'm assured that they will not,' he says, but he doesn't sound certain. He tells me that there will be 24-hour shopping some days, so it won't be in Grosvenor's interests to prevent access. 'People going about their lawful business have nothing to worry about,' he tells me.

So will Grosvenor be preventing people from wearing hoodies on their streets, like Bluewater does? I ask. 'I don't think they'll be allowed to do that,' he says. But, again, he's not sure. I ask him if the rights of public access to the area will be exactly as they were before. 'I would think so,' he says. Again, there's no certainty. He's a nice guy is Peter Mullen, but what he tells me is not exactly reassuring.

What's happening in Liverpool city centre might sound like an extreme case, or an isolated one. It isn't. One of the things that Peter Mullen was keen to tell me, in fact, was that Paradise-style arrangements were 'nothing new'. He was quite right: they are, in fact, becoming increasingly common all over the country, as cash-strapped local authorities hive off increasing amounts of public space to private bodies.

The results, as Liverpool illustrates so well, are clear. Not only do the civil liberties and public access implications start to get worrying, but the kind of organisations which can afford to splash out hundreds of millions on redeveloping areas and then maintaining and monitoring them tend not to be very interested in the character of places or in the small, subtle human relationships that create that character. They tend to be interested in money, and how to get more of it. They tend to be massive, unimaginative, top-down corporate behemoths, which apply the same equation to every project they undertake: expensive apartments + chain stores = regeneration.

In 2006 the venerable Royal Institution of Chartered Surveyors (RICS) produced a landmark report on precisely this subject. *What Kind of World Are We Building?* examined the growing private ownership and management of the public realm all over England and it showed that Peter Mullen was right: the Liverpool experience is by no means unique. In fact, places like Paradise – 'over-controlled, sterile places which lack connection to the reality and diversity of the local environment'[9] are proliferating.

In London, the Broadgate Centre, adjacent to Liverpool Street station, is a 30-acre site owned and managed entirely by development company Broadgate Estates, which also manages other such estates elsewhere in the capital. The Broadgate Centre is patrolled twenty-four hours a day by private security, and is aimed specifically at attracting 'high earning people' and their high earnings. Also in London, 70 acres of land in the King's Cross redevelopment area has been farmed out to Argent Developments, which hopes to control, brand and market the public spaces as prime destinations for visitors.

Then there are Business Improvement Districts – or 'BIDs'. You may be hearing a lot more about these in coming years, as councils all over the country are excitedly adopting them. BIDs are a way to get more private finance into urban areas. A tax is raised from local businesses and is spent on improving the local environment: providing more of those private security officers, cleaning up graffiti, providing new street furniture and improving the look of shops. In return, the businesses decide what the environment looks like. Local councils rave about them: Peter Mullen wanted me to know all about the BID that is currently operating in Liverpool, entirely separate from the Paradise Project.

But BIDs are also a means of homogenising and controlling that environment: focusing it on consumption and taking the day-to-day running of it away from publicly accountable authorities, placing it in the hands of private corporations instead. The RICS report quotes one city-centre BID manager, who 'made it clear that he is keen to encourage more high earning shoppers and fewer less affluent customers. "High margins come with ABC1s, low margins with C2DEs," he said. "My job is to create an environment which will bring in more ABC1s."'[10] This job frequently involves, for example, moving homeless people out of BID areas for fear that they will deter wealthy shoppers.

You are, in other words, not a free man: you are a number. You are a carefully calibrated demographic. Seen in its wider context, said RICS, this was starting to look like the beginning of 'a quiet revolution in landownership, replicating Victorian patterns'. The next decade or so could see the very nature of our urban public spaces changing, as they are increasingly sold off, controlled and made risk-free and profitable to their private landlords, who run them at their own discretion. Our urban streets are becoming 'malls without walls', a trend that has been evident in the United States for decades and is now beginning to take off here. The end result of this, suggests RICS, could be very unfortunate indeed:

Today's developers are more concerned with the principles of the shopping mall than with creating places able to stand the test of time... This is because they are too narrowly focused simply on creating places that would generate maximum returns in terms of shopping and spending... the drive towards creating a place purely as a consumer product contradicts the creation of that sense of place, as the aim of property-led regeneration is higher property prices and higher rents, out of reach of local residents and local shopkeepers.[11]

What is happening in Paradise looks like a clear indication of where many more of our urban public spaces could be heading: not just clone towns but private clone towns, where you will behave as instructed, you will shop sensibly, and you will leave at the designated time. Or, to put it another way: Place = Profit. The equation is a simple one. And it works.

Upton Park, East London
March 2006

The café is small, cold and bare. It serves Indian food straight from hot plates behind a glass screen. There are no frills here. Like the rest of the place, it works but it's not much to look at.

I'm sitting at a plastic table eating rice, chicken and spinach and drinking a lot of water from plastic cups. It's hot stuff. Around the table with me are three men. Mark Jones is a local history teacher. Balding and with piercing eyes, he's friendly, well-informed and passionate. John Peasnall has a small moustache and grey hair, and has something of the air of the brigadier from *Dr Who circa* John Pertwee. Saif Osmani is in his twenties; an artist and local Green Party activist, he's clean-cut, in cords and dark winter coat. They're all eating too, and talking at the same time.

This is Queen's Market. There has been a market on this site for a century, and in that time it has changed a lot, as the area around it has changed. Today, it is one of the most ethnically diverse markets in London: 140 shops, stalls, barrows and kiosks serve a mind-boggling array of ethnic and cultural groups, from traditional East Enders to recently arrived Somalis. As a result, it is one of the most weird and wonderful places in the capital: a dazzling medley of colour, languages, shops, stalls, merchandise and movement. It is a lifeline for people on low incomes: the things that are sold here, from halibut to haberdashery, are almost unbelievably cheap. The whole is a strange, twenty-first-century extension of the kind of chaotic street market that has been at the centre of English life for thousands of years.

Mark Jones can wax lyrical about Queen's Market for hours. He is passionate both about what it is and what it stands for. 'One of the attractions of this place,' he tells me, as we eat, 'is that it's not just an environment where people can buy affordable food, it's a social space where people feel natural. Nobody is channelling them, shovelling them in a particular direction. They're not being monitored. You go to Stratford Mall a few miles away, it's a new, modern shopping mall, and you compare it to this place – you know full well there are about fifty cameras on you, there are security guys everywhere. There's a sense of menace. Here there's none of that.'

Saif grimaces when Mark mentions Stratford Mall.

'Listen,' he says. 'Listen to this place. There's noise everywhere. People talking all sorts of different languages. You go out there, everyone's shouting "bananas" and "apples" and God knows what. It's a real market atmosphere. You go to Stratford Mall, it's silent. It's tragic. I've lived in this area for twenty years. I moved here when I was five. Maybe there's a kind of nostalgia about it, but I think this is a real space for people to be part of, a very public space. Almost a communal one. All sorts of people get together here, and I think that's what they're afraid of. They don't want that. It's not the kind of place you can control.'

'They' in this case is Newham Council, whose plans for Queen's Market have sown seeds of anger and resentment widely among the local community. It intends to knock down the building in which the market is currently situated and replace it. Few people would have a problem with this: the building is ugly and badly maintained – largely due to its neglect by the same council over a long period. The trouble is that the council, led by its ambitious Labour mayor Sir Robin Wales, is going to replace it with something quite different.

See if you can guess what's going to happen here. Go on: just hazard a guess at what sort of development is going to replace this messy, affordable, human scale, popular place. If you've managed to read this far, it probably doesn't require a great effort of the imagination.

Newham Council has farmed Queen's Market out to a developer called St Modwen, which calls itself a 'prestigious, city-oriented regeneration specialist',[12] on a 150-year lease. The Council asked St Modwen to 'breathe new life into the area', which it plans to do by demolishing the existing market. It will replace it with a new market building, 370 'executive apartments', an eighteen-storey block of flats and a new library. It will also be demolishing a popular local pub, The Queens, next door.

St Modwen and the council say that this will benefit the local community. The new market building will have just as many market stalls as the existing one, and will be much more pleasant for everyone involved. Stallholders' rents will be frozen for five years to make sure that they are not priced out. Lots of new people will come to the area to see the new market, which will be very near the site of the 2012 Olympics. It will be an 'Olympic visitor destination', in fact.[13] There will be much-needed new housing, and the whole thing will be cleaner, safer and better than it is now.

Oddly, though, many local people think otherwise. Mark, John and Saif are just some of the Friends of Queen's Market, a local campaign set up to oppose the redevelopment. Virtually every market trader and stallholder in the market at present supports them. Every opposition party on the local council supports them. Campaign groups, ethnic minority organisations and local churches support them. Hardly anyone, in fact, seems to support the mayor and his council. Apart from St Modwen.

The reasons are numerous but, as so often, they stem from a lack of consultation with local people when this 'regeneration' scheme was being drawn up by the politicians and businessmen who were steering it through. The result has been twofold: first, an enormous backlash against the council and the developers has been generated. The Friends of Queen's Market have managed to put together a 12,000-signature petition – the biggest in Newham's history – and to gather around them a formidable alliance of supporters.

Secondly, the developer has had to change its plans as a result. Initially, the redevelopment plan included a branch of Asda. Shoppers and market traders were astonished. The Council, having produced a plush document designed to soothe those who believed it was set against the embarrassingly scruffy market's very existence, were now sanctioning something which would effectively destroy it. The Friends of Queen's Market mobilised. They produced research showing that everything you could buy from Asda which was also available in the market was considerably cheaper in the market. St Modwen got the jitters and announced that the supermarket would be smaller than originally suggested – too small for Asda, it seemed, which then pulled out of the deal.

But it's the future of the market stalls themselves that really raises blood pressures around here. The council and the developer stress that the new market building will contain just as many spaces for market stalls as the existing one, and St Modwen has made a lot of noise about how keen it is to ensure that the market remains as diverse and popular as it is now. It has made a similar noise about its rent freeze commitment, supposedly putting paid to claims that existing stallholders will be driven out in favour of wealthy incomers.

That, anyway, is the theory. The practice looks like being a little different. Firstly, Queen's Market is made up not just of market stalls, but of shops and kiosks too. The new development, while guaranteeing the same number of market stalls, has space for fewer shops than currently exist, and while rent on the stalls will be frozen for five years, rent on the shops and kiosks will not. It seems likely that the rents on the new shops will shoot up, to bring them in line with commercial rents on the nearby streets. The shopkeepers at Queen's Market currently pay around £10,000 a year rent to the council; a shopkeeper on the nearby high street will pay at least three times as much. If this kind of 'readjustment' takes place in the new development, none of the shopkeepers currently providing a vital, cheap and popular service to low-income people here is likely to remain in business.

Furthermore, while the market's stallholders currently pay a single rent payment to the council, St Modwen intends to split this into two payments – rent and service charges. Rent will be frozen, but service charges will not. There is no guarantee, in other words, that the operating costs for everyone here at the moment will not spiral way out of their reach, indelibly killing off the character of the place. To top it all, St Modwen admits that it still has no idea what it will cost it actually to run the market – and consequently how much it will have to charge the people who want to do business in it.[14]

It is probably not surprising, then, that both the shoppers and the sellers at Queen's Market are unhappy. This unhappiness is magnified even further by the fact that Newham Council has neglected this place for a long time. For seven years there was no market inspector, meaning that no one monitored the declining conditions in the building. Those conditions included a leaky roof, tatty awnings, hardly any litter bins, rarely washed floors, squalid nearby gutters and pavements, a barely functioning system of refuse removal and no redecoration for over a decade. Talk to many traders here and they'll claim that the council has been deliberately running the building down to provide a justification for replacing it with something more profitable.

'All we are really saying,' says Saif, 'is, look, if you want to do the market up, just consult us! Ask people what they want, let them be part of the process. Whereas the whole thing has been manufactured. Where's the vision? Where's the participation? The council had an option on the table when it first started to consider the future of this market – it was to refurbish this market itself at a cost of £6 million. They rejected that option. They never had any real intention of doing it.'

'As you can see,' says John, 'it's not a single issue here. Queen's Market is an open space where each community can operate. They overlap, but what they get out of it is quite different. In my view, though it is not perfect, it works very well. People who at the moment use it as a social space, who spend a lot of time here talking and shopping and meeting up – they won't be able to do that if the council and St Modwen have their way.'

'It's about identity,' chips in Saif. 'The identity of the East End, and of minority ethnic communities. Sixty-five per cent of this area is ethnic minority, and much as we like to lump them all together, that is lots of different people and cultures. There's all this debate now about multiculturalism and ghettoes and cultures trying to seal themselves off, but here they don't do that. That's what's so important about it. You've got African shops next to Asian shops next to East End barrow boys. I'm not romanticising it, it's fragile, but it's also real. And it works.'

Mark, whose eyes are shining now, couldn't agree more.

'I compare the market to a coral reef,' he says with passion. 'It's a place that has grown up organically, slowly, layer by layer over a long period. It's an incredibly diverse ecosystem but it's also very delicate. After the 7 July bomb attacks on London, this place should be celebrated as an example of how all these different cultures can rub along together. Instead, what are they doing? They're destroying it.' He looks intensely frustrated.

'It's not a beautiful place,' he concedes. 'But what it says about humanity is beautiful.'

*

A market is a complex and nuanced kind of space. It is public and private, communal and commercial, free to move through yet with a price on everything. At the heart of virtually every society for millennia, it is probably the most common type of public, or least open, urban space there is. A gathering point, a place to buy, sell, meet, do deals, argue, wander, take in the sights: a market is all of these. A town or an area of the city with a thriving market is usually thriving in a wider sense too. And the reverse is also very often true – dead or declining markets are often an effective signifier of a dead or declining community.

In England, the market as an institution has shaped our towns and cities – often literally, as high streets and squares were modelled around its presence. It has given them names: the Old English word for market is *ceap*, as in Chipping Norton, Chipping Barnet or Cheapside. It has shaped the mentality of the people. The market has even lent its name to the global economic ideology which is now, with heavy irony, bearing down threateningly on places like Queen's Market. We live in a market economy, but markets themselves are not always safe from it.

Walk through Queen's Market and you are given a fascinating lesson in how markets and communities interweave. There's no harmony here, but there is co-operation. The building itself is a classic sixties concrete precinct: run down, water-streaked, ugly, badly maintained. I wouldn't want to run a shop or a market stall in a building like this. Bins have been set on fire and the resulting mess not cleaned up. Shop roofs are strewn with litter – old cardboard boxes, bin bags, refuse. Vegetable waste gathers in corners and the ceiling is grimy, creaky-looking, missing panels.

It's easy to see how you could look at this place and question why anyone would oppose its regeneration. Yet if you look closer, you can see how a misapprehension has occurred. This building is grubby and grimy and ugly, but what happens within the building is probably irreplaceable. Replace this with something new, shiny and cleaner and consequently more expensive and closely monitored, and the delicate balance of that coral ecology Mark described would most probably be destroyed, never to be replaced.

And looking closer is a revelation. Here is an Afro-Caribbean hairdresser selling insanely multi-coloured wigs. There is a haberdashery, a silk stall, a linen kiosk with vast rolls of material, all of different colours, all lined up next to each other, with women busily sorting through them. Here is a chemist shop. There is a pound store. Here is a shop selling catering goods. There is a butcher, offering cows' feet, curry meat, turkey wings, ox tails, chicken legs, turkey gizzards. The butcher thuds them heavily into separate pieces with a huge chopper on an even huger chopping-board.

Next door a Caribbean fishmonger is doing a roaring trade, as is the Asian greengrocer opposite, selling vegetables I have never seen before and couldn't begin to name. Here's another fishmonger's, where you can treat yourself to octopus, squid, mackerel, snapper, coley, milkfish. Milkfish? I have no idea. There is a fancy curtain shop, a kettle stall, another haberdasher's, entirely populated by Bangladeshi women with scissors sorting through the material, taking it home to make things themselves.

This couldn't be further away from a supermarket. There are no ready meals in sight. Here you buy the ingredients, whether they be fish or silk, and you take them home to make the finished product yourself. The diversity is remarkable enough, but maybe even more remarkable are the prices – everything is eye-wateringly cheap. Asda's Price Promise would be laughed at here. In an area like this, with so many people living on very low wages, this is not just convenient, it is vital.

As I walk and watch, it strikes me that places like this can perhaps best be understood by seeing them as a confluence – a meeting point of different tribes. Quite literally in some cases – there are Eritreans, Somalis and other Africans here, according to Mark Jones, from quite distinct tribes within their home countries. But there are also Jews, Muslims, Hindus, Christians and atheists. There are football fans, passers-by, old people, young people, visitors from Up West and families who have come in from the outer suburbs specifically to shop here. There are flat caps, baseball caps, Afros, perms, burkas, headscarves and turbans. Skin colours range from deep black to pale pink and most shades in between. The sounds range from bhangra to barrow-boy. It shouldn't work, and yet somehow it does.

Danny Woodards is old East End and proud of it. Though he now lives in Billericay in Essex, as so many old East Enders do, his family has run a fruit and veg stall here for five generations. In his leather coat and flat cap, Danny looks like an East End market trader would be expected to look, and sounds like one would be expected to sound. He knows his work and loves it, he is proud of where he is and he feels he belongs here. And he is furious.

'I'm fifth generation here, OK?' he says. 'We've been through two world wars – got it? Two world wars and God knows what else my family's gone through. And now one man, this mayor, ruins everything. No one asked us, you know? All of a sudden it was on us.'

Unprompted, like so many others, Danny tells me what he thinks this is about at its heart – individuals versus the machine.

'It's the same old thing, isn't it?' he asks, rhetorically. 'They're gonna clone it. I'm serving people here, their grandchildren are coming to me. You know, "Nan said come here, and Mum said come here". And we're supposed to say, "Oh, all right, St Modwen, come and take us over. Kick us up the studs and we'll take whatever you give us." Well, I'm sorry, I won't.'

Down at the other end of Danny's stall, as we're talking, his partner is selling a massive bag of onions to an Indian woman. Danny nudges me and points at her.

'Here, look at this,' he says. 'You won't see anything like this after St Modwen have come in. She's buying a whole pallet of onions there.

This isn't wholesale – this is normal, what these people buy. They'll buy 10 kilos of onions and 10 kilos of potatoes and then come back next week and get another lot. These people I deal with, their wives are indoors cooking. They're not going to work. They're cooking and feeding their families. But the way the developer looks at it, they want to put white people in these new flats they're gonna build – yuppies, you know? Get down the station, go to work in the city, come home and sit in their flat with the door closed. These people here, they've got nothing that St Modwen wants.' He looks disheartened, but not broken. Danny is insistent that he will not be broken.

'I been doing this for a lifetime,' he says. 'I know what I'm doing. And my family are being slung to one side by a borough we've served for a hundred years. They're fucking gangsters in suits. We could never get away with what these people are gonna get away with.'

Danny's voice is plaintive as he speaks these words. This is not the voice of a man romanticising this place – Danny doesn't look like the romantic type. But neither is it simply the voice of a man who makes money from it. It is the voice of a man who, for all its faults, believes that it is his place and that he belongs to it, and that he deserves a say in what happens to it. Put like that, it doesn't seem very much to ask.

'I'll tell you something,' says Danny. 'This market's a foothold in business. It gets you on the ladder. Most of these people trading here, there's no way they could afford St Modwen's prices. You watch, when this market is rebuilt there won't be a quarter of these shops trading. One Asian guy in a shop over there, he turned around to me and you know what he said? He said this is ethnic cleansing. Ethnic cleansing, the man reckons. And I reckon he's got a point.'

So here we are again. Again, emotive, extreme language which originates in something real and painful. It originates in displacement. Is this ethnic cleansing? Obviously not in the original, terrible sense of that term, no. But it could, through accident or design, result in the washing away of this messy, chaotic, ethnic diversity and its replacement with a monocultural money culture.

Whether or not you want to use the term 'ethnic cleansing', there is another term that could be used about what is happening here – and what has been happening in so many of the places I have visited across England. The term is class war. A war waged, as ever, by the landed and the wealthy against those they would educate, civilise or simply shove out of the way.

This kind of thing is not supposed to happen in England any more. We are supposed to be a middle-class nation, at ease with itself, weekending in European cities, shopping at Ikea and cooking Nigella's recipes. Class war is so very unhelpful a concept in this age of caring capitalism. So very aggressive, so very unnecessary, so very 1970s.

In which case it is still the 1970s here in Newham. With a vengeance.

Manish Patel is in his thirties. He's articulate and energetic. He wears stylish steel-rimmed glasses and runs a shop called Kirti Gifts; a shop set up by his father in the heart of Queen's Market. Manish is also the founder and leader of the Queen's Market Trade Association, which is fighting the corner of the shopkeepers here in the whole redevelopment saga.

Kirti Gifts is a maze of cheap, useful things which appear to have no relationship to each other. I have to wait about fifteen minutes to see Manish because he's so busy, and in that fifteen minutes I watch him behind his counter. In front of a wall hung with plastic clocks, he serves a woman in a headscarf buying a squeezy yellow mustard dispenser, an African guy buying half a dozen saucepans and a middle-aged woman who wants to know how much the ashtrays cost. He serves a long line of people buying a wide array of things. The shop is packed and buzzing, and Manish has to work hard to keep on top of it.

'The Association started off with about three or four shops,' Manish tells me during a brief lull in business. 'It's turned into the whole market. We were all worried about what was happening, because we weren't being asked. The way the council treat us… whatever we do they know how to counter it. We went to a meeting recently and all we wanted to do was ask questions, but by the time we got into that meeting the people had already been told, "That Manish Patel, he's just a troublemaker." '

Manish doesn't look like a troublemaker. He looks like what he says he is – a businessman. He sounds like one, too.

'When I go to a meeting and ask a question,' he says, 'I want a yes or no answer. I don't want "I'll get back to you", and then I never hear from them again. We sat down with them. They asked us to compromise: we compromised. I just simply asked them, what kind of lease are we going to get? Is it going to be five years? How much is it going to cost us? I've got no answers to any of these questions. How can I run a business like this? So I've cancelled all the meetings with the council. I said to them, "Until I get answers to the questions I've already asked I'm not prepared to meet with you any more." I don't see the point. So the council has put it around that we won't meet with them and we're not co-operative. We're just troublemakers.'

Manish has found himself thrust into the role of campaigner, but it's not a role he really wants. As he keeps telling me, he's a businessman first and foremost. He is here to make a living for the three generations of Patels who run, have run and perhaps will run Kirti Gifts. It's not a charity. And yet the shop is also part of a social, cultural and economic web. It serves people at the bottom of the economic pile – the overworked, the underpaid, the illiterate, the non-English speaking. They need Manish, and he needs them. It's not to exaggerate the role of shops like this to say that they are rooted in their community, and that those roots put out suckers and feelers that cannot be seen above the soil, but which nourish the place and its people.

'I would say,' estimates Manish, 'that about 80 per cent of the traders are now asking themselves, "Is it worth going into the new market?" They said to me, "If you want a place in the new market we can place you." Fine, but the new shops are going to be smaller than the ones that exist now, and the rent is going to increase two- to three-fold, according to the estimates they gave me. I was laughing because I knew we had no future in this market. If they increase our rent by three times I have to increase my prices by three times, and then I get no customers.'

I wonder what he thinks he's going to do. Realistically, honestly, how does he see the future here?

'First of all,' he says, 'my fight's not finished. We're trying to set up Queen's Market Online. I've bought the domain name and we're going to try and sell things that way. Other traders are joining in. Because, to be honest, if things go ahead as they're currently planned, we'll probably have to pack up and go somewhere else. This is a family business. I've got a little kid. I know it sounds nasty saying "We'll just go", but this is everything to us. Most of the traders I've spoken to have said the same. And look at people like Danny, his family has been here for generations, it means even more to him than it does to me.'

He means it. I can see it in his eyes.

'I've got to make a living,' he says.

I need to leave, but before I go I want to say goodbye to the people who have shown me around. I find Saif up near Danny's stall. In front of the stall is a big plastic bin. It's crammed with boxes, bags and vegetable waste, and below it are scattered a few wooden boxes full of cast-offs: rotten bananas, cabbage leaves, split clementines. In these cast-offs, three people are rummaging.

One of them is Saif, in his trenchcoat and trainers. Later in the day, the Friends are doing an installation as part of an art exhibition in the University of East London nearby. Saif is in charge, and thinks a display of cast-off cabbage leaves and banana skins would add to the ambience.

But two other people are also gathering up old cabbage leaves and filling a wooden box with them: an Asian man and his young son. This, I think to myself, is real poverty – the sort a sheltered bourgeois type like me can only imagine. The sort I have seen, and expected to see, in Delhi or Jakarta, but am now seeing two hours from my home. Guilt and empathy hit me like twin pistons. This man, and his fresh-faced son, reduced to eating cast-off cabbage leaves they've scraped from under a bin. How can this happen in twenty-first-century England?

The man straightens up, his box full, and turns to leave. He sees me looking at him. He smiles and indicates first his son and then the leaves.

'For pet rabbit,' he says.

There's something very English about the way the politics of public space is developing. By 'English' I mean suspicious of ideas, 'no-non-sense', unpretentious. Being English myself, I'm prone to the kind of practical anti-intellectualism that is often said to define our national character. Often it can be refreshing and necessary. Sometimes, though, it can be limiting, because it inculcates a tendency to focus on the here and now rather than thinking about the implications for the future.

Look at our national political debate and you'll see plenty of examples of this. Take civil liberties. The English seem to rather like having hundreds of security cameras posted all around their streets, because at a local level they are said to deter crime. England is the most camera-surveyed country in the world, but nobody really complains. It's not much of a leap from this to the government's proposed system of national identity cards and an accompanying national database, upon which the personal details of every citizen in the country will be placed.[15] It will help catch criminals, so what's the problem? If you've got nothing to hide, you've got nothing to be scared of.

It's not hard to see where this kind of live-for-the-moment attitude starts to lead us when we consider the future of our urban public spaces. New security guards policing the streets? Sounds like a good idea if it keeps the hoodies away. Privatisation of the same streets? Well, so what? It doesn't make much difference to me, and who wants to pay more council tax? Bullying corporations? Welcome to the real world: the rich will always be with us.

Don't think about the consequences if there's no immediate reason to: that seems to be the English mentality. And we pay for it. We didn't think about the consequences when we all started driving to the out-of-town superstores to do our shopping. Now we complain that all the local shops have disappeared. We didn't think about the consequences when we ran gawping towards the Gap sales and the new branches of Starbucks. Now we complain about the cloning of our high streets.

Now the English are at it again. We're not thinking about the consequences of what we're doing – or allowing to be done – to our urban public spaces. They are being locked up, privatised, sold off and cleared not only of colour and character but, in a more sinister development, of poverty, homelessness and inconvenient social groups. To use Mark Jones's imagery again, those delicate, organic, complex coral reefs are being blasted into shards with dynamite. Then the seabed is being beam-trawled and an oil rig erected on the dead sediment. And what are we doing about it? Very little. Perhaps all those clone towns, superstores and business parks have colonised not just our landscapes but our minds.

Whatever the reason, we seem happy to let millionaire developers and metropolitan architects loose on the very heart of the public spaces in our towns and cities. It will not be the ordinary shopkeepers, or even the ordinary shoppers, who benefit from this. Why should it be? I talked earlier of class war, and I don't think I was exaggerating. And when people talk to me of 'ethnic cleansing', while the language may be unpleasant, the sentiment behind it is not exaggerated either.

Come back in ten years, said Don Lee, and see where we are. Time will tell whether he was exaggerating too, but if things go on as they are, I suspect that his fears will begin to come true. The English are sleepwalking towards a colonisation and corporatisation of their urban public spaces. As usual, we will properly wake up to this when it's almost too late. We like to boast lazily about being the birthplace of liberty and the home of the freeborn Englishman. Freeborn we may have been, but liberty is currently looking pretty sick, and its defenders don't seem inclined to do very much about it.

As we say in England: you get what you pay for.

The White Horse Inn
PATRONS
CAR PARK
LEPHONE
TELEPHONE
BRADFORD · ON · TONE
POST
OFFICE
AND
VILLAGE
STORE

7

The Village Green Preservation Society

The townsman envies the villager his certainties and, in
Britain, has always regarded urban life as just a temporary
necessity. One day he will find a cottage on the green and
'real values'.

Ronald Blythe, *Akenfield*, 1969

Ashford, Kent
July 2006

It's been a long time since I was here last. Twenty years, perhaps? It's
hard to say. My parents brought me here when I was a kid – a couple
of times, I think. There's still a photo in their album of me standing
next to the sign which announces the village name on the road in.
I'm not much bigger than the sign is.

Things were different then, I should think, though I can't remember much. Just the name of the village, which at the time was quite
exciting because it was the same as mine: Kingsnorth. This, as far as
there is one, is my ancestral home, which makes it sound a lot
grander than it actually is. Our family history comes back to this village and its environs, where generations of my ancestors worked in
the fields, doing nothing obviously spectacular: living their lives,
working for their rulers, surviving.

The history of my family, in this sense, is a history of the social mobility of ordinary folk in England: a history of how change and opportunity transformed lives. For centuries we remained in and around the Kentish village from which we took our surname. In the nineteenth century, with the expansion of industrialism, some of us moved to London to seek our fortune in its factories. By the middle of the twentieth century we were living in its new suburbs, where I spent my early years. Now we are all over the country; all over the world, in fact. Some of us have university degrees and cook our food in olive oil. Welcome to the new England.

Things have changed in Kingsnorth too. Not as much as you might expect in the old heart of the village, perhaps. This is a conservation area, tucked away behind the medieval church in whose grounds some of my ancestors lie. Its old, white weatherboarded Kentish houses probably haven't changed much in outward appearance for a century or two. But this is no longer where the action is: conservation areas rarely are. Outside this protected little heartland, with its great oaks and hedge-lined lanes, Kingsnorth, like many other English villages, is being transformed.

A mile to the north of the village is the town of Ashford. For a long time this, too, was unremarkable. These days, though, Ashford is a 'hub'. The government has plans for it. The high-speed Channel Tunnel Rail Link, due to open in 2009, goes straight through 'Ashford International' – next stop, London. It has become a middle point between the capital and the Continent, and a potential home to those who work in both or either places but don't want to live there. Ashford is still an unremarkable place. But if the government has its way, it will become a much bigger unremarkable place.

Ashford has been designated one of four 'growth areas', in which a process of 'urban intensification' will take place. This is shorthand for a massive programme of housebuilding. The government has a problem: the population is rising, largely due to an increase in immigration, at the same time as the number of people per household is falling: more people stay single longer and more get divorced. At the time of the last national census, in 2001, 30 per cent of households across the UK were only occupied by one person.[1] The housing market, partly as a result, is overheating so insanely that in many parts of the country – especially the south-east, where the population has increased by 10 per cent in twenty years[2] – people on anything close to the average salary simply cannot afford to buy a home.

In an attempt to tackle this ever-growing problem, the government is demanding that 200,000 homes be built every year across the nation until 2016. This, runs the logic, will cool the pressurised housing market and solve the housing shortage problem. In reality, it may have little effect: even such a massive increase in housing construction – the biggest wave since the end of the Second World War – will probably not provide enough supply to dampen down an increasingly frantic demand. In any case, that demand is largely concentrated in the south and south-east: nationwide there are actually more houses than households,[3] and in some northern cities thousands of old terraces are being knocked down for lack of residents.

Nonetheless a total of 200,000 new homes will be built in the four 'growth areas' – Milton Keynes, the London-Stansted-Cambridge corridor, the 'Thames Gateway' and Ashford – by 2016. By this date, Ashford will also get a network of new road and motorway improvements, a new railway station, a new bus interchange, a new park-and-ride scheme and increased train services. It will get an 'urban renaissance' in its town centre, so that it can promote 'new urban lifestyles'. It will get lots of new jobs – theoretically, at least – and new water supply and drainage systems to help cope with them. It will get new education, health and community facilities.[4]

Crucially, though, it will get those houses. The government wants Ashford to absorb 31,000 new homes between 2001 and 2031, 13,100 of which are to be built by 2016.[5] What this means for the village of Kingsnorth is laid out starkly in the government's regional planning guidance document. '[Ashford] is relatively unconstrained by high quality agricultural land or other landscape designations on its southern side,' it reads, 'and there is significant potential for developing the town to take advantage of its manifest locational advantages, and all that has already been achieved.' After all, Ashford is 'well located as a nodal point for sub-regional, national and international communications'.[6]

What this gibberish means in plain English is simple: Kingsnorth is going to get it. Ashford will effectively double in size over the next twenty years, and if everything that is planned comes to pass, Kingsnorth will no longer be a village: it will be a suburb, located in something called 'greater Ashford'. Its conservation area will doubtless remain much the same, but once you step outside, it will be into a very different world.

Not everybody is happy about this. One of those who is less than pleased is Dr Hilary Moorby, a Kingsnorth resident for twenty years. A former chairman of the local branch of the Campaign to Protect Rural England, she lives in the village and has spent much of the last decade battling plans to suburbanise it. I arranged to meet her in a car park by the village hall, from where she promised to walk me around the village and show me what's happening. But first, in her car, she's showing me the official documents, and the colourful maps that go with them, which lay out the village's future in black and white and red and blue.

'They want three "urban villages", with 6000 houses in each, then another 13,000 houses in the centre, and in the outlying villages,' she explains, leafing through the glossy document. 'The number comes from the government. They tell you how many houses you have to have, and you can fight that for a while, but you won't get very far. So that's the plan for Ashford. They're phasing it, and the "urban village" that will incorporate Kingsnorth will be the last phase, after 2021.' She looks out of the window across the fields beyond the car park.

'So that's how they're going to totally destroy Kingsnorth,' she says.

Not that Hilary, and others like her, haven't tried to stop them. She says she had a 'big argument' with those responsible when the plans came out. Hilary seems to have a lot of big arguments with local politicians and developers. She likes to keep them on their toes.

'We had a workshop,' she says, 'with these consultants, and we played a silly game with different coloured tiles – honestly, the things these people think of – and we were moving the tiles around to decide where things should go. It was called a "strategic growth model workshop". So everybody put these tiles where they thought things should go, and eventually we came to a decision.' She snorts.

'What nonsense!' she says.

The first place Hilary takes me is the new housing estate that was built near the village about fifteen years ago. You have to walk across some fields to get there – fields that Hilary and others fought hard to retain. The original plan had been to stick the new houses directly onto the edge of the village – on a flood plain. Instead, a wildlife 'buffer zone' now exists here, providing valuable green space for the villagers and those who live on the estate. Beyond it, a line of red roofs creeps towards us from Ashford; a taste of things to come.

'When I came to the village in 1986, none of this was here,' says Hilary. 'It was just open countryside. The trouble with estates like this is that they're all the same, aren't they? We're working hard to make sure that the newbuild won't be, and so far we're being quite success-ful. These old estates were very badly designed: no shops, no facilities, and all these cul-de-sacs coming off one circular main road that inevitably gets used as a racetrack. That won't happen this time. The new estates will have a proper street with shops and things on it. It will be a bit more like a real community than a dormitory, so in that sense things have got better.'

When we reach the estate, I can see what she means. It's a maze of cul-de-sacs, all leading onto a wide, streetlamp-lit road which shears off, past a fenced-off remnant of ancient woodland ('absolutely incredible with bluebells in spring' says Hilary), towards the nearby

Tesco which squats on the edge of the village. What's most interesting about this estate, though, is the style of its houses. They're all big houses – large, detached, pricey, built here to provide a little bit of almost-countryside for people who, as Hilary puts it, 'want to live in the village, and in the countryside, but also want all the comforts of the town. You can understand it, but it leads, in the end, to suburbia everywhere'. But the styles: they're all over the place. Quite literally. One house is made of flint: the kind of vernacular style you'd find in parts of Norfolk, or in the Chilterns. Next to that is a mock-Tudor effort, all dark beams and whitewash. Next comes a house in the old Kentish wood-and-tile style. Then one made of red brick. It's like a regional housing styles theme park, or a very big model village. Off-the-shelf regional consumerism. Our landscapers have erased all history and knowledge from this place so that you may replace it with your own, at a price which, we feel sure you will agree, is very reasonable indeed.

'It would be nice to think,' says Hilary, as we walk on, 'that by 2021 everyone will come to their senses a bit, and they won't want all these thousands of houses. Otherwise, this will all be Ashford. Actually they're trying to call it Ashford now. They're constantly referring to Kingsnorth as being in the "greater Ashford" area. It's a very subtle sort of conditioning of people to think of themselves as not Kingsnorth but Ashford, and not rural but urban.'

In any case, she says, housing or no housing, the character of many villages in this part of Kent is being lost to encroaching development.

'A lot has changed in twenty years,' she says. 'You get different types of people in the village now. The people are more urban or sub-urban, used to home comforts, not really understanding they're in a different place. I've been doing a traffic count in the village since 1996. Back then, you'd get 2500 vehicles a day down our road. I did one the other day and it's just under 6000. The village shop and post office closed down about eighteen months ago... it all adds up.'

Up a rise and down a footpath hemmed in by garden fences, we come to a pond in a small area of green space. The pond is fringed with lilies and rushes and full of large, lazy fish. The surrounding shrubs are hopping with noisy goldfinches. Houses overlook this place from all sides and a well-maintained footpath winds past it. Signposts instruct you not to fish or swim. There is a life-ring on a stand. It's like a small version of the kind of suburban park I played in when I was a kid.

'Now, this is interesting,' says Hilary. 'This pond was here long before this estate. It's an old farm pond. When I came up here originally it was really lovely. It was just this pond on a little hill completely surrounded by fields. You can scarcely believe it now, can you?' She looks around her.

'It was the village fishing pond,' she continues. 'And they'd been coming here for generations – all the village boys, they came here to fish, and the fishing was good. They didn't see why they shouldn't continue to come, and neither did I. But when they built this estate, the people in these houses here made *such* a fuss about it. They said the boys were being rowdy, and disturbing their Sunday afternoons. So now they're not allowed to fish. You can see how they've planted all these spiky shrubs all around the edges so that you can't get down to the bank, and there's a sign up there saying you can't fish. See? It says "Area to be kept tidy at all times". It's quite sad, I think. The fish are still here, and so are the water lilies. But the place is dead, really, isn't it?'

In 1969, a Suffolk writer called Ronald Blythe published a book about the village he lived in. Times were changing in the village, and in the countryside as a whole. Mechanisation and intensification were rapidly changing the landscape. Farm subsidies and new urban incomers were transforming the nature and character of rural England and, for better or for worse, it was clear it would be for ever. Blythe envisaged his book as a portrait; 'a kind of natural conversation with three generations' of his neighbours. A snapshot of an ordinary, 'not particularly striking' English village at a particular moment in time.[7]

As writers will, Blythe took a liberty or two in the creation. The village which he chose to call 'Akenfield' was actually two nearby villages, melded into one for the sake of literary convenience. The rest of the book, though, was about as true to life as a non-fiction book can be. Blythe chose simply to interview village residents and to record their words verbatim. The result would be a literal transcript of the views, opinions and experiences of the people of one English village at the end of a turbulent decade.

Unexpectedly, *Akenfield* was a huge success: a bestseller all around the world. The story had touched something. After the turbulence of the 1960s, it seemed to take a step back and shed some light on the true roots of England.

And those roots were withering away. Many of the contributors to *Akenfield* talk about the decline of rural life and dwell on their fears that they will be the last of their line or their profession. Most of those fears came true. This was revealed most poignantly when another writer, a generation later, decided to find out what had happened to this most famous of English villages.

Twenty-five years after the original's publication, journalist Craig Taylor went back to the area in 2004 to write a follow-up book, which he called *Return to Akenfield*. Taylor was not a Suffolk man; in fact, he was Canadian. But he was curious about what had happened to Akenfield. On visiting the villages, and interviewing the residents, using the same techniques as Blythe had nearly four decades before, he found some marked changes.

The population was bigger for a start: 358 inhabitants rather than 298. The two shops and the post office were gone and the vicarage was empty. The village pub looked like the inside of an Ikea and Akenfield now had broadband internet access. Accents were changing, from broad Suffolk to estuary English. But there was a wider change too – one more permanent and meaningful:

All of the villagers who worked in the old professions – the wheel-wright, the saddler, the blacksmith – are dead, and most of their professions have gone with them... In their places now are commuters and entrepreneurs and retirees from other parts of the country. The family names in the local graveyard are no longer the surnames of the people living in the houses.[8]

Between Ronald Blythe and Craig Taylor, Akenfield had become a village finally detached from the land that surrounded it. The original book's interviewees include horsemen, orchard workers, farriers, blacksmiths, forge workers, shepherds, thatchers, saddlers, ploughmen: the legions of the land. Craig Taylor's population is very different. There are still a few orchard workers and farmers, but there are also entrepreneurs, retirees, pub managers, college lecturers, students and walkers. Even those that do work the land are either getting on in years or, like the migrant farm workers and itinerant sheep shearer, are just passing through.

In this, Akenfield is typical. Like so many other English villages, it has become a place for retiring to, visiting, weekending in, passing through. Taylor's probably unintentional but nonetheless overwhelming theme is the tearing up of roots which previously kept places like this, and the people in them, connected to the land. Not that everyone thinks this is a bad thing. One of Taylor's interviewees is Blythe himself, now eighty-three, who warns about romanticising those roots. 'People then were extremely poor,' he explains. 'Their houses were uncomfortable and damp. Children left school very early... it was very hard to get away, to do anything or to be yourself, and people worked and worked until they died.'

Yet even the old writer can't help regretting some of what has been lost. 'When this last generation is gone,' he says, 'there will be a break from people who have had any experience of this life. Some of it will be missed: the part that cannot be put into words.'[9]

*

The part that cannot be put into words. It's become a familiar refrain to me – and sometimes a frustrating one for someone whose job is to do just that. Also familiar have been many of the other factors which have contributed to the changing character of villages like Akenfield and Kingsnorth: agricultural decline, shop closures, pub company power, soaring house prices, wealthy incomers, the death of place-based culture.

A village, though, is a complex place: a nuanced community with many influences from within and without. It's hard to define. What, after all, makes a village? What does it need to be what it is? A church? A farm? A pub? A certain number of houses? Even the *Oxford English Dictionary* isn't sure: it rather spinelessly defines a village as 'a group of houses and associated buildings, larger than a hamlet and smaller than a town, especially in a rural area'. Since it goes on to define a hamlet as something smaller than a village, and a town as something larger than a village, this is not tremendously helpful.

But perhaps it tells us something about the diversity of English villages. Perhaps they are that hard to pin down. Villages in Yorkshire look very different from villages in Sussex. A Devon village is not the same thing as a Norfolk village. The small, local, subtleties make the difference. Kentish villages tended to grow up along main roads, for example: they're long and straggly with no obvious centre. Hertford-shire villages tend to be focused around a green, Buckinghamshire villages often have a pond at their centre. The architectural styles and materials used, from thatch to flint to stone to slate, vary from region to region and sometimes from village to village within them.

In parts of the northern uplands there are no villages at all, only isolated farms and small hamlets. Some villages will date back to pre-Roman times, others be products of population shifts caused by the fourteenth-century Black Death or the eighteenth-century Enclosure Acts. Some were even created wholesale by landed aristocrats who wanted a picturesque view, or Victorian industrialists who wanted to give their workers a decent place to live.

Yet the *idea* of the village is central to the English idea of themselves and their nation. We continue stubbornly to think of ourselves, in some vague way, as a rural nation. The country which invented both capitalism and industrialism more than two centuries ago, and whose merchant classes imposed them brutally on its population – and later that of half the world – still imagines that it lives in a Constable painting. It still wanders lonely as a coach load of tourists through Grasmere every August; still dreams of that early retirement to a cottage with roses round the door. Over one hundred thousand of its people move from urban to rural areas every year, in search of that dream.[10]

No matter that we have been a predominantly urban nation since 1850 and that 80 per cent of us live in cities or towns. No matter that both Constable and Wordsworth worked at a time of rapid and confusing change themselves, and often reacted against it. No matter that the rural idyll today is increasingly affordable only to the wealthy, or that the supermarkets we shop in and the economic model we buy into are responsible for the decline of the countryside we profess to admire.

No, the English still want to think of themselves, somehow, as villagers, in their hearts if not in their everyday lives. More often than not it's an unexamined, Marie Antoinette version of country life: a comfortable, dirt-free vision of rurality, where cocks never crow at 4 a.m., roads are never covered in slurry, cows don't shit on the footpath and farmers doff their caps in the low-beamed pub. An easy vision, appealing in its way but not connected to any kind of reality, past or present.

Yet perhaps it's too easy to condemn it. Humans have lived on and from the land for 99 per cent of their history. They have moved with the seasons and the wider natural world of which they are still a part, however much some of them might like to imagine otherwise. In the grand scheme of things, a couple of centuries of urban industrialism is a drop in time's ocean. Maybe this is what fuels those dreams. Our heads may have broken with the countryside, but perhaps our hearts are still there.

Whatever the reason, if it is villages which make up the true heart of England – and we long to believe it is, regardless of where the truth might lie – then taking the temperature of the English village today might give us some idea of the health of the nation and the culture. Or, if that sounds too ambitious, it might at least give us a reality check.

Portscatho, Cornwall
August 2006

The best way to get to the Roseland peninsula is to take the King Harry Ferry across the wonderful, wide River Fal. There's been a ferry service operating here, between Trelissick and Carlannick, since at least the time of Henry VI; hence the name. Today's version is one of only five chain ferries left in England, and likes to boast that a national newspaper once voted it one of the top ten ferry journeys in the world. I can see why. It's a beautiful summer's afternoon and we are moving slowly across the Fal, steep green tree-shrouded banks sliding down into deep green waters. Terns dip and skim over the mud-flats beneath the receding bank as, ahead of us, individual trees begin to separate from the green whole.

On the Roseland, not far from here, is the small seaside village of Portscatho, a place which has all the necessary prompts to take me back to childhood caravanning holidays in the west country. The screeching of gluttonous gulls. The stone harbour, tide out, fishing boats sitting askew on mud and bladderwrack. Tourists eating pasties. Kids in shorts with nets made of bamboo canes. White-painted houses, low old pubs, art galleries. It's the August bank holiday week, the sun is out and half the country is here, enjoying it.

But it's not always this crowded, or this lively. As the afternoon draws to a close I find myself standing on the harbour wall with two local residents. Julian German is an independent local councillor: early thirties, blond-haired, in a green T-shirt and jeans, he runs the local grocer's. John Nicholson is in his sixties: white-haired and weatherbeaten, as a Cornishman should be, he is from the hamlet of Bohortha, a mile or so over the hill. They have come to show me the village behind the pasties and the fishing nets.

Julian raises an arm and points to a pretty row of seafront houses to the left of the harbour.

'Along this road here,' he says, 'I think there's five lived in. Along this other road here' – he swivels around to point at the seafront on the other side of the harbour – 'there's two. That's out of about forty houses in all. In the whole of the Portscatho harbour area, there is only one child at the local school. Every other house is a second home or a holiday cottage.'

Portscatho has a problem. It is a problem it shares with the whole of Cornwall and many other equally beautiful parts of England: local people are being priced out of the villages their families grew up in. Madly spiralling houses prices, a lack of affordable homes and the enormous increase in the numbers of houses sold for second homes or holiday cottages in the last decade has created a housing crisis that is hollowing the heart out of Cornwall's villages. Portscatho becomes a very different place when the tourists go home.

'What you might call the resident population lives in a council area up the hill, which you can't see from here,' says Julian. 'The houses aren't so nice to look at and it doesn't have the views. Within the harbour area here, we're now looking at 80 per cent holiday or second homes. No one local lives here unless they're very wealthy, and not many of them are.'

'In Portscatho,' chips in John, 'there are more second homes than holiday lets. In Bohortha we have more holiday lets than second homes, but we have a similar problem. Young people in particular just can't afford to live here now, with these prices. The decline of the farm economy has contributed too, and the difficulties in finding jobs. Whether it's too many second homes or too many holiday homes is not really the point – the point is that together they mean there's a lack of affordable housing, which is just killing places like this.'

Julian points at the seafront road again. 'You see those two houses there? The creamy one and the white one? They were both council houses. The one on the right was recently sold for £400,000. Three bedrooms, no parking, just a 1950s semi, needed a massive amount of work inside. But look at the views. That *was* the affordable housing. They're building new ones to replace it, but they're on the town allotments. Also, it's much harder to get planning permission to build a new affordable house than to build a holiday let. There was a case recently in a smaller village down the road, where a woman wanted to convert a building for a relative to live in. The planners said, no, you can't, there's no amenities, there's no bus route – but if you want, you can turn it into a holiday let.'

'Happens all the time,' agrees John, glumly.

'And now we've got a newer phenomenon,' continues Julian, 'which is investment property. Traditionally people bought second homes, and quite often they would let them out for holiday homes as well. They probably needed to get a mortgage to buy it so they wanted to get some income back. But now you're talking £300– £400,000 for a house down here, and the people who can afford that sort of money, with their city bonuses and stuff, they're buying it purely as an investment. They don't even come down at all to live in it. Some of these houses just stand empty every day of the year.'

For a moment, nobody says anything. The gulls scream.

'We're not saying we're against tourism,' says John. 'We just need affordable houses for local people as well. People need to be able to afford to live here and work here. Otherwise the place dies.'

*

The writers of Cornish tourist brochures – in line with an apparent policy adopted by the writers of tourist brochures everywhere on Earth – like to chirrup about 'a land of contrasts'. The most striking contrast in Cornwall, though, is one which none of them mentions: the extreme and growing gap between the county's poverty and wealth.

Think about poverty in England today and you'll probably visualise some grim, inner-city estate. Think about homelessness and you might think of *Big Issue* sellers or rough sleepers in Leicester Square. You're unlikely to think about the land of clotted cream, donkey rides, quoits and golden beaches; a general lack of awareness which seems to be part of the problem.

According to the homelessness charity Shelter, Cornwall is the least affordable part of England in which to live, including London.[11] In 1996, the average property price in the county was just under £56,000.[12] Ten years later it was over £195,000[13] – a staggering 348 per cent increase in just ten years.[14] This is the fastest rise, and to the highest level, of any county in England, but it is just the beginning of Cornwall's problems. The county is also the poorest in the country: earnings per head of population are 62 per cent of the national average[15] and the region's economy has suffered from the disappearance or decline of its traditional sources of jobs and income – mining, fishing and farming. Tourism, in fact, is about the only major 'industry' Cornwall has left. Such is its poverty that it is the only region anywhere in Britain which still receives 'Objective 1' funding from the EU – the budget slated for areas of extreme deprivation.

This combination of poverty, unemployment and inflated property prices has led to a painful and peculiarly Cornish form of inequality which is achingly apparent in places like Portscatho. By the sea, and in the beautiful old areas of countryside, the homes are absurdly expensive. Those who buy them are usually from elsewhere, and many don't live in them. Almost a third of Cornish property changes hands for cash – the highest proportion in England and one which reflects the extreme wealth of many of the purchasers. In the very western tip of the county, where Portscatho lies, the proportion rises to almost half.[16] Meanwhile, the Cornish live on the cheap estates and in the ugly, just-about-affordable places, far from the eyes of the quick-buck City investors and the holidaymakers who come looking for the Real Cornwall.

To compound the problem, the continued sale of properties for second homes and investments in the county is not matched by any significant construction of affordable homes, with the result that more homes are leaving the market than come onto it, pushing prices up even higher. The right to buy council homes, introduced by Margaret Thatcher, has been a boon for the rich here and a curse for many of the poor. Cornwall's proportion of social housing is just over 11 per cent, compared with a national average of 19 per cent, and in the first years of this century more affordable homes were sold than constructed. In the same period, the number of people on housing registers in the county nearly doubled, to over 15,000.[17]

People like John and Julian have had enough of all this, and they're not the only ones.

Twenty-five miles west, in a small semi on an estate in the equally picturesque seaside village of Porthleven, a Cornish nationalist is telling me what she'd like to do about it. Councillor Jane Acton lives in one of those affordable but not picturesque houses that Julian and John were talking about. Its chief distinguishing characteristic is a sticker on the front window that says 'Cornish Assembly Now!' Porthleven is very similar to Portscatho, and hundreds of other villages around the county's coastline. It too has a little stone harbour, and the village centre is inlaid with higgledy-piggledy old houses, lots of tourist shops and narrow streets with views across the Atlantic.

Hence it too has that same social apartheid. Jane has just handed me a map which shows how the various parts of Porthleven are faring with regard to holiday lets and second homes. In the Harbour Road, in the prettiest bit of the village, 83 per cent of the houses are not inhabited by local people. The average for the village's coastal area is 74 per cent. The estate in which Jane lives is not even on the map.

Jane belongs to a political party called Mebyon Kernow. Translated from the Cornish, this means 'Sons of Cornwall'. It's not a party that gets much attention on general election night, but it's more than half a century old and has a respectable, if small, political base in the county. Mebyon Kernow – MK as it's locally known – sees Cornwall as a 'historic Celtic nation' – one of six, the other five being Ireland, Scotland, Wales, Brittany and the Isle of Man. It's trying to popularise this idea, at the same time as it popularises the idea of self-government for Cornwall and the rebirth of the Cornish language.

Some measure of self-government has some support in the county, which has consistently expressed majority support for the idea of a Cornish Regional Assembly; 55 per cent of the population were in favour in the most recent MORI poll on the subject.[18] But the ballot box does not favour MK. At the 2005 general election, its four Parliamentary candidates garnered just over three and a half thousand votes between them; and that was their best ever result.

They do have a handful of district councillors, though, and Jane Acton is one of them. I'm not sure she's quite what I was expecting from a Cornish nationalist, though – she has a Lancashire accent for a start. She moved to Cornwall when she was a young child, she tells me, which means she doesn't have any Celtic roots herself. This doesn't stop her promoting the economic and political case for Cornish self-governance, though. It is, she says, a strong one, whatever your views on the Cornish language or the Celtic nations. And the erosion of Cornish village life by second homes and the tourist trade is a good example of why it is needed.

'What we want, politically, is a clearly defined Cornish region, with its own Assembly,' she tells me, as we sit in her front room sipping tea. The room is homely and slightly chaotic. There are political posters on the walls and folders and sheafs of paper on most of the surfaces. Jane is friendly and eager to talk about her cause. She wears a green cardigan and a denim skirt, with long earrings hanging beneath her curly brown hair. She sits on an unfolded futon across from the shell-bedecked fireplace and cradles her mug in both hands.

'We want a Cornish region,' she says. 'It's a popular demand. We put together a petition which gathered 50,000 signatures from people in Cornwall, and it's got cross-party support. The basic point is about responding to the needs of people here. At the moment we're part of the South West region, which goes from Swindon all the way down to Land's End. It's the largest region in the country. The problem with this is that the economic needs of Cornwall, which is the poorest area in the country, get subsumed within the wider economic needs of a very large and very different region. Obviously the needs of Swindon are very different from the needs of Truro. We're a very poor area here, and we have very specific needs and a very specific history and contemporary situation. It's ridiculous to fold us up together in this huge great region.'

What Jane is talking about here is something which few people know about – English government's best-kept secret, perhaps. It is something which, when I first began to look into it, I found quite astonishing.

In 1998, Parliament passed a dull-sounding and largely overlooked piece of legislation called the Regional Development Agencies Act. It was to have serious implications for the way the country was governed. The Act divided England up into eight arbitrary regions, drawn up in Westminster: East Midlands, Eastern, North East, North West, South East, South West and Yorkshire and the Humber. For each region, it created something called a Regional Development Agency. This was to be – indeed, still is – an unelected quango, directly appointed by the government and with no accountability to the people of its region.

The purpose of these agencies is to further economic development, promote employment and growth, push for more 'regeneration' and 'enable the regions to improve their relative competitiveness'.[19] In pursuit of these aims each agency may, according to the Act, 'do anything which it considers expedient for its purposes',[20] subject to government approval. They act and are structured like businesses, each with a Chief Executive and a Board, producing slick annual reports and focusing on 'growth' and 'regeneration.' Each one is run by a 'business leader' appointed by government.

The same Act also set up regional assemblies for each of the eight regions of England. The assemblies, too, were to be appointed bodies, unaccountable to, and in many cases probably unknown by, the people they governed. They were to take over many of the functions of existing local, district and county councils. They were to work with the Regional Development Agencies to push a region-wide agenda, much of which was dictated to them beforehand by Westminster or, some say, Brussels (the 'regionalisation' of England was first proposed by the European Commission in 1971. They even drew up a map of how it might look, which bears a spooky similarity to what actually happened three decades later.[21]).

The unelected members and support staff of England's regional assemblies cost the taxpayer around £360 million every year,[22] despite the fact that most taxpayers have never heard of them – and, unlike local councillors or MPs, don't get the chance either to appoint or to sack them. This is somewhat unfortunate, as their powers are significant. They prepare the 'spatial strategy' for their region – which in English means that they plan the future of its transport, its waste management, its planning and its housing, overseeing budgets of tens of millions of pounds as they do so. It is the South East Regional Assembly which decides how much new housing Ashford and Kingsnorth are going to have to swallow, for example.

In short, they are a serious – and seriously undemocratic – force to be reckoned with. And they will soon become even more so. Soon after Gordon Brown became prime minister, he announced the scrapping of the regional assemblies. Not, it seems, because they were undemocratic, but because they weren't undemocratic enough. From 2010, their powers will be handed over to the Regional Development Agencies. Planning, transport and housing decisions across the English regions will be in the hands of unelected businessmen and other Westminster appointees.

The Cornish have, for some years, been running the most effective and popular campaign against this top-down, unrepresentative regionalisation anywhere in the country. They are spurred on, as Jane Acton says, by how very different Cornwall is – in both economic and cultural terms – from the other counties which have been artificially forced together into the South West region. No body this big, this unaccountable and this driven by central government imperatives, says Jane, is ever going to able to deal with issues like Cornwall's housing crisis in any kind of serious way.

'Which is why,' she says, 'we want our own Assembly. In the end, it's about democracy. A Cornish Assembly would turn its attention to Cornish problems – it would have to. And the impact on places like Porthleven of the second home invasion would be an issue in the way it simply isn't now.'

Mebyon Kernow, Jane tells me, has its own answer to the Cornish housing crisis: a cap on the proportion of homes that can be sold to non-residents in any community.

'We are very explicit about capping,' she says, 'which no other party is. If over 5 per cent of housing stock in any community is second homes, no more second homes will be allowed to come onto the market. Properties could only be sold as permanent homes. That includes holiday lets. It's not that we're not up for tourism as a valuable part of our local economy, but there has to be a way of balancing it with the needs of the local community.'

In Porthleven, she says, the same problem as Portscatho is manifesting itself: the village is dying, because the social mix is fading away.

'If you want to meet large numbers of Cornish people in one place you have to go to the large horrible housing estates,' she says. 'You won't find them in any of the picturesque parts any more. They've all been picked off. Think about the message this sends to young people here: even if you stay down here you're not going to get a decent job, and even if you do get a decent job you're not going to be able to afford a house to live in. This means we lose our young people, we lose our young families.'

Jane, like John and Julian, sees either myopia or a deliberate turning-away on the part of national politicians, many of whom, perhaps not coincidentally, have second homes.

'Whitehall just hasn't grasped this,' she says. 'They don't see rural poverty. We have an issue here of what is called hidden homelessness. The overcrowding in Porthleven – you wouldn't believe it. Just two doors down, my neighbour had her daughter and her son, and another daughter with her husband and three children, all living in a three-bedroom house because they couldn't afford to buy anything, despite having OK jobs. They had to do a makeshift conversion of the cellar, which probably wasn't legal, but they had to accommodate everybody. After five years of this, they still haven't come to the top of the housing list. Similar things happen in the worst inner cities, but they are at least recognised by policy-makers, and they get in the media. Down here, though – the government really hasn't got a clue.'

Jane sometimes feels, she says, as if the destruction of rural communities in Cornwall is seen by government as a done deal – too late to do anything about, and too many vested interests to tackle in any case. It angers her because, accent or no, she feels she belongs here.

'I've lived in Cornwall since I was a little girl,' she says. 'And despite all the problems, I love living in Porthleven. There are local peculiarities, a real sense of place and a real sense of community as well, which I don't think we would lose too easily. There would be a lot of uproar for any loss of that. And that's what I love about a lot of Cornwall. It has all these very real, very difficult problems, but in so many places that real sense of community and identity and strength still holds it together.' She sighs again.

'We just really need the power to stop this,' she says, 'before it gets any worse.'

While the housing situation in Cornwall is dire, it is actually just an exaggerated version of the rural housing situation across the nation. An apartheid of wealth is being played out in most of England's villages, and the prettier they are, the more pronounced it is. The government's Commission for Rural Communities, set up rather belatedly in 2005 to 'tackle rural disadvantage', provides some stark figures and some stark predictions. Of the 9.5 million people who live in the English countryside, most of them want to remain there: almost 70 per cent of people living in villages want to stay living in villages. In the country's urban areas, meanwhile, over 40 per cent of people would like to move to a village or a hamlet. 'Most people,' says the Commission's annual *State of the Countryside* report for 2006, 'seem to have a clear preference to live in small settlements of some form.' [23]

This explains why the government predicts a 20 per cent growth in the population of the 'most rural' areas of England by 2028: the greatest rate of population growth anywhere in the country. This means that the same forces which are affecting Cornish villages could come into play across the nation. In general, the government's figures show that the smaller and more rural a village is, the more expensive it will be to live there – with obvious consequences for the community's health. *State of the Countryside 2006* sums up the problem sharply – and suggests a radical solution:

> Recent work… has estimated that over the next five years, 45 per cent of newly forming households in all rural areas will not be able to afford to purchase or rent on the open market. The research calculates that to meet the needs of these households up to 22,000 new

affordable homes will be needed per year. In addition, over 8,000 homes are required to meet the current backlog of need, for example to help those in overcrowded accommodation or without self-contained accommodation. The government's Affordable Rural Housing Commission, which used a different methodology, concluded that a minimum of 11,000 new affordable rural homes are needed over the coming few years. Under either estimate, current levels of provision are insufficient to meet needs.[24]

It's a stark assessment, and it calls for a lot of rural housebuilding to save rural communities from becoming playgrounds for the rich. Meanwhile, over in Kent, and in many other places across England, housebuilding is identified as precisely the force which is destroying rural communities – ravaging their countryside, destroying their cohesiveness and identity and turning them into urban ones. It seems that the defenders of village life have a serious contradiction on their hands.

Promoters of mass housebuilding in rural England – chiefly its beneficiaries, the building firms – are certainly keen to highlight it. 'Anti-housebuilding groups,' declares the Home Builders Federation, the lobby group for private housebuilders, 'are responsible for shaping planning policy on the basis of fanciful claims about Britain being "concreted over" whilst championing themselves as environmentalists. Nothing could be further from the truth. They have no interest in the wider environment, only their backyards... their views are seriously damaging the lives of the moderately paid.'[25]

Business lobby groups often pretend to be selfless charities to shame their opponents, but in this case there is a vital difference between the construction of private-sector housing and affordable housing. Constructing thousands of new open-market houses somewhere like Cornwall is unlikely to have much impact on the county's affordable housing problem. They will be priced way out of the reach of most people, and many of them would immediately be snapped up as yet more holiday lets, second homes or investments for the rich.

Building affordable homes, on the other hand – houses in which prices are kept deliberately low – and confining their sale to people who live and work in the area or to those doing key jobs, as is already practised in some of England's national parks and inner cities, could make a real difference to the social mix and the health of a village. There is, in other words, no contradiction in opposing the construction of thousands of homogenous market homes on green fields and, at the same time, promoting the responsible construction of affordable homes in desperate rural areas. In fact, championing both is vital for the future health of the English countryside.

Back in Portscatho, Julian German put it well. 'The government's approach is all wrong,' he told me. 'They aim to sort out the housing crisis by building thousands of new homes in towns like Truro, which don't have the infrastructure to cope with them anyway. It misses the point. I'd rather see two affordable homes built in every village in Cornwall than thousands of open-market homes plonked on the edge of towns that can't cope with them. That would really get to the heart of the problem.'

It's a good idea, but it's not what the authorities have in store for rural England. Instead, we will get vast new estates of mostly open-market homes built on the outskirts of towns, destroying their character and barely making a dent in the problem of rural poverty. This is the easy option, the way things have always been done. The alternative would be to challenge vested interests and to change the policy habits of decades.

Yet think what could be achieved if affordable homes were made available in every village in the country. Not just by building, either, but by requiring the owners of some of the country's 350,000 second homes either to live in their properties or to sell them on to people who need them. Think what could be achieved if numbers of second homes or holiday lets were capped by local authorities.

Think what could be achieved, in other words, if the stranglehold of the rich on England's villages was loosened; if politicians had the guts to tackle the moral outrage that is represented by the existence of thousands of empty 'investment properties' owned by absentee millionaires in the midst of rural poverty and homelessness. Villages could become living places again, rather than canvases for the rural fantasies of the Mercedes-owning classes.

But, no; that would be revolutionary, and the English don't do revolution. It sounds a bit too French. Besides, virtually every minister and shadow minister in Parliament has a second or third home up their sleeve. Best to just keep doing what we've always done, and hope for the best, eh? How many marginal seats are there in Cornwall, anyway?

Sulgrave, Northamptonshire
July 2006

Sulgrave is a nice little place; the kind of picture, at first glance at least, that a tourist might paint if asked to describe a 'typical English village'. It has an old pub, The Star, which is owned by the nearby Hook Norton brewery. It has a green, with two great beech trees towering above it and a pair of stocks at its centre. It has little lanes and old stone houses, and is surrounded by green and yellow fields which glow in the light of high summer.

The first impression you get of Sulgrave is of a wealthy place: large, well-appointed period houses of the kind that dentists or consultants might live in. But that's not quite fair. When you look closer, you see that Sulgrave is actually quite mixed in character, with a fair number of affordable, pebble-dashed semis complementing the mix. Socially, and in terms of age and class, it's a fairly mixed place too. As a village, it still lives. This might explain how it is managing to swim against the tide.

A few hundred yards down the road from the village green is a shop. It is closed, and its blinds are drawn down. The red plastic 'Post Office' sign that once hung on its frontage lies scratched and battered under a nearby bush. Squint through the gaps in the blinds and you can see empty shelves, the old post office counter, a pair of dusty scales, an unplugged phone. A collection of unopened post is piled up on the mat. The door itself is smeared with white-wash, in which someone has written with their finger:

CLOSED FOR EVER.

It's a melancholy sight. Sulgrave's shop closed in 2002. The landlord raised the rent and the shopkeeper couldn't afford to keep it going. With it went a gathering place, a community focus, a lifeline for older villagers, and a valuable commercial service. With it went part of what made Sulgrave a village.

A typical village has – or had – a few key gathering points: the church, the pub, the shop, the village hall, the post office. All of them are currently experiencing what might accurately be described as an existential crisis, as villages themselves struggle to redefine themselves for a new century.

Churches still retain some of their previous role, but as religion declines in popularity so does their function as places where all can come together, and a funding crisis within the Church has led to some being sold off for (expensive) housing. Village halls have also been shutting in many places, as the demographic changes from mixed community to commuter dormitory. Those which do remain tend to be used only on special occasions. Village pubs, as we've already seen, are in decline too.

This leaves post offices and shops, which in most villages were combined in the same building. As in our towns and cities, village shops perform a social as well as an economic role; but in the countryside that role is still more pronounced. If you live somewhere which is several miles from the nearest town, and only has one shop, its value as a place to buy your staples, post your letters, meet your friends and pick up the latest village gossip becomes all the more important.

But rural post offices and shops are both in steep decline. Most villagers now do their shopping in towns, at the supermarket. Rising property prices mean rising rents, hitting the thousands of shop-keepers whose premises are rented rather than owned, and pushing many over the edge. The government withdrawal of many services from post offices, combined with a long-term programme of branch closures, has hit them hard too.

Like the village pub – and perhaps the village church too – the village shop is thus in trouble. Hundreds of them have closed in recent years, and they continue to do so. Ninety per cent of rural post offices now fail to make a profit, and one in five have less than forty visits a week. Despite a government subsidy of £150 million every year, 1000 rural post offices have gone out of business in just the last five years. Almost 8000 remain, but a national programme of closures will see more of them close by 2009, and government support for those remaining will end in 2011.[26] From collecting the pension to meeting the neighbours, post offices have long been acknowledged as lifelines for the elderly in particular, and their decline is having a particularly serious impact on the lives of vulnerable pensioners across rural England.

All of which makes Sulgrave an intriguing place. Two hundred yards across the road from the sad, whitewashed shell of the old shop, soon to be converted into housing if its owner has his way, is a small stone building. It was built in the 1720s as the village school – there can't have been many pupils at the time, because the place is tiny. It's big enough, though, for what it has become – Sulgrave's new, com-munity-owned shop.

Sulgrave is a village that refused to die. When the old shop closed, a handful of villagers got together to discuss what could be done about it. What began as discussions ended up as an ambitious, and so far very successful, project to raise Sulgrave's village shop from the ashes. Inside this tiny building is a popular and successful new shop, which sells local produce, supports local farmers and producers, has its own in-house bakery in the attic, and has been nominated for national awards. Most interesting of all, it has been set up, is run and is entirely owned by the village.

Inside the shop, fighting for space with organic apricots, cinnamon and sugar, fresh baked bread, baked beans and racks of chocolate bars, is Robin Prior. Grey-haired and distinguished, wearing chinos and blue shirt, he is friendly and posh, in an English country village sort of way. When I walk in, he's talking to Jean, who has just finished baking the morning's bread. Robin has promised to give me a tour of the shop. It looks like it will take about thirty seconds.

'The effect on the village of the old shop closing was quite surprising,' he tells me. The shop tour, in the end, took about ten minutes. Now we've retired to Robin's garden, at the rear of a large stone house just up the road, where we are having a cup of very English village tea.

'You would see far fewer people just walking around the village,' continues Robin. 'People would just get up, go to work, come home, close their doors. When the new shop opened all that changed. People now wander off around the village, meet up, have a chat. The effect on village life is noticeable. As a social function, it's been hugely important, apart from its obvious economic benefit. Even though we're a small community, people who didn't know each other before have now got to know each other through the shop, by working together or just shopping there. It's a very good hub for the village.'

Robin is the treasurer of Sulgrave's community shop. Getting it set up was a risk, but it has paid off so far. The villagers set up an Industrial and Provident Society to establish the foundations of a community-owned shop. Acquiring and doing up the building cost them about £100,000, and equipping and stocking the shop cost them another £30,000. Then there was planning permission, forms to fill in, bureaucratic hurdles to leap. It wasn't easy.

But they had support from their parish council, which owns the building and rents it back to them. They were given grants for community projects, and villagers and their friends made loans or donations. Finally, shares were sold. Retailing at £5 each, they cannot be sold on and they produce no financial return, but they do mean that anyone who owns one has a stake in the running of the shop, and elects the management committee that runs it.

'There's a very widespread feeling of ownership,' says Robin, stirring his tea gently. 'It's sometimes difficult to know how much of the success is because people are so determined to support the project, or whether it's just operating on its merits. But I think that had it been done any other way it wouldn't have worked. The community involvement has really been key, but it does require a huge amount of commitment. The place is basically run by fifty volunteers. We have a full-time manager, but everyone else is working for nothing. It's a pretty intensive effort.'

What is happening in Sulgrave is quite exciting. It's just a tiny shop, in one sense; hardly the basis for a revolution. But the fact that fifty people choose to give up their time to make it work, the fact that people buy shares and expect no financial return, the fact that this village was so determined to keep its shop and its community alive, promises greater things. It suggests that some of my occasional cynicism about people's willingness to be the change they claim to want to see is perhaps misplaced; that, actually, people – or some of them, at least – really do care about the place they live in, and are prepared to make sacrifices for it.

And Sulgrave is not alone. This is one of around 150 community-owned village shops in the country; a number which some think could double in the next five years. Taken together with examples like the Old Crown, the co-operative pub in Hesket Newmarket, and an increasing number of co-operatively owned village halls and other village services, this starts to look like the beginnings of a tentative community revival in English village life – just when it is needed most.

'We do seem to have come along at a moment when there seems to be a lot more interest in community ownership, local shopping, that sort of thing,' says Robin. 'There is a sense that rural communities are slightly forgotten and have lost out. Centralisation, rationalisation, internationalisation of businesses and government services and everything else means that all of this trickles away from small communities and from the countryside. I think this has opened people's minds to the possibilities of how we could do more for ourselves as a village.' He finishes the last of his tea. A wood pigeon begins hooting gently in the trees at the bottom of the garden.

'You know,' says Robin, 'I think there's a real belligerence, almost, about communities like this. A kind of "We'll do it despite them!" I think there's a general feeling of, why stop here? If the pub were to close, for example, that would be another issue for people, and maybe that could become another community project. Who knows? I think the main point is that people now feel that anything is possible. In fact, they *know* it's possible, because they've done it. It's made the community stronger.'

Perhaps it takes adversity to bring a community out of itself. Maybe, in the case of England's villages, it takes the loss of a shop, a pub or a decent amount of affordable housing to test its mettle: to test whether it really is a community in anything but name. In places like Sulgrave, that community clearly exists – and is enlarged, reinforced and emboldened by its successful challenge to the supposedly inevitable forces of rural decline.

Perhaps anything – or at least something – is, after all, possible. But village communities need a fair crack of the whip. Money and a lack of local democracy are choking the life out of many of them. In what other country in the world is the countryside so expensive that, in many places, only the rich can live there? In what other country is a collapse in village services – and with them a collapse in village life – widely and blithely tolerated, if it's even noticed?

Over one hundred thousand people move to England's villages every year, and many more would like to. Not just to live that dirt-free Marie Antoinette life, but to experience, and contribute to, the countryside. The wheelwrights and the farriers have gone, along with the blacksmiths and the shepherds, and they're not coming back. Life, and society, has moved on. England, like most of the world, is now an urban, not a rural society, and the swing to the cities is only going to continue.

But this doesn't mean that England's villages have to die. With some foresight and effort they could be reborn as communities again; communities of people who may work the surrounding land or may not, but will certainly contribute to the life of the place. It's not a question of whether we as a society are going to 'go back' to rural life. It's a question of whether we can evolve by building on the best of our rural past to make our rural present live. The alternative is a countryside of soulless commuter villages studded with the odd theme park experience of Olde Worlde charm.

There are millions who would like to help make England's villages live again, if they had the chance. But they can't afford it, and that problem is getting worse. England's villages could be reinvented, or they could be killed off: death by a thousand BMWs. Making the right choice won't be easy; but, then, nothing easy is ever worth having.

8

The Orchard on the Hill

What can your eye desire to see, your ears heare, your
mouth to taste, or your nose to smell, that is not to be had
in an orchard?
William Lawson, *A New Orchard and Garden*, 1618

Tenbury Wells, Worcestershire
December 2005

It's a bright, cold December morning in the Marches. I've driven through rising mist, past great fields of hop poles and settlements of timbered houses, across the river Teme and into the little town of Tenbury Wells. It's chocolate-boxy here: it looks like a Victorian scene from a naff Christmas card. The redbrick higgledy-piggledy High Street is strung with dozens of independent shops and hung with Christmas lights. It gives me a warm feeling.

Off the High Street, by the river, is the site of the town's old cattle market, which was operational until very recently. There are two enormous black iron sheds with corrugated roofs and a system of metal bars to hold the cows in. There's a redbrick office building, the old market's headquarters, and a green corrugated-iron hut, which now serves as a café. We need a café, because it's freezing. I have a Styrofoam cup of steaming tea in one hand and a bacon roll in the other. It's early in the morning, but many people have been here much longer than me.

The place is milling with characters. Scowling, weatherbeaten old men in wellies and cloth caps. Bearded country geezers smoking pipes and grinning at nothing in particular. Determined-looking men in overalls. They are all here to do business. The giant sheds which once housed cattle are today sheltering a complex layout of Christmas decorations, all made from local flora: ivy crosses, holly bosses, holly wreaths, fir wreaths with red ribbons, and dozens of combinations thereof.

But the real business of the day is in the big concrete square outside the café, where vast mistletoe bundles are lined up in rows. Men walk between them judging their quality, knee-high in white berries and slender leaves. Old chaps in tweeds and leather gloves push trolleys stacked with more of the stuff. Tenbury Wells is the self-appointed 'Mistletoe capital' of England, and this is one of its three annual mistletoe auctions. They are the only mistletoe auctions in the whole of England, and the people of Tenbury Wells are not about to let you forget it.

The auction begins just after ten. The holly and the other wreaths are sold off first, with the mistletoe – the main event – saved until last. A man in dark glasses and a wax jacket, with a shepherd's crook in one hand, takes bids. He sounds exactly like an auctioneer should. 'One pound sixty – *eighty* – do I hear two? Two? *Two* pounds!' A crowd of wholesalers gathers around him, wrapped against the cold, their breath rising like smoke into the winter air.

Over by the café is a huddle of journalists. Reuters is here, so are a few Fleet Street titles and so, curiously, is the Canadian Broadcasting Association. It's here, like me, because this is not just the only mistletoe auction in England – it could also be the last. The cattle market site is – surprise surprise – to be sold off to a developer. Tenbury English Mistletoe Enterprise (TEME), which organises the auction, is unhappy about this and has managed to whip up a storm of media interest.

But this isn't really why I'm here. I've had enough of covering stories about developers trying to destroy cattle markets. Anyway, it's Christmas. I want to eat bacon rolls and look at the lights and not think about destructive, rapacious tycoons for a few days. No, I'm chasing a slightly different tale.

TEME seem to me to be a pretty effective bunch. Even if the old cattle market is sold off, I bet they'll find another local site for the auction. What I'm possibly less sure of is whether there will be enough mistletoe to auction in coming years. Because if there is a threat here, it's a longer term one, and it stems from a wider phenomenon than the selling off of a single town centre site. The journalists aren't writing about it, but they should be.

Less than an hour later, I find myself opening a five-barred gate at the bottom of a grassy hill on the other side of the river. It's part of an old Teme Valley farm. Confused sheep scatter before me, and three penned-in dogs bellow their objections fruitlessly from the back garden. Everything about this valley seems warm: the light, the worn-down shape of the old buildings, the curve of the hills, the colour of the hop husks. And the trees.

I'm not alone here. With me are three people from TEME. There is Jonathan Briggs: by day a humble employee of British Waterways, but by night – or in the evening, at least – possibly England's leading mistletoe expert. There's Alec Wall, TEME founder and retired detective, whose searching gaze is presumably a hangover from years in the interview room. And there's Reg Farmer, appropriately named, who has farmed land in this valley for most of his life. Jonathan is perhaps in his forties, but Alec and Reg are both in their seventies. Like the other founders of TEME they are people who have lived in a 'mistletoe town' all their life and want it to stay that way.

We are here because this is where the mistletoe in the market originates. Mistletoe is a curious plant, which is still not properly understood by science. It grows wild on certain trees in certain places at certain times. Nobody quite knows why it prefers some trees to others, or why it is abundant in some parts of the country – like this one – and non-existent in others. Its mystery has contributed to its mythology. The 'golden bough' was famously a sacred plant of the Druids, and its elegant and hardy life in the midst of dead winter has given it a special place in the religions and mythologies of northern Europe for thousands of years.

In England, this is its heartland. Worcestershire, Herefordshire, western Gloucestershire and Somerset – with Tenbury Wells at their confluence – account for the vast majority of mistletoe growing in England. Despite the plant's mysteries, one thing that is clear is that mistletoe seems to grow best in ancient orchards; and some of the best ancient orchards in England, if not in the world, are found right here.

'None of our mistletoe is cultivated,' Alec tells me, as we walk up the gently sloping hill towards the fruit trees that crown its brow. 'It's all naturally occurring on soft-bark trees, apple trees are the most common. The seeds are spread by birds. There are over a hundred varieties of mistletoe globally, but ours is the best. Our plant is more attractive than the others, the size and the pearl-like qualities of the berry, the shape of the leaves… the curve of the leaves.' He looks contented just talking about it.

'It's all very pleasing,' he says.

At the top of the hill is an ancient orchard. This farm belongs to one of Reg's friends, but even he doesn't know quite how old the orchard is. The trees are wonderful: apples, plums, damsons, cherries, twisted and gnarled, covered with lichen, some hung with mistletoe. Grasses and wild flowers grow around their base. The place is a haven for wildlife, Reg tells me, and it seems natural that it should be so. On all sides, the Teme Valley is lit by December sun. Hop poles stretch away towards banks of trees on the horizon, around which the shallow, fast-flowing Teme curls.

Reg can identify every tree in the orchard, and take a good guess at the age of each. He can remember this place from his childhood. He has a lovely old Worcestershire burr – he says 'yuur' instead of 'here' – and talks quietly, but with authority. His words are shot through with realism rather than sentimentality, but it somehow makes them sadder.

'This orchard,' he says, wandering between the trees on the brow of the hill, 'contains what might be the only Normington apple tree left in the country. A farmer I know has an orchard with over a hundred different varieties in it. The old orchards around here are amazingly varied, and you'll get varieties in them that people have never heard of. There might be apple varieties even here today that aren't written down anywhere. Look at this tree here' – he ambles over to an ancient, hunched specimen – 'It's a Casey Codling. Insignificant as an apple; it's a cooker, and commercially it's no use at all. But that's a very rare old apple. Here' – he moves to the tree next to it – 'we have a Bramley, the most common cooking apple. I do like a Bramley. The original Bramley tree is still going in the garden of a cottage in Nottinghamshire, you know.'

Reg can talk for hours about apples. He knows these orchards and this valley, because they are his own. He knows, too, that much of that knowledge will soon be lost. These orchards are on their way out: commercially useless now, in this age of supermarkets and globalisation, they are being levelled daily, and the old apple trees destroyed. With them go centuries of accumulated knowledge, rare or possibly unique fruit varieties – and the mistletoe they support.

'Of course, we've lost a lot of orchards,' says Reg when you ask him about it. 'This whole valley was once covered in orchards and hop yards. But as you will see if you go to the supermarkets, it's mostly foreign apples now. The market has gone because Sainsbury's and all these people don't want it. It's all about eye appeal, isn't it? Tenbury used to have a market every Tuesday and it used to be full up with fruit. It's gone now. That's just the way it is.'

Jonathan, who has been poking about in the upper branches of the Casey Codling, backs Reg up.

'There is definitely a decline in this sort of orchard,' he says. By 'this sort' he means old, localised, full of very specific diversity: probably entirely unique and, once gone, irreplaceable. 'This is going to lead, if it hasn't already, to a decline in the quantities of mistletoe available. This isn't just an English issue, it's northern European. We import a lot of mistletoe, most of it from France, and that's also harvested from neglected old orchards. But if you keep on neglecting your old orchards, in twenty years' time there won't be any left... there is that worry.'

Reg looks out between the trees across the valley. He points out large houses that stand in the fields or are surrounded by orchards. There are still hop poles and fruit trees to be seen on all sides, but Reg has seen most of them disappear over the years, and the process that has taken them is not finished yet.

'Look,' he says. 'I can say that 95 per cent of those houses were bought out of fruit – out of the orchards. We used to have Bulmers Cider based here, they bought up a lot of this fruit. They've gone to Newcastle now, and their contracts have gone with them. Look at the ground, you'll see the fruit in this orchard wasn't harvested this year. It wasn't last year either. The owner's planning to sell out. He said to me, about the mistletoe, he said, "Strip it all out, Reg, I won't be here next year." Probably the trees won't be either. I expect it will all go.' He scans the river valley inscrutably.

'Things change, don't they?' he says.

By the time you read this the orchard on the hill, with the Casey Codling and the Normington and the Bramley, the badgers and the butterflies, the centuries of layered history and meaning, the roots both physical and metaphorical, will probably be gone. The trees will probably have been grubbed up and burned, and the land put to more profitable use. Everybody has to make a living, and there's not much living in damsons now, or in rare apples or mistletoe. Things change.

If you ate a different variety of apple every day for six years, you would still not have exhausted the list of those which are, or can be, grown in England.[1] The apple is our national fruit, and the country's orchards were once famed across Europe for the diversity of their produce. Introduced to England by the Romans, who had somehow themselves got hold of the fruit that originated in the Caucasus and has been cultivated by Man for 4000 years, England's damp, temperate climate and excellent lowland soil is possibly the best in the world for apple-growing. Certainly no other country has, over the course of many centuries, created such a stunning and curious diversity of this fruit.

Every county, every soil type, in some places every village, grew its own variety of apple, in orchards whose twisted trunks and un-ploughed ground provided havens for wildlife – badgers, woodpeckers, bees, butterflies, songbirds – as well as fruit for people. Eggleton Styre. Scarlet John Standish. Laxton's Superb. Gravenstein. Kirkston Pippin. Foxwhelp. Lady Henniker. Cornish Honeypin. Keswick Codlin. Yorkshire Greening. These are just a few of the varieties of apple that were once grown across the country: at least 2500 of them, accounting for more than a quarter of all the apple types on Earth. These are names that tie locality to people to history to ecology, but which few of us know or could recognise today.

Orchards, and the fruit that grow in them, are intimately tied to the distinctive character of local landscapes. Different apples are associated with different counties – Ashmead's Kernel with Gloucestershire; King's Acre Pippin with Herefordshire; Blenheim Orange with Oxfordshire; Ribston Pippin with Yorkshire. The main commercial fruit-growing areas of England – Kent, Somerset, Devon, Cambridgeshire, Essex, Herefordshire and Worcestershire – each have their own specialities. Kent is famed for eating and cooking apples, cherries, pears, plums and cob nuts; the eastern counties for dessert apples; the south-west for cider apples and perry pears. Every region has its own apple-based recipes, from pies to puddings to ciders. The apple is to the English what *fromage* is to the French – an identifier of place, a creator of culture, a symbol of the nation.

Walk into any of the supermarkets which sell 70 per cent of all the apples bought today, though, and the story they tell about the state of the nation won't be a happy one. If you can tell which apples are home-grown and which are imported, you may be able to spot an English Royal Gala or a Cox's Orange Pippin. Those you do find will often be foreign varieties grown in the UK (like Royal Gala). They will be grown in vast industrial orchards and packed in factories by machines which will measure their diameter and 'colour ratio' to the nearest millimetre. They will be selected not for taste or seasonality, but for their ability to travel long distances without bruising, and look identical on the shelves. And they will be on the shelves all year round, whatever is growing outside the sliding doors.

In the early twentieth century, almost 80,000 hectares of English agricultural land was dedicated to growing fruit trees. Today, it is just over 20,000, and of this, a maximum of 2000 hectares are estimated to be genuinely ancient orchards, managed in the traditional way by grazing animals under the trees for half the year. In 1987, there were 1500 government-registered apple and pear growers; now there are 500.[2]

It is possible to drive down roads in Herefordshire or Kent that even five years ago ran between blossoming trees, which today are surrounded by empty fields or sorry, shrivelled stumps. Wiltshire has lost 95 per cent of its orchards since 1945; Devon 90 per cent since 1965;[3] East Anglia 80 per cent since 1950.[4] The amount of land taken up by apple orchards has halved in the last decade alone, and the amount of fruit they produce has halved in the last five years. The reason is simple: there's no living in it any more.

The orchards of England are a map of local character, lined and contoured in the colours and flavours of the fruit they produce. In the apple we have a happily symbolic fruit; a product of nature that symbolises the country it grows best in. The state of our apples, in other words, could be said to point to the state of the nation.

Ludgershall, Buckinghamshire
October 2006

'I think you'll find,' says Derek, surveying the tabletop before us, 'that most of these are officially extinct.'

We're standing in Derek Tolman's low, ancient Buckinghamshire barn. It's freezing cold. Motes of dust dance in the light that creeps through the pattern of gaps in the walls and doors.

'What am I eating here?' I ask. In my mouth is a slice of a small, hard, slightly spicy yellow apple. It fits neatly into my palm; more the size of a plum, really. Its colouring is mottled and its shape untidy. In my right hand is a knife. On the table in front of us are lines and lines of apples, pears and quinces; almost a hundred in total, their names written on small cardboard labels beside them: Gooseberry Pippin, Ashmead's Kernel, Wyken Pippin, Pitmaston Pine Apple. Those that don't yet have names display suggestions, possibilities, places or simply question marks.

'We don't know,' says Derek. 'Yet.'

Derek and his wife Judy have run Bernwode nursery from this site for over two decades. Their nursery is named after the old royal forest of Bernwode, which once covered over 400 square kilometres of the surrounding land. Most of it is now gone, but Derek and Judy are carrying on the region's link with ancient trees. They are some of the foremost experts on historic apple varieties in England.

The apples on the table today are just the latest of the many strange, rare, unusual or entirely unidentified varieties that they collect or are sent on a regular basis. Derek has made the cataloguing and the tracing of England's apple heritage his life's work. The results have been surprising, to say the least.

'That's quite an interesting apple,' says Derek, picking up a small, green musket-ball of a fruit and rolling it around between his fingers. 'Look at that one. I've got no idea what that is. It was sent to me. I get this all the time: people post me fruit from trees in their garden or wherever and ask me what it is. Much of the time I just don't know, because it's not been identified. There's a whole rogue industry dealing with apple identification out there. They're a bunch of charlatans. They know they can't really identify half of the apples around, but they take a best guess so they don't appear ignorant.'

He lifts the apple to his nose and inhales.

'Lovely smell, this one, too,' he says. 'Yes, the trouble is that most of the apple experts out there are really not aware of how many apples there *are*, because they're not going and doing the business of looking and seeing and finding out on the ground. So they'll get an apple, and look in the few basic books and say, "It looks like that one, so it must be one of those." But it doesn't work. There are many varieties that look like other ones. I've been doing this for years, and what I've found is that the number of apple varieties in this country has been massively underestimated.'

Derek is an apple fanatic. When he started Bernwode he was selling all kinds of plants, trees and shrubs, but he soon started to zero in on fruit. These days he sells mostly apple trees, many of which are old varieties; he has 600 different ones at the moment, and more are on the way once he can name them. And in his spare time, he pursues his mission: to catalogue every known variety of apple ever grown in England, and to show the 'apple establishment' that the country is even richer in its national fruit than is generally assumed.

Derek takes me to his office to prove it. Past lines of young trees and polytunnels of saplings we walk to a loft above another barn. The walls are lined with books and magazines, journals and historical documents, every one of them about fruit. *Scott's Orchardist*, from 1873. *Hogg and Bull's Herefordshire Pomona*, from 1878. *Apples and Pears* from 1911. Old fruit catalogues from 1826. From among them, Derek takes down a large volume.

'This,' he says, 'is the *National Apple Register*. It was published in 1971 by what was then the Ministry of Agriculture, Fisheries and Food. It basically records certain ancient books and documents, and tries to put in one place all the apple varieties that were known in Britain. It didn't include cider apples, and it didn't have access to all the books that were available. It also didn't go outside London to look at local varieties. So although it's an excellent work in many ways, and took seven years, it was far from complete. Yet it's the only full register we have.'

Derek puts down the book and moves to his desk, where he sits down in front of his computer and hits a key. The screensaver disappears.

'Basically,' he says, 'the *National Register* is *way* off. This is the database that we're building up. Every single one of these apples listed here is a distinct variety with a distinct name. I'm doing global and national databases, and both of them are way higher than anything official. Look at this.' He brings up another screen, and a number: 16,163.

'That's the number of distinct varieties we've tracked globally,' he says, 'and we're not finished yet.'

'Really?' I say. 'But I read somewhere that there were about ten thousand types of apple in the world.'

'No, that's way out,' says Derek, with certainty. 'You probably got it out of a paper somewhere, did you? People are always using figures like that because they just don't know. All of these apples here have been researched by us. They're distinct, they're not just names we've plucked out of the air and stuck down there. I've found over sixteen thousand already. That's globally – in this country, we've traced 5700 varieties. My best guess of the number of distinct apple varieties that have been grown in this country is something like ten thousand. But we just don't know, and perhaps we never will.'

This, to any apple enthusiast, is gobsmacking news. Derek has identified almost six thousand British apple varieties: more than double the official, widely quoted estimate. Each of these, says Derek, is a variety of 'UK interest' – not necessarily developed here, but grown here at some stage, and mentioned in at least two pieces of apple-related literature. It sounds astonishing, I say. Derek smiles.

'Nobody else is doing this,' he says, 'If you go out and find an orchard that may be up to 200 years old, you just *know* that some of the trees in there are some of the ones missing from the *National Register*. But so many of these orchards are disappearing, they're taking varieties with them that maybe were never known about at national level, or listed in a book written by someone sitting in a library in London. Maybe some old man bred a new variety when he was younger – he's dead, and the knowledge of what that tree was is dead with him.' He stands up and walks across to the window.

'We've maybe got a ten-year window before they're lost for ever,' he says. 'Globalisation, the way the countryside is changing – none of this is going to go away. And to be honest, as the population keeps on storming up, climate change starts biting, and everyone wants more comfort and possessions… there's a limited time to collect these old fruits before they're just wiped out of history, out of the national memory.' He looks around the room, at the books and the database and the apple paraphernalia that covers virtually every surface.

'We're doing a Noah's Ark job, really,' he says. 'Somebody has to.'

I can't remember whether an apple a day was supposed to fend off the attentions of the doctor or the dentist. Perhaps it was both. My grandparents used occasionally to say this to me when I was a kid, but its effect was rather ruined by the fact that they not only ran a sweetshop but also lived above it. I ate apples – always have, and liked them too – but I was hardly an aficionado. Who is?

Derek is, of course, but he's unusual. The rest of us – well, we're mostly restricted to a choice of two apple varieties: crunchy or fluffy. They might have a few official names between them, but shop-bought apples now are basically selected to be one or the other. Supermarkets think that's all we're really bothered about, and for quite some time they seem to have been right.

In the last few years, though, things have changed slightly. In line with the general consumer trend towards all things local, seasonal and organic, and because of increasing pressure to reduce their carbon footprint, even the big supermarkets have started to stock more English apple varieties. They've started, belatedly, to feel slightly embarrassed about importing apples from South Africa in the middle of the English autumn. Prominent Union Jack stickers have started appearing on the fruit, and the big four supermarkets have even had the cheek, having stocked up on three or four English varieties after a twenty-year hiatus, to pose as the saviours of an English apple industry which they have played an enormous role in bringing to its knees. The government's official National Fruit Collection, at Brogdale in Kent, which is supposedly the biggest collection of varieties of fruit trees in the world (Derek scoffs at its mere 2300 apples) is now sponsored by Tesco.

But how many varieties of apple can anyone eat? And why does it matter much if the historical richness of fruit varieties begins to shrink? It's easy to assume – as I did for a while – that our palate has homogenised over the past half-century; that we're no longer attuned to the richness of what is out there; that our ancestors ate a glorious diversity of apples, while we're happy with a soggy, yellow Golden Delicious. But this is probably not true. Over the centuries in which that glorious diversity of varieties were developed, most people lived in one town, region or village all their life. If they ate apples, they would be the varieties grown where they lived – maybe half a dozen at most. Nationally there was – and remains – a stunning diversity of apple types. But there was never a time when the average English citizen sampled them all – or even knew they all existed.

So why does it matter if fewer varieties exist? What if Derek is right, and there are 10,000 varieties of English apple? If this fell by half it would still be more than most people could really even conceive of. Most can't be sold, and most won't be bought. We could stick preservation orders on a few old trees or orchards but, realistically, we can't expect hundreds of thousands of hectares to be used growing fruit that no one wants, just because they're rare. If we're over-supplied with apple varieties, maybe some will have to slip away. Who will even notice?

But there's another way of looking at this. If we have 10,000 varieties of apple in England – or even 5,000, or even 2500 – we have something very special indeed. We have a piece of living history. We have the literal fruits of the efforts of thousands of people over hundreds of years. No one is really suggesting that Sainsbury's should sell them all. What people are suggesting is that these old fruits, and the old orchards they grow in, should be preserved – at least in part, at least as examples – just because they are so wonderful.

The apples themselves are intriguing: they connect us to our past. The orchards are beautiful landscapes, both productive and astonishingly diverse in their wildlife value. They provide havens for birds, insects and other species that have been having a hell of a time of it in the increasingly intensive, chemical-soaked agricultural countryside of the last few decades. True, there is often little or no money in them. But then there is little or no money in opera, seashores, badgers, fritillaries, moors, statues, tumuli or red telephone-boxes, and we don't seem to have a problem preserving those. It is, probably, simply a matter of priorities. What do we value? And what do we overlook?

Marden, Kent
April 2007

On top of a clay hill in Kent, surrounded by tall trees, hop poles and ancient marlpits, stands what could be the future of England's orchards.

It's a low, overcast spring day, with spots of rain gusting occasionally across the Weald. But this 4-hectare field, hemmed in on all sides by green, is busy, as it has been all week. Seven days ago there was nothing here but yellow clay and the sound of the tree sparrows. Today there are over ten thousand trees, and by the weekend – it's a Thursday now – there will be almost eleven thousand. The trees are small; eighteen-month-old saplings, they are planted in dead straight lines, between tall concrete poles whose tops are connected with wires.

The trees themselves are less than a metre apart, the better to squeeze in the maximum number. They have been expertly bred by specialists to produce far more fruit than the average tree of their kind could manage. In a far corner of the field, a small yellow digger is moving along the last line, drilling holes in the solid clay with what looks like a giant corkscrew. A tractor follows behind, pulling a trailer loaded with saplings. Half a dozen Polish workers busy themselves planting the trees in the holes which the corkscrew has made.

'It's fantastic, actually, isn't it?' says Peter Hall. Peter is standing next to me, dressed in a jumper and shorts. His greying hair is wind-blown, and he has a deep, plummy voice. Peter is the owner of this land – a farmer for decades, he has mostly grown hops, but is now branching out. He has never seen anything quite like this before. Nobody has, in England at least.

This is only the country's second Concept Orchard – a new, well, concept in apple growing that its progenitors hope will revolutionise the business. One of them stands on the other side of me from Peter, in jeans and a sweatshirt, squinting slightly into the spots of rain. Mike Jobbins is as keen as Peter to explain what is happening here. Mike is Technical Director of OrchardWorld, a company which, for two decades, has been one of the country's major suppliers of fruit to the big retailers. OrchardWorld works with a number of growers, like Peter, from all over the world. It hunts down fruit produce from around the globe, markets it and supplies it to the big retailers.

Or, rather, to just one of them. In the eighteen years that OrchardWorld has been in the business, the number of suppliers has contracted, as fruit grower after fruit grower has gone out of business. At the same time, the number of companies like Mike's working with the big boys has contracted too. These days, OrchardWorld has just one customer: Sainsbury's. The country's third-largest supermarket now gets all its 'top fruit' – apples, pears, plums and the like – from just two companies. Mike's is one of them.

This means competition is fierce, and innovation is important. Sainsbury's has started to express a serious interest in English apples, after a very long hiatus. It looks green and wholesome, and the more they sell, they more they realise that their customers really want to buy them. So they are looking to OrchardWorld to supply it. Here, in the Kentish Weald, in the slight rain, OrchardWorld is obliging.

The Concept Orchard is an ambitious attempt to steal a march on other companies, and to adapt traditional fruit-growing methods for a globalised, computerised, supermarket age. The trees still smell gorgeous in flower, and the apples they produce undoubtedly taste pretty good too. But that is perhaps all that this place has in common with the old-style apple orchards that still litter this Garden of England.

'The key to this whole thing,' Mike is telling me, 'is attention to detail, and it starts early. First you select your site, which is crucial. We had soil analysis done to understand precisely what we have and what we don't have here. We started preparation of the soil a long time before we arrived at where we are today. Plant spacing is obviously a lot tighter than in a traditional orchard – they're between 0.8 metres and a metre apart. Usually it would be a least 4.5 metres. The height between the soil and the grafted union – that bit you can see there at the bottom of the tree – is critical. It has to be a certain number of centimetres. Each tree must be pruned to leave between six and eight branches. All of this is dictated to us according to the model.'

The model. This is the key to what I am looking at. When the Concept Orchard gets going – and despite only being planted now, these trees should be providing fruit next year – it will be a fearsomely efficient system. A traditional orchard around these parts will produce around 20 tons of fruit for every hectare of trees. The Concept Orchard will produce three times as much. It has been planted with about half a dozen favoured varieties which sell well – Cox, Braeburn, Royal Gala, and one or two new experimental ones, including the Fuji, which is currently flown in from China.

The whole thing has been extensively researched, tested and developed to the point where, in effect, what I see here can be run by following instructions in a guidebook produced by a specialist apple-grower based in Holland who developed the Concept Orchard for Mike and his colleagues. Everything that will be done here will be done according to that guidebook. Nothing will be left to chance. This is apple growing as a slick machine. Peter and Mike can't wait to see it in action.

'The real key to this,' enthuses Peter, 'is that one person calls all the shots. They've got the system and from the word go, it's been done to their recipe. There's no "Oh, perhaps I'd like it a bit more salty than that". It's their recipe. Every aspect – the trees, where they come from, exactly how deep they go, exactly how the ground's prepared, exactly how many boughs, the ratios and relationships – it's all completely prescriptive, and that's why it works.' Mike nods in agreement. On the other side of the field the tractor has stopped, and the workers are taking a break.

'It's discipline,' continues Peter, warming to his theme. 'My God, it's discipline. One of the other things, of course, is that because it's a relatively simple recipe you can teach anyone to do it. None of this stuff about having people who have been thirty years in the business. You can take someone who's never seen a tree before and say, "You do this, this, this and this." In fact, even that is probably too many instructions. I'm a farmer, but increasingly we spend more time in the office these days. I really don't come out pruning trees. The guy who does it for us, he has five sons who help him with it. He talks to the agronomist, they decide exactly what to do and I promise you, when they've all pruned an orchard, you can't tell which person has pruned which row. They are all consistently the same.'

It's a funny thing. Part of me revolts against this imposed, top-down, industrialised system of supermarket production. Another part of me is impressed. Yet another part is curious about the farmer's attitude. I can see, in one way, how he would love such a system – one that reduces his workload, reduces the chances of a bad harvest, gives him more of a guaranteed income. Who wouldn't? On the other hand, it doesn't sound much like – well, like farming.

'To be honest,' says Peter, when I say so, 'the idea that chemistry hasn't moved on in fifty years is quite frankly nonsense. My view has always been that one should be looking at using the best of grandfather's husbandry in combination with the best of modern technology. And we've got to interpret it, after all. We know the ground, we know what does what, we know the conditions, where the springs are... but what we're doing is reducing the margin of error. You can see why it's so exciting. You know, when we finish this we'll have a weather station in the orchard which will transmit onto the internet, and the guys in Holland will be able to look at it at any time. Soil temperature, soil moisture, air temperature, wind... and because of their models of scab and mildew prediction, they will dictate what we do exactly and when. Everything. It is a total system.'

We stand and watch the Poles munching their lunches at the side of the woods. Mike, who has been listening keenly to Peter, and nodding frequently, explains how passionate he is about English fruit. When OrchardWorld first saw similar systems to this being developed in Holland, he explains, they asked themselves how they could make it happen here.

'We took this idea to Sainsbury's,' he says, 'and they grabbed it with both hands and said, "That's fantastic." They genuinely want to support their supplier base and British agriculture. Supermarkets get the blame for an awful lot, you know. Some of it is obviously justified, but some of it is completely not. There's clearly political PR kudos for them in selling English fruit, but they've actually realised that this is what consumers want and that it's a good thing to do.'

It seems that what Sainsbury's has done here, as it has started to do in other areas of English agriculture, is to make something of a commitment to its suppliers. Their 'Farm Promise Scheme' is intended to get more organic, British food onto the shelves. Farmers who convert to organic crops – as Peter has done with this new orchard – will get the costs of doing so covered by Sainsbury's.

The supermarket commits to work with the grower for a certain amount of time. Sainsbury's gets a helping hand to cash in on the fast-growing organic market and the supplier gets some security. But, in return, suppliers must produce as much as they possibly can, in order to meet the supermarket's demand. Hence the intensive growing in the Concept Orchard. Only maximum productivity will do.

We stand looking down the long, long row of Estival apple trees, stretching off towards the hedge 5 acres away. Spots of rain land on my glasses. Somewhere on the other side of the hill a tractor engine chugs into life.

'Yes,' says Mike. 'I think this is the future of the English orchard.'

Putley, Herefordshire
November 2006

Apple season is almost over. Most of the harvesting has been done in those orchards which will be harvested this season. A few trees still bear fruit, and the grass beneath them is scattered with those that didn't make the grade. Driving here, down roads still lined with trees on both sides, evidence of work recently completed can be seen. This is a land of apples: its heartland, still beating despite the retreat of the wider empire.

At the entrance to Dragon Orchard, a pig munches on semi-rotten apples under the trees that bore them. Two dogs bark from the house at the top of the drive. Sun streams through the straight lines of apple trees that crawl up a slope away from me. It's a beautiful place. Up at the top of the drive, in the garage next to the house, a man is sorting through a bag of quinces. They smell gorgeous: sharp, fragrant, addictive. The man turns when he hears my approach. He smiles and offers me his hand.

Norman Stanier is in his fifties. He has short grey hair, his trousers are bright orange and his shirt is green. He looks almost like a piece of fruit himself. And he has another way of looking at the future of orchards.

'Quinces,' he announces, 'are the original air-fresheners. You don't need to buy any of those horrible sprays if you have a quince. Take a couple and put them in your car and it'll smell wonderful all the way home.'

Norman, with his wife Ann, own and run a traditional English orchard, set deep in the heart of traditional English apple country. It has been here for 150 years and has been subject, in recent decades, to the same pressures and problems as all the other orchards in the area – indeed, the country. But Ann and Norman are doing something very interesting with Dragon Orchard. They are making it survive; flourish, in fact. And their methods may have something to teach other beleaguered lovers of the English apple.

In the large, airy kitchen of their house, which the Staniers built themselves, Norman makes tea and tells me their story. Ann is currently away, at a conference, telling it to others. She travels a lot, says Norman, and gets many more invites she can't take up. Dragon Orchard is beginning to make waves.

'This orchard has been in my family for four generations,' says Norman. 'A hundred and fifty years ago, the squire of what was then this estate decided to try an orchard on a commercial scale, and he planted it here. My great-grandfather was his overseer in the 1850s. A lot of the village was planted up into orchards at that time. But a lot of the estate was split up after the First World War, and that was when my grandfather bought his bit. He built his house here after the First World War. You can see it over there, just beyond the trees, see the roof? We wanted to kind of follow in his footsteps. My parents took it over after him, and now we run it.' He busies himself with the kettle and the water. Like everyone else I've spoken to, Norman genuinely loves apples and apple trees, and his enthusiasm is infectious.

'In our village there're still six functioning fruit farms, and they're still second and third generation,' he says, 'which is very unusual. Ours is a relatively small orchard. It's 9 hectares. A big orchard might be about 24 hectares around here. But even with the bigger orchards, nowadays it's getting harder and harder to make a living.' If you're going to supply supermarkets, he says, you need to be large scale and very centralised. There was a time when there were plenty of other outlets for your fruit – but not any more.

'Back in the 1950s, you could just about make a living from an orchard like this,' says Norman, 'You could sell everything you produced. When I was a kid it could go for cider, it could go for pot fruit, there was a local jam factory in Ledbury, there were lots of local canning factories. There were small cider places that would take small amounts early in the season. Now the cider mills don't open until late autumn and the big buyers only want the top-grade stuff, so the rest is wasted. Everything became centralised, all the small guys disappeared. Having said that, there has actually been a revival of it in recent years, with local craft cider-making, so that's some good news. But it's a very small quantity of stuff really.'

This meant, says Norman, that his parents needed to do other things as well as running the orchard. They could not live on apples alone.

'We had pigs, we had turkeys, we had chickens,' he remembers fondly. 'We used to grow gooseberries and raspberries and strawberries: all those sorts of things to try and extend the season. We actually used to process food on the farm. We had an apple-peeling machine

and a little canning operation. A key point was that we had to diversify and we had to add value to the fruit we produced. And, actually,
that's exactly what we are still doing, just in a slightly different way.'

Norman and Ann moved away from the orchard in their twenties
and spent a couple of decades living and working elsewhere, in
London and Birmingham, far away from apples. But in 1993 they
came back. Norman's parents could no longer keep the orchard
going, and they made a decision to take it on themselves. For a while,
it seemed like they might preside over the last gasp of a long-standing
family business.

'It was just getting really difficult to sell the fruit,' remembers
Norman. 'To begin with, they would go to the local cider factory, but
then that closed down. Then the local wholesaler got taken over
about three times. It was classic stuff. It was a Herefordshire company
and we knew the buyer, then they got taken over by another company, and the old boy who was a buyer went. Then a bigger company
took that over. Now it's a multinational and it doesn't want to send its
lorry out twice a week round four or five small orchards in Herefordshire when it could just get a container-load of Bramleys in from
Holland. So it stopped. And much of the rest of the apple trade now
is with supermarkets, and they don't have mechanisms for dealing
with small producers either.'

This is the great weakness of the giant corporation; it is a lumbering beast, rather than a small, agile animal. It crushes everything in its
path, whether it intends to or not. The story that Norman tells me
next, about the Bulmers cider company, is a brilliant example of
exactly how this phenomenon discriminates against the small, the
local and the rooted.

'Bulmers was a family company,' he explains. 'I went to school
with three Bulmer boys in Hereford and they treated their growers
very well. They had wonderful schemes – if you planted an orchard,
you got an interest-free loan, that sort of thing. But they got ambitious and tried to mix it with the big players in the drinks industry –

with the Heineken's and Carlsberg's and so on. They aggressively marketed their stuff, and they started to sponsor Leeds football team.' He smiles grimly at the memory.

'Leeds!' he says. 'It always sticks in my throat, because the season they sponsored Leeds – they spent £5 million on it, and the team did very badly – in that same year, they ran into cash-flow problems. The whole of the bill they paid to Herefordshire growers was £3 million, and they couldn't pay us. They took all our crop and they couldn't pay us. They did eventually, but very slowly. Anyway, they got taken over by Scottish & Newcastle, who are primarily brewers. They put all of their transport and marketing systems together and centralised it all. The chief executive of a big brewing company based in Edinburgh really isn't terribly interested in what's happening in small Herefordshire orchards. So that was the end of that.'

It's a typical story, highly representative of the way that small producers and suppliers all over the country, from shops to farms to orchards, lose out in the face of the triumph of big business. It's particularly piquant, as Scottish & Newcastle became notorious among campaigners for beer and pubs at around the same time, when, as part of a rationalisation scheme (their slogan these days is 'driving growth, driving value') it sold off its historic breweries in both Edinburgh and Newcastle, leading CAMRA to drily re-christen it 'Ampersand Breweries'.

'Earlier,' says Norman, 'we'd taken out the lot of the dessert apple trees and replaced them with cider apples, because that was what was selling. When Bulmers went down, it seemed like a very bad idea, but now Magners have come in and we have contracts with them. Do you know Magners? The new Irish cider, you must have seen it, it's all over the place. They've pretty much revolutionised the cider industry. It's been a real shot in the arm, and the knock-on effect in Hereford has been fantastic. Of course, it's called Irish cider, but they're using English apples. If you think about it, what is Irish cider? It's a marketing ploy, but it's a very successful one.'

But this still isn't enough to keep the orchard going, and in any case there is no guarantee that a contract with Magners will be any longer-lasting than a contract with Bulmers. As the Staniers saw it, they had two choices. They could let their orchard die, killed off by the demands of big business – or they could use their imaginations, and work out a way to save it. It wasn't a hard decision to make. They put their minds to it, starting with the basics – what did they have that other people might want, and be prepared to pay for?

'There is a tradition, a weight of history,' explains Norman. 'And we were producing some lovely apples, some lovely dessert apples, that we wanted to keep. We tried selling some at the farmers' market, but apples aren't very good at farmers' markets, because they're very low value, and by the time you've loaded the van and taken them all down there, you don't make much. But what's special here is what you see when you look out of the window. We have this little corner of Herefordshire, in a pretty idyllic rural surrounding, with fruits that we know people really enjoy, and an orchard that we know people really love when they see it. So we thought, how can we connect people back to that, how can we make them feel part of the landscape as well as wanting to eat the fruit?'

The answer Norman and Ann finally came up with was an intriguing one. They launched a 'cropsharing' scheme, designed to bypass the supermarkets and go straight to the apple-buying public – and to find people who cared enough about the place the apples came from to be a part of it themselves and to pay to keep it going.

'We didn't know if it would work,' says Norman, 'it was really an experiment. We produced our first brochure; we did it on recycled newspaper. We booked a stand at the Ludlow Food Festival, and off we went. We said we'll try it for a year, if it doesn't work, we haven't lost a lot of money. We thought, really, if we're going to have to end this tradition, then let's go out with a bang.'

That was five years ago. The Dragon Orchard cropsharing scheme was born out of necessity, but it has done a lot more than simply keep the orchard going. It has retained the diversity of fruit within it, and it has connected a whole new collection of people to its history and its landscape. Crucially, it means that the trees are still worked. This is not about conservation or time-warping those lines of trees. It's about a new way of making a living from a very old landscape.

The principle behind it is a simple one, and one that is increasingly practised all over the rich world, where farmers are having a hard time surviving: it's known as community-supported agriculture. It gives the farmer a reasonably guaranteed income, and it gives those who buy his produce not only the produce itself but a link with the land it came from, and a part to play in the running of that land. Schemes vary – you can sign up for vegetable boxes, or even sponsor a cow – but the principle remains the same.

In the case of Dragon Orchard, cropsharers pay an annual fee to join up. In return, they get a hearty amount of fruit and fruit produce from the orchard every year. They also get to visit four times a year, to take part in the harvesting, to listen to talks, to visit canning factories and cider mills, to bring their kids to play under the trees, to meet the Staniers and to feel as if they are a genuine part of the life cycle of Dragon Orchard.

'Think of fair trade,' says Norman. 'A lot of people pay a little bit extra for fair trade products. I know in some ways we're elitist middle class and we can afford to do it, but many people are happy to say, "If I pay a bit more, I know that bit more is going to the producer." People are now wedded to fair trade for the Third World, and actually I think that people could become committed to fair trade for the rest of the world too. If they paid a penny more a gallon on milk, for example, dairy farmers would be all right. Our biggest dessert apple producer around here has 60 acres. At the moment he can just about survive. If he got a penny a pound more for his fruit, he could invest substantially in his organisation. If he got 2p more it would turn him around.' Most people, Norman reckons, wouldn't mind paying that penny if they knew that the impact on the producer and the land-scape would be a positive one.

If they can take part themselves, of course, they have even more of an incentive. At Dragon Orchard, you get a pinch of fair trade with a dose of participation thrown in.

'You get to come for four weekends of the year,' says Norman, 'one for each season, and every weekend is different. On the autumn weekend, you get to take away your share of the crop. It's a car boot-full, all sorts of apples and pears. Another fruit-farming family in the village runs a juice-making business, so they make juice from our apples. We have local cider- and perry-makers too, so people get a case of each, and of a single variety apple juice, which is very different from the mixes you'll get in the shops. Annie does jams and jellies and chutneys, with plums, apples and quinces. A neighbour has a home canning-machine and he cans some of our pears. Then we usually put in something like a recipe book or a mug. It costs £300 a year.'

Norman, obviously, thinks this is good value. But the value, he says, is not just in the produce, but in the experiences – in reconnecting to the land, and to the traditions that have sprung from that land. In rediscovering what plenty of people used to know, but most have now forgotten.

So successful has Dragon Orchard Cropsharers been that other initiatives have been launched on the back of it. You can sponsor a tree in the orchard now – visit it and even help to plant it. There's a new 'fruitshare' scheme for those who are keen on the fruit but don't have four weekends a year to spend at the orchard. Small things, says Norman – though things that take a lot of work – but things which make a very big difference, both to them and to the people who join up.

'There's nothing more seasonal than an orchard,' he says. 'It delineates the seasons absolutely spot on. Winter is cider, it's wassailing, it's bare trees, it's shotguns, it's going out in the dark. Then you come at blossom time, in spring, for cider-tasting, and the orchard is in blossom. There's maypoles and morris-dancing. You walk through that orchard when the trees are in flower – phew! – it's a total sensual overload. And in the summer it's an evening barbecue, little apples on the trees, the smell of mown grass. Autumn is harvesting, the deep colours, the smell of the fruit, fungus walks… It is a real connection to the land.' He smiles into his tea.

'I think that's why people appreciate it,' he says. 'Because so many of us simply do not have that any more.'

When I was in my early twenties, I worked for an environmental campaign group in London. We used to do a lot of work on rainforest protection. Everyone was talking about rainforests back then (they seem to have forgotten about them now, even though the rate of their destruction is much the same. Environmental fashions come and go. Whales, like wide lapels, were big in the seventies. These days, whales are old hat: it's all carbon-rationing and airline boycotts. Sometimes it can be hard to keep up.)

Anyway. I wrote a lot about rainforests in those days, and the need to protect them from destruction. And I found that there were – still are – many different arguments for why we should do so. I found also that the easiest ones to get across were the utilitarian ones.

It was simplest, when someone asked why we should bother protecting, say, the Amazon, to explain that it was a 'carbon sink' – it helped stave off climate change, which was good for all of us. Failing that, I might say that rainforest plants had been used in the past to create medicines for us, and that the cure for cancer might be out there somewhere, and how would we feel if we logged and burned that before we even knew about it?

But I was always uncomfortable with this, because it was always, to me, beside the point. We were, in essence, saying that the rainforest should be preserved because humans found it useful – that we might even, one day, be able to make some money out of it. Whereas to me

— naïve as I was, and probably still am — its preservation was an end in itself. It was enough to say that it was an entirely unique marvel; a place like no other; something remarkable that made the world a better place. It was enough to say that it was a home to hundreds of thousands of other species, and that to raze it to the ground for the sake of toilet paper or soybeans was self-evidently criminal.

Orchards are not rainforests — they're entirely man-made landscapes, for a start — but the same principle can be applied. That we have, in this small and not especially naturally diverse country of ours, such an amazing variety of a single fruit, such a remarkable result of a collaboration between people and the rest of nature, is a wonder. It is a marvel; something we should be boasting about, and holding on to tight. To let it all slide away simply because we can't cash in on it right now or because we'd like the land to grow biofuels or housing estates is equally, obviously wrong. It is something we would later regret, and mourn.

It would be, it seems to me, a genuine folk tragedy. It would be a loss to English culture and to English people on a par with the ongoing collapse in breweries, pubs and regional beers, or with the death of small farms and the knowledge and traditions that go with them. Preserving these things, ensuring that they continue to live, would not help us in our slavish and unquestioning journey up the global economic ladder. None of them makes quick bucks, and some make no bucks at all. And when we finally become a nation in which that is reason enough to shrug our shoulders and let them all go… well, you decide whether that makes us a global success or a local failure, or whether the two are strangely interdependent.

'All great civilisations are based on parochialism…
Parochialism is universal; it deals with the
fundamentals. To know fully even one field or one
land is a lifetime's experience… A gap in a hedge,
a smooth rock surfacing a narrow lane, a view of a
woody meadow, the stream at the junction of four
small fields – these are as much as a man can fully
experience.'

Patrick Kavanagh, *The Parish and the Universe*, 1952

9

Know Your Place

We shall not cease from exploration
And the end of all our exploring
We'll be to arrive where we started
And know the place for the first time.

T. S. Eliot, 'Little Gidding', 1942

I think I might leave soon.

I went to the pub tonight with a good friend of mine who's moving out of town after seventeen years. It was a valedictory kind of occasion. We've visited this pub a lot over the last few years, to drink and talk and play bar billiards. It's set back behind its beer garden on the banks of the Thames, a few hundred yards from one of the locks I used to work on. In high summer it's clogged with tourists and people eating weekend lunches. It's winter now, though, and on winter evenings it's at its best.

The pub has never been gastro'd or corporatised. It's an ordinary, unremarkable little place, which is why we like it. The landlord has two enormous old English bulldogs that look like they want to eat you but actually want to be scratched under the chin. A gang of old boys gathers for darts tournaments every week, to play, smoke too much and cackle at private jokes. The walls are hung with badly stuffed fish. There are armchairs and an open fire.

Or there were. We got there tonight to find the stuffed fish, the stuffed armchairs, the bulldogs, the dartboard and the regulars all gone. New tenants. They've cancelled the darts tournaments and chucked out the board, so who knows where the cackling old boys will go now. Worst of all, they've thrown out the bar billiards table. Bar billiards is a weird and wonderful old pub game that's only found in a few southern English counties. It's the very essence of local distinctiveness. They've replaced it with a pool table; the kind you'd see in a roadhouse in America or a bar in Bangkok. And I am suddenly weary.

I've lived in this city for over a decade, and this has been creeping up on me. I could just be getting old and grumpy, but most of the changes I see now are for the worse. Oxford is being cloned before my eyes, and it's hard to watch.

The old canal is all but gone now, its character buried beneath canyons of brick and money. The meadows are being turned over to fake Georgian executive homes. We have four Starbucks, two Subways, a branch of every chain store you can think of and any number of pubs undergoing conversion into 'exclusive apartments'. The last-but-one independent record shop closed down last month. Most of the independent bookshops – in this supposed seat of learning – have gone too, replaced by sandwich bars which all sell baguettes with the same four or five fillings.

A vast new multimillion-pound Bury St Edmunds-style shopping mall is to be built in the city centre over the next five years. Its 750,000 square feet will double the city's 'retail space', sucking more traffic into the already gridlocked city so that we can compete with Reading and Bicester. It's a hundred yards from the Norman castle and the old Victorian prison, which themselves have recently been converted into a matrix of corporate wine bars and clone stores. And I'm so bored with it all. Bored and tired and sick of complaining.

When I look back at my journeys through England, and ask myself what I feel about what I saw, the emotion that claims primacy now, perhaps unexpectedly, is anger. I am angry about what is being done to my country, about what is being lost and what is being deliberately erased.

I am angry because to me, as to the many people I have met, the things that are being erased have a clear value, a detail, a meaning, an irreplaceability. Yet they are easily destroyed, by people and institutions who see nothing of this. Everyone I have met – that you have now met too – is working so hard, for little personal gain, to save these things and to teach others of their value because they have come to understand what that value really is.

And we are not a society that appreciates value. We appreciate speed, instant gratification, primary colours, simple answers. We appreciate celebrities and shopping and media scandals and premium rate phone lines. We appreciate investment properties and email on the move and only the finest ready meals. We are losing sight of who we are and where we have come from. And we don't care.

Or do we?

I am hardly the first to examine the ongoing destruction of place, meaning and culture in this country. For better or for worse, people like me have been around for centuries. In that sense, I'm just the latest in a long line to point out what is happening, and to make a plea for things to be different. If I look over my shoulder I can see them all lining up to intimidate me: William Cobbett; H. J. Massingham: G. K. Chesterton; Clough Williams-Ellis; Ian Nairn; J. B. Priestley; George Orwell. Angry, every one, at the same process which now angers me.

These were writers who, in their day, railed too against the plastic world that was ruining what they valued, against the rape of the landscape, the primacy of the market, the power of thoughtless 'developers', the unholy alliance of big business and big government that was chewing up people and places and spitting them out like used-up tobacco, drained of colour, taste and any kick it might once have had.

But what does this tell me? Perhaps that the one constant over the last few hundred years has been writers railing against change. Or perhaps that I am simply a contemporary scribbler in auspicious historical company, analysing the latest phase in a process that has been under way for centuries and is now merely more advanced; dug in deeper, harder to dislodge. Perhaps all I can do is record what has not yet gone, before it, too, is blasted clean by an unstoppable tide of Bluewater.

But there is a more optimistic view to take. This is that I am not merely a recorder of the soon-to-be-lost; not merely a Canute standing ankle-deep in a money-coloured sea that has some way to go before it reaches the high-tide line. This view sees this book as part of a process of changing things; for the better, not for the sake of it. At their best, books can do that. They can reflect wider trends in society, and help make things happen. It was once seen as inevitable that monocultural farming would spread to every corner of England; now it looks like the past, not the future. The flow of brutal, modernist concrete in the sixties and seventies is now seen as a mistake; much of it is being demolished. From socialism to Thatcherism, things that once seemed solid and inevitable have melted away, often quickly, and unexpectedly.

There is no reason, in other words, that the currently accelerating homogenisation of our landscapes and cultures needs to continue. Inevitable and unstoppable as it can often seem, it can be changed, if enough people want to change it. And one thing I have learned in my travels is that people *do* care. Most people don't want to live in a nation of clone towns, mega-malls, privatised streets, gated communities, ex-farms and eight-lane motorways strung with revolving billboards. They don't want to do the things that endless growth requires of them. They don't want to lose local distinctiveness, peculiarity and difference. They have an appreciation of character and place, culture and history. They value it. They want it to remain. Not everyone, but a hell of a lot of people; enough of them to change the way things are going, if they really want to.

The question is: do they want it enough?

The Margin and the Machine

These days, Richard Mabey is regularly referred to as 'England's greatest living nature writer'. A quarter of a century ago, though, when he hadn't yet earned this epithet, Mabey wrote a book called *The Common Ground*. It was 1980, at the height of the destruction being wreaked on the English countryside by industrial agriculture which, for the past few decades, had been utterly dominant. Big was beautiful, chemicals and computers were the future, and anyone who thought otherwise was an embarrassing throwback.

Mabey was one of those throwbacks, and his book was a passionate plea for the preservation of the special, the particular and the beautiful in the countryside. Today, the arguments he was making are widely accepted, and the dominant agricultural ideology of that time is increasingly discredited. Back then, though, Mabey was crying in the wilderness as he explained that virtually the only areas in which wildlife and natural diversity remained on the chemical-soaked farms of the time were the margins, where the sprayers had not reached, and where the unprofitable wildlife had holed up, expelled from the fields it had once made home:

> Time and again we have seen how most of the naturally rich areas that remain on the farm are now confined to land that is agriculturally marginal... It is intrinsically low in productivity, and the investment needed to raise its output usually greatly exceeds the overall social benefits, and in some cases even the agricultural returns.[1]

Everything of value, in other words, had been confined to the edges; to the odd bit of scrub, the long grass, the stony soil beneath the hedges. It was a value that remained entirely unrecognised by the agricultural masterminds of the time. Real value was in the crops themselves: in their ever-increasing yields. Never mind that the crops were not wanted; that more often than not once grown they were piled up in mountains, or dumped cheaply on the economies of poor countries, destroying their farmers in the process. What mattered was efficiency, productivity. What mattered, quite literally, was growth.

What was then true of agriculture is now true of society as a whole. What I have seen through my travels can be looked at as the results of a process of intensification. The attitudes then applied to farming – the narrow focus on high-yield monoculture; the careless use of chemicals which provide a short-term boost at long-term expense; the destruction of landscape features and wildlife in pursuit of those goals; the total failure to question where it was all leading – have now left the fields and taken to the streets. Across the country, we are confining real life to the margins; pushing it beyond the balance sheet; dismissing it; destroying the valuable and the irreplaceable.

We are doing so because we must grow. We must develop, and regenerate, and push forward. We must consume and profit and invest and the end goal, while unclear, must not be discussed, and must certainly not be questioned. We are in competition with other nations who must do the same things, and there is no time for questioning. We are UK plc, and we compete in a global marketplace. We are serious people now, with no time for whimsy. Whimsy does not pay, and never has.

As we move forward in pursuit of the siren of growth, we unleash a flattening of our history, heritage, landscapes and cultures. We tear up our orchards, bulldoze our markets, sell off our farms and our public squares. Big government and big business combine to steamroller people and places, for the good of the country, and those who object are pushed out to the margins, to cling to what remains of colour and character. That character clings on where it is not, yet, worth the time and effort it would take to extinguish it. But its time will come. It will be regenerated, because there is no other way.

As I pointed out in the first chapter, the changes that are affecting England are no accident, and neither are they anything unusual in global terms. Global consumer capitalism is unleashing the same forces on every nation on Earth, and each of them, in its own way, is experiencing the same sandblasting of the special, the same razing of the real.

It is seen in the empty strip malls of America, surrounded by car parks which sit at night like dead oceans of concrete, populated only by teenagers with nowhere else to go but online. It is seen in the identical city centres on separate continents, and in the matching interiors of offices and business hotels, the same from Siberia to Singapore. The world's landscapes are being efficiently remade in the interests of business, not people. People are merely players in global business's 'flexible labour market'; we must go where we are needed.

In return, if we are some of the global chosen, we will be given access to this season's look, and access to credit to buy it. At weekends, we will be given time off, which we may perhaps choose to spend visiting one of the theme-park manifestations of our landscape which have replaced the real thing and which, for a small entrance fee, we can enjoy with the benefit of a guided audio tour and a latte-to-go.

Recently, it was announced that Delhi is to ban its legendary street food vendors, in preparation for the 2010 Commonwealth Games. Indian officials cite health and safety concerns, and the need to 'modernise'. Already some people – the vendors themselves, of course, who will lose their livelihoods, but also those to whom they represent a real and vital part of the life of India's stubbornly chaotic capital – can see what is coming. Stubborn chaos is not the modern way. The fields must be sprayed, the weeds put down, the poppies pushed to the margins, the fields made safe for McDonald's, Starbucks, Apple, Dell, HSBC.

In twenty years' time, when all of Delhi's street vendors, tailors, small shopkeepers, kettle-menders, cobblers, machinists, hawkers and cooks are but a memory, and in their place is a productive, modern, profitable, sterile and inhuman maze of plate glass and chain stores, then the success of India's development and modernisation will be hymned by business editors and politicians. All of the gains will have been tallied up and none of the losses, except in the hearts of those who understand what is missing. The fields will have been cleared of weeds, the butterflies which remain will be confined to the hedge banks, and India, according to all the benchmarks that matter, will be a better place.

The Thing

Most of the people I've met during the course of my journey have not bothered to explain their politics to me; whether they're Left or Right or neither. And I've not bothered to ask, because I'm not much interested. Politics, in theory, is a way of both understanding the world and changing it – or at least managing it. Yet when I do talk to people who are very clear in their minds about which side they're on, be they red or blue, yellow or green, it can be curiously revealing. The issues raised in this book are often not quite understandable to them. Somehow, they don't quite get it.

It's easy to see why. Politics, in the tiresome adversarial sense in which we currently understand it – choose a side, chuck bricks at the other one – is a process not of understanding but of simplification. Doubts must be quashed, soft edges knocked off, areas of agreement played down and areas of disagreement magnified. It's a boys' game, fighting over power, and in boys' games, things get broken.

I have been searching, as I travelled England, for the things that get broken. For subtlety, complexity, diversity and colour. For things that don't fit into boxes. For things that neither traditional politics nor conventional economics has any way of quite dealing with, or really understanding. We have a problem, you see, politically, and it's an increasingly global one: the old lines drawn in the sand are of no use to us any more. There has been a sandstorm, and the dunes have shifted. The old words don't work. The old spells don't function.

What is killing the real England? The Left blames corporations and the Right blames Europe. The Left blames under-regulation and the Right blames over-regulation. The government must save us from capitalism. Capitalism must save us from the government. They both have a point – they're both right in their own ways, and yet they only see part of the picture. The bunkers remain occupied long after the armistice, and the soldiers on both sides still think they're winning. But another, bigger battle rages: one which they refuse to fight because they haven't yet won the last one.

Delhi, England, Beijing, Prague, Melbourne, anywhere else you care to look… this 'development' – this beast which crushes all before it and calls that crushing progress – is the real enemy now. It existed before Marx, before Adam Smith, before trades unions, before the stock market. Back in the 1830s, Cobbett called it simply 'the Thing', but it was ancient even then.

This is not about Left versus Right. This is about the individual versus the crushing, dehumanising machine, whether that machine is represented by the profit-hungry corporation, the edict-issuing state or – today's global reality – a powerful alliance of the two. The machine may come at us from 'Left' or 'Right'; the twentieth century has given us many examples of both variants. But wherever it comes from, it always overshadows any mere individual who stands near it.

If Cobbett were here today, he'd recognise the Thing immediately; grown bigger and smarter than in his day, but the same creature nonetheless. The government wants your fingerprints on a central database. Tesco wants to know exactly what you buy and when. Subway wants your local high street. CCTV cameras shout at you in public. Millionaires buy up the countryside. Corporations privatise the streets. Legislation forces the little guys out of business but does-n't touch the clones. Everywhere you look, the results are the same – top-heavy, selfish, elephantine power is crushing the life out of people and places. The Thing is still with us, and it's still hungry.

The Things that Don't Count

On a regular basis – once or twice a year – a story appears in the media about happiness. It's the same story with a different news peg: usually a survey carried out by a university or a think-tank. The survey will tell us soberly that, although people in England are richer today than they have ever been, they are also less happy. It will explain that, while our GDP is at record levels, while consumer borrowing is high, while we all have more holidays and white goods and cars and houses than ever before, it doesn't seem to be doing us much good.

It will explain, often in a puzzled tone, that we are also, as a society, more stressed, more fearful and less optimistic. Although things are officially better, unofficially we feel worse. Levels of mental illness and family breakdown are higher than ever. Personal relationships are suffering. Levels of depression are rising, levels of trust falling. Something is wrong, but no one ever quite resolves it.

For my part, the reason we are less happy seems clear, and it is not despite our levels of growth, success and development, it is because of them. We are less happy because many of the things that matter in people's lives are not measured. They do not count. As long as we use crude economic measurements to measure success, we are always going to miss out many of the things that make life actually worth living. None of them goes onto any balance sheets, but all of them have an emotional resonance that make our lives complete.

When your local pub closes down and is replaced by a Starbucks, if it shows up on the balance sheet at all, it shows up as a positive. A free house run by a landlord making a living for himself contributes little to the economy. Another outlet of a giant corporation, which is much better at squeezing profits from its customers, will certainly be marked down as a plus.

And yet, self-evidently to anyone who knows the reality of the situation, it is not an improvement. The people who work there have lost their jobs. The people who drank there have lost a community space and a bolthole. Their choice has been reduced, because nowhere else will be quite the same; unlike the branch of Starbucks, which will be a deliberate replication of every other branch of Starbucks, what was there before was unique. The wider community in the area will therefore be affected. People's relationships with each other will be affected too. None of the losses will be measured, but everyone will feel them.

We need to think differently, invent a new way of speaking – or perhaps just re-invent a very old one. A way of speaking that is not smothered in figures and does not need jargon to justify itself. We need to speak from the heart about what matters, what makes us happy and unhappy, what makes a place live, what we feel about our landscape. Our challenge is to break free of the dead economic language that both Right and Left use to justify their opinions. It has manacled our minds and destroyed the places that we live in. It has let the Thing loose to feed on our contentment.

Landscapes of the Mind

A few days ago, I was lying in bed listening to a current affairs programme on the radio. A presenter was interviewing a woman who was angry with Tesco. At first, through my fug of half-sleep, I thought this sounded promising. I wondered what was bothering her: the death of her high street, the crucifixion of local farmers, over-packaging, junk food… there was so much to choose from. But it wasn't any of those.

The woman was angry because Tesco had refused to accept her brand of credit card when she went shopping. She was so angry, she wanted to tell the nation. She thought it was an outrage. She couldn't see why a big supermarket like that couldn't accept every credit card there was. 'It's my right,' she said – and Tesco was violating that right by telling her to pay some other way. She was going to start a campaign. I felt a strange and alien emotion: sympathy for Tesco was coursing through my veins.

Some on the political right used to talk a lot about the 'dependency culture' created by the welfare state. Generous benefits gave people no incentive to look for work, they said; instead they just 'sponged off the State'. These days, with benefits much harder to get, and peanuts when you get them, they've gone a bit quiet on this. But while it's useful to watch your language sometimes, for fear of being stuck in the wrong box, there is, it seems to me, something in the phrase. Increasingly, as the Tesco woman showed, we do live in a 'dependency culture' – of a different kind. We depend on the consumer machine to provide for us – to give us what we want, when we want it. This is our 'right'. The Thing has dehumanised us, and we are all increasingly dependent on it for succour. We expect. We demand. We are like children. Everything must be instant and, if it isn't, somebody must pay.

Perhaps we don't know what's real any more. Consumerism, after all, specialises in creating a fake world, in which new 'needs' are created every day by fashionistas and marketing gurus, who will then meet them – at a price. In this fake world, age, pain, misery, insecurity, loneliness – all can be fended off or overcome with purchases. Animals die out of sight, and their meat comes to us shrink-wrapped and washed clean of blood. Apples fall from the trees twelve months of the year. Plastic landscapes, designed in distant office suites, come between us and the reality of place. We are cut off from the land, from seasons, from geography, from the dirt and hard work and complications of the world outside the bubble. Enough of this, and the bubble itself becomes the reality.

In this world we are prepared to brave a pre-dawn crush on Oxford Street to get hold of a shopping-bag we saw hanging off the arm of someone on the telly. We become narcissistic, self-absorbed, atomised. All that is real seems unreal; all that is false seems sublime. Everything is controlled – including us.

Anyone who starts to talk like this has to brace themselves for a backlash. The good thing is that the backlash is often quite predictable. So, there are two cardinal sins which, having made these arguments, I can now expect to be accused of.

The first is nostalgia. Many of the people I met all over England would often get their pre-emptive defence in early on this charge. 'I'm not just being nostalgic,' they'd say to me, unprompted; or 'I might just be being nostalgic, but…' In a world in which it is incumbent upon us all to be progressive and forward-looking at all times, nostalgia is a serious misdemeanour.

It's always struck me that dismissing people who see any value in the past, or draw any lessons from it, as simply 'nostalgics' is a reaction born of fear. Fear that our blind march towards an uncertain future might not be leading us where we expected to go. Fear that it might be true, after all, that learning from the past rather than seeking to obliterate it could be useful. Fear that – whisper it – some things might actually have *got worse*. 'Notice the shrill wail of anger,' wrote George Orwell in *The Road to Wigan Pier* in 1937, with which the simplistic defender-of-progress 'meets the suggestion that his grandfather may have been a better man than himself'.

Certainly there was no past Earthly Paradise known to us to which we should be aspiring to return. But what makes us think there will be one in the future? The bombastic narrative of human history which we are all taught as little children explains that mankind started off grunting in the swamps and will end conquering the stars, disease-free and immortal. This is no more realistic than imagining that every swain in pre-industrial England inhabited a world of bucolic bliss. At least we know what the past was like: we have no idea what is waiting for us in the future. In that context, a blind belief in the promise of 'progress' starts to look rather silly.

It is possible, in a strange way, to be as nostalgic about the future as about the past. I don't believe in a Golden Age, and even if I wanted to 'go back' I know it wouldn't be possible. But what is characterised as 'nostalgia' is often, in fact, a recognition that something valuable that once existed is in danger of being lost; and that it doesn't have to be. A recognition that we all live in history, and that the best of it should be carried with us on our journey. To dismiss that observation as unrealistic or backward-looking is not wise or brave or 'progressive': it is ahistorical, and culturally naïve.

Which brings us neatly on to the second criticism: that of being 'against change'. This is another potential line of attack on all those who defend local distinctiveness, and it's even more primitive than the 'nostalgia' line. It is the ultimate get-out clause for those who want to impose their destructive schemes on others. Don't want that new motorway, that expanded airport terminal, that housing estate, that nuclear power station, that windfarm in the wilderness? You're just against change.

This is closely tied up with the use of the word 'nimby', which most of the people I met on my travels have had thrown at them at one stage or another. Imported, like so much else, from America by the Tories in the 1980s, 'nimby' is the insult of choice which developers throw at their opponents. Nimbies are, by definition, 'against change'. They put their own interests ahead of those of society as a whole. If you can make the word stick, you can dismiss those who foolishly choose to defend their locality from the depredations of distant profiteers.

There is no doubt that some people do have their own selfish reasons for opposing genuinely useful change at local level: lowering the tone of the area, spoiling the view from the window and so on. In this sense, the 'nimby' does exist. But there is also no doubt that the word has become an extremely effective propaganda tool in the hands of those who, in turn, have their own selfish motives for imposing unpopular change onto local communities; usually motives associated with financial gain. For this reason, it's always worth being suspicious when you hear it used. Often what you are actually hearing is the whining of the thwarted lobby group or the frustration of the man from the ministry, brought up short in his grand designs by the tiresome objections of people who will actually have to live with them.

Taming the Thing

I carry one deep, lasting and entirely unexpected impression away from my journeys around England. Growing, unspoken, but nonetheless real, that 'class war' – or at least class division – stays with me, and unnerves me. Since 11 September 2001, and the consequent debate about Islam and the West, there's been a lot of discussion about the dangers of 'ghettoisation' across England. But it's not Muslim ghettoes we should be worrying about – it's moneyed ones. From commuter villages to executive apartments, I have seen these ghettoes growing everywhere, and the divide between the haves and the have-nots is widening daily. The haves, in this case, have not just money but power, and they are using it ruthlessly for their own advantage.

Where is this going to lead us? Gated communities with private police forces, surrounded by deserts of debt, monitored by security cameras. Four or five superstores selling us everything we could possibly need, and a lot of things we don't. A twee, dead countryside packaged as a rural idyll and sold to bankers and retired civil servants. Developers and 'regenerators' stalking the land like hyenas, picking off the weak and the defenceless. A wide corporate blandscape in which money will buy you what looks on the surface like character but underneath is nothing of the kind. Everyone out for themselves, everyone blaming it on someone else. Is this what we're in for?

It doesn't have to be. In the first chapter, I identified three forces which are combining to scour life and character from the landscape: the state-corporate machine; this new class war; and the reluctance of the English to talk about themselves, their culture or their nation. You have now seen the first two in action all across the land. You've seen, too, that many people are beginning to talk about it and daring to describe – and act to create – an alternative.

The question now is: what can be done to help them succeed? How we can we save the real England? Firstly, it seems to me, we all need to take back control of our own lives. We need to break that dependency on the Thing and take responsibility for our places. If we care about small shops, we need to stop going to Sainsbury's. If we care about farms or orchards disappearing, we need to support them. If we care about our local area, we have to stand up and be counted. Blaming everyone and everything else won't cut it. Societies are made up of people – people like us. It's people who make cultures thrive or die. Blame the government, if you like, and blame Tesco too: they certainly deserve it. But don't think that doing so is a substitute for looking in the mirror and asking yourself what you have done, and what you can do.

It seems to me that, though the many problems I encountered on my journeys were diverse, complex and often very place-specific, there was one overall principle which tied them together: at a local level, people did not have enough power. If this is the problem, then the solution suggests itself very clearly: re-localising that power, and trusting people to use it.

This would provide us with any number of new possibilities. Most crucially, perhaps, it would allow people to feel what they should have been feeling all along – a sense of ownership of their place and their community. Then they could begin to feel again that political action is worthwhile, because what they do will actually make a difference: they have the ability to re-shape their place as they want it, not as the distant demands of business require it.

I have seen, in many places, what happens when communities are given – or take – real power at local level, things which would have been thought impossible start to happen. For years, politicians have been biting their nails over the 'apathy' of the electorate. Their proposed answers – voting by text message, anyone? – have often been laughable, because they have been asking the wrong questions. People are not apathetic. They are just sick of voting. Locally, the people they vote for have been stripped of so many powers by central government that it's hardly worth the bother. Nationally, you can choose from one of two groups of market fundamentalists in suits. The things that aren't counted will continue to be overlooked, and what happens to your neighbourhood will continue to be out of your hands. Why bother?

The urgent task is to tame the Thing; to bring power back home, to local level. And out there, something is beginning to stir. Not just in the myriads of small, local battles fought by the people I have met and many more like them but, curiously, at the top too. Recently, both major political parties have begun cautiously speaking a new language. Both are starting to talk of the need to give power back to local communities. They are throwing words like 'empowerment' and 'enabling government' and 'local power' around like confetti. Both parties say they want to get central government off people's backs. They never talk of getting big business off people's backs, of course, but you have to start somewhere.

Who knows how much they mean it? What's significant, though, is that they feel the need to say these things at all. All over England – and Scotland, Wales and Northern Ireland, come to that – people increasingly want power back. Politicians sense this and they know, too, that unless it starts to happen, their positions will be increasingly de-legitimised. What they can do, and how much they are prepared to do, remains to be seen. But the language is changing, and so is the atmosphere. We may just be in with a chance.

I hope so, because if things are going to change it's our friends in

Westminster who are going to have to make the first moves. This may sound paradoxical. After all, if we're looking for a widening and a deepening of power at the local level, it's surely local people who need to be acting, not the usual suspects in London. But this isn't quite right. The system as it currently operates militates against the small and local and in favour of the large and centralised. The playing field is nowhere near level and the referee is looking the other way.

If we are to see our landscapes and cultures rejuvenated – if we are to see the real England survive and thrive – then those in government have a job to do. It's not their job to make these things happen – they couldn't even if they wanted to. Their job, rather, is to clear the decks. To loosen the chains which tie local communities and prevent people from acting. To rein in the people and organisations and laws and directives which do the damage. To create an environment in which local power can flourish again.

A flowering of local power is not a panacea. Local communities can make mistakes, can be venal or even corrupt, just as central government can. There will always be a tension, too, between the need for more power at local level and the necessity of doing some things at national and international level; international policies on climate change, for example, or national ones on affordable housing or healthcare. But local democracy is always more responsive to real on-the-ground needs than its national equivalent, just as a Cornish Assembly would be more responsive to the needs of Portscatho than one based in Swindon. And real local democracy is what we need. The task of government should be to provide it.

Democracy in England is in a parlous state. Local councils were denuded of much of their power by the Thatcher government. The Blair regime continued the process of centralisation, crowning it with the setting up of the unelected, anti-democratic 'regional assemblies'. The Brown government removed even this fig leaf, handing power to the corporate placemings of the Regional Development Agencies which now make many of our decisions for us, in the shadows.

Meanwhile, post-1997 devolution has created a situation in which the English are uniquely ill-served by British democracy.

The Scottish now have a Parliament, with elected members, a large budget and significant powers to run their own nation in their own way. The Welsh have the same to a lesser extent, as does Northern Ireland. All of these nations also have representatives in the British Parliament at Westminster. The English, meanwhile, now have the worst of both worlds. Instead of our own, elected Parliament or Assembly, we have undemocratic regional government. And at the British Parliament in Westminster, Scottish and Welsh MPs can make decisions about the future of England to which they will never have to answer to their constituents – though English MPs cannot do the same in those countries. Thus Scottish, Welsh and Northern Irish MPs at Westminster can vote, and have done, to impose controversial policies such as university tuition fees or foundation hospitals on the English which their constituents at home will not have to suffer and for which they will not be answerable at the ballot-box.

England is the only British nation without any form of democratic devolution. It is the only nation in Europe without its own parliament or government. It has fewer MPs per head of population than the other British nations, and regularly receives less money per head from the treasury than either Scotland, Wales or Northern Ireland. The British government has ministers for Northern Ireland, Wales and Scotland – despite devolution – but no minister for England.

Constitutionally, in fact, England does not even exist. The Acts of Union between Scotland and England in 1707 removed the constitutional identity of both countries; they became, along with long-conquered Wales, a new political entity called 'Great Britain'. In the late 1990s, Wales and Scotland rightly regained their political nationhood, with the creation of devolved governments for both countries. England remained in limbo. It still does.

What I have seen has convinced me that England needs to be re-democratised, from the top down. The clumsy, secretive and unaccountable regional structures should be swept away, and an English Parliament created (a measure currently supported by almost 70 per cent of the population[2]). It could then begin to act on the issues that concern the English, as the Scottish Parliament does for the Scots.

Who knows where this could lead us? In my idle daydreams, the first debate held in the new English Parliament (which would emphatically not be based in London; I quite fancy York, the old Viking capital) is about the dominance of multinational corporations within our society, the impact on our landscape and culture, and what we can do about it. And one of its first laws takes its lead from the pioneering Land Reform Act passed by the Scottish Parliament in 2003, which ended feudal land ownership and gave communities the right to buy the land on which they live and work. The possibilities of a new era of genuine democracy in England, after so many decades of increasingly centralised government, often in the interests of corporate power, are exciting.

Such a devolution at national level would need to go hand in hand with the devolution of significant powers to local authorities too. These powers would give them the right to make far-reaching planning and land-use decisions, decide how or if big corporations operate in their area, protect their street markets, promote their farms and local shops and businesses, and rework their local economies to give priority to the local and the distinctive.

But even that's not adequate. Local authorities need more power, yes – but that power needs to be genuinely available to local communities as well. It's not good enough just to expect councils to do it; this can be almost as disempowering as waiting for central government. A new settlement needs to ensure that every street, every neighbourhood, every village and every town has a voice. It needs to involve genuine public participation.

This is not the same thing as the sham 'consultation' processes that all recent governments have indulged in whenever they had a big infrastructure project or new housing development to push through. This usually involves deciding what will be done, asking the public what their opinion of it is, and then doing it anyway. Participation is very different. It necessitates people taking decisions about how their local budget is used, if and where housing will be built, what to do about transport and shops and the totality of the local economy. It means a daring reaching-out to citizens: not just asking their opinion but handing them the power to turn their opinions into change.

If this sounds like idealism, it is anything but. It is possible, and it is already happening elsewhere. I have seen genuine public control of local affairs all over the world. In Brazil, I've visited cities which were running 'participatory budgets'. There, the citizens, in a series of public meetings, workshops and votes, decided themselves how their local authority budget would be spent. They allocated the money to the things that mattered to them and were involved in the decisions about what could and could not be spent.

In the US, I've visited towns in which local laws had been changed, through citizen pressure, to give the people control of their town – how their high streets look, which corporations operate there, and how they are run. All over the world there are schemes similar to this taking off, becoming more popular. When people are given responsibility, they rise to it. They make their places live again, better than any corporation or government department could ever manage, if it was even interested.[3]

Curiously enough, there is currently a Bill going through Parliament which aims to enshrine a re-localisation of power in law. With the support of over four hundred MPs, including the leader of the opposition, the Sustainable Communities Bill might even have a chance. The brainchild of a coalition of organisations and politicians dedicated to reversing local economic and community decline, the Bill would return considerable powers to local people. Councils would have a duty to promote 'sustainable communities' – defined as communities in which the local economy and environment flourishes, as does the participation of the people – and national government would have a duty to help them do so. Genuine participation by local communities would be at the heart of the new arrangement. It aims, say its organisers, at 'bottom-up government'.[4]

Naturally, this Bill has received virtually zero attention from the media and the commentariat. And as I write this, another Bill, which has a much stronger chance of becoming law, has been proposed by the government. This one will 'streamline' the planning system, by taking decisions about big development projects – motorways, airports, power stations – out of the hands of elected politicians and putting them into the domain of a new, unelected, government-appointed quango of technocrats. It contains a 'Tesco clause', designed to make it easier to build out-of-town superstores, and, if it becomes law, it will make the United Kingdom the only Western country in which citizens and their elected representatives have no say over major planning decisions. The Confederation of British Industry has been pushing for this for years, and is very pleased indeed.

In other words, we still have a huge distance to travel, and we have barely started walking. Some of us are determinedly walking in the wrong direction. And until we can lever our elected governments out of the grip of corporate interests and calm our obsession with endless economic growth and development for development's sake, we are not going to move far.

This is not just a question of what laws are passed – it is about how politics, power and democracy works in England. It is about our increasingly rotten system of government, trusted by fewer people each year, in hock to money and influence, governing for the Thing rather than the people. It is about whether and how we can ever become a nation in which the small, the local, the particular and the real matters as much to us as the Dow Jones Index, this season's man-bag, or the value of our property portfolio.

Geography and Biology

Recently, I was having a conversation with a Scottish nationalist. He was telling me how successful the Scots had been in creating a renewed sense of national identity since devolution. It puzzled him, he said, that the English couldn't do the same thing. 'Why can't the English talk about their identity or their culture?' he asked me. 'We just can't understand it.'

I didn't really know what to say. I couldn't quite understand it either. The English, perhaps uniquely among European nations, are becoming almost a de-cultured people. From the shops on our high streets to the vocabulary we use, we are becoming a cheap and nasty imitation of the worst of consumer America. We can't sing our own folk songs or, increasingly, cook our own national foods. We don't know what grows in our local area. We sneer at morris dancers while we sip skinny lattes. We are cut off from who are and where we have come from.

The English – or the English intellectual classes, at any rate – have long been renowned for this kind of rootless shoulder shrugging. George Orwell was railing against it during the Second World War. Taking 'their cookery from Paris and their opinions from Moscow', he wrote, the average English left-wing intellectual is entirely cut off from popular culture: so much so that 'it is always felt that there is something slightly disgraceful in being an Englishman and that it is a duty to snigger at every English institution, from horse racing to suet puddings'.[5]

Not much has changed: even suet puddings are making a comeback in the nation's gastropubs. Mention Englishness to an English intellectual today and you can still count the seconds before they start mentioning the horrors of Britain's imperial past (horrors which are never, oddly, anything to do with to the Welsh or the Scots). They are usually much happier hymning the virtues of England's ethnic minority communities – communities which, ironically, draw much of their strength from their strong sense of cultural identity – than discussing English culture as a whole.

Often they will go on to deny that 'English culture' even exists. Morris dancing was invented by the Victorians, they will proclaim, incorrectly, St George was Lebanese, and in any case, we're all 'multicultural' now, so talking about it will probably offend somebody. Discussions – let alone, God forbid, celebrations – of English identity are to be regarded with immediate suspicion, whereas those of virtually any other community on Earth (except probably America) are to be welcomed as positive displays of ethnic diversity. Even the tarnished ideal of 'multiculturalism' often seems to involve the positive celebration of every culture in Britain except the largest one – English culture.

This cultural self-denial has had two dangerous consequences. One is that the far right has been able to colonise Englishness for itself, conflate it with whiteness and make us all even more nervous about discussing it. The other is that the door has been left wide open for the Thing to trample over what remains of the English landscape, both physical and cultural.

Debates about 'Englishness' might seem esoteric, and in the wrong hands they can be. But if the right questions are asked, this matters. Many of the people I met during my travels exhibited a solid, quiet Englishness that had nothing to do with pained intellectual definitions and everything to do with belonging to the historical landscape they were part of. This, it seems to me, is crucial. Landscape and belonging are tied inextricably together. Englishness as an identity comes not from institutions or vague ideas about 'values' but from *place*.

In this context the reluctance, or the inability, of the English to discuss who they are is a key contributor to the decline of our landscapes, places and cultures. If we don't know what England is, or what made us, or what we value, then how do we know what to retain, protect and develop? How do we know what matters and what doesn't? If the English cannot be English, then what makes up England will cease to exist. There will be no good reason not to replace the lot with homogenous outdoor malls and executive lofts.

The English need to talk about themselves again – and be happy to do so. Regardless of their skin colour, religion or politics, the English need to be able to belong to and to cherish their places and their identity, to talk about who they are and to defend it, without fear of being associated with racism or xenophobia.

We need, perhaps, a new type of patriotism, benign and positive, based on place not race, geography not biology. One which seeks to make the best of what we are and what we have. A national mission to reclaim the land and the landscapes for all the people who live in them and care about them.

In Roman mythology, every place was distinct, and every place had its own guardian spirit. This guardian, usually in the form of an animal, was known as the *genius loci*. The identity of the guardian represented the character of the place. These days, the phrase has come to mean the spirit of a place in a different sense: its distinctiveness and character. As I have seen on my journeys, and as I hope I've managed to communicate to you, the *genius loci* of most places in England still exists. It is weaker, undoubtedly, than it has ever been, but it is still there, watching, waiting to see what we will do; whether we will notice it again, even consult it, or whether we are content to bury it forever.

And maybe I am being an idealist now, but when I close my eyes and look back over where I've been and what I have seen, it is possible to visualise a future in which England wakes up again and steps back from the precipice. It is possible to visualise a future in which the many wonderful things I have seen are not wiped out but are preserved, promoted and enriched as part of a living landscape.

It is possible to imagine a future in which England is not a vain consumer monoculture, but a patchwork of living communities, inhabited by people who care enough about them to make them live. A future in which we realise that global success and local failure will always go hand in hand: that we can grow, grow, grow, to compete with China, or we can nourish our landscapes, cultures and relationships – but we cannot do both.

The reality or otherwise of this vision, though, lies with us. All of the work done by the people I have met stands or falls on whether enough of us not only support it but are prepared to do similar things ourselves. To make things happen, rather than wait for others to do it for us. To battle for what matters and what is ours, rather than to watch it pulled out from under us by money and self-interest.

Because, ultimately, whatever central or local government does, whatever laws do or do not exist, such a country can only be created by the people who live in it. If we are to move away from that dependency culture, hole the Thing below the waterline, or at least cripple it momentarily, then it is up to all of us.

We embody the *genius loci* – we create or destroy it. It is in us all, and we hold in our hands the future of our landscapes and communities. There is still a real England. It can live or it can die. We can be surrounded by plastic or be part of something real. We can be Citizens of Nowhere or we can know our place – know it and be prepared to stand up for it, because we understand how much it matters. The choice, as ever, is ours.

Taking Action

How to get in touch with some of the people and organisations featured in this book – and some other interesting pointers.

Pubs and Beer

Campaign for Real Ale
230 Hatfield Road, St Albans, AL1 4LW
01727 867 201
www.camra.org.uk

Freedom for Pubs
PO Box 5, Bristol, BS10 7DA
www.freedomforpubs.com

Waterways

Save Castlemill Boatyard
www.portmeadow.org

Regents Network
20 Oval Road, Camden Town, London, NW1 7DJ
020 7267 7105
secretary@regentsnetwork.org

Save Our Waterways
www.mike-stevens.co.uk/defracuts/

Independent Shops

Knights of St Edmund
www.knightsofsaintedmund.com

Tescopoly
www.tescopoly.org

Friends of the Earth
26–28 Underwood Street, London, N1 7JQ
020 7490 1555
http://community.foe.co.uk/campaigns/real_food/supermarkets/index.html

Farms and the Countryside

Small Farms Association
Ley Coombe Farm, Modbury, Ivybridge, Devon, PL21 0TU
01548 830302
www.small-farms-association.co.uk

FARM
www.farm.org.uk

Countryside Restoration Trust
Barton, Cambridge, CB3 7AG
01223 262999
www.livingcountryside.org.uk

Urban Public Space

Save Chinatown Campaign
Min Quan, 14 Featherstone Road, Southall, Middlesex, UB2 5AA
07940 514 268
http://minquan.squarespace.com/save-chinatown

Open Spaces Society
25a Bell Street, Henley-on-Thames, Oxfordshire, RG9 2BA
01491 573535
www.oss.org.uk

Friends of Queen's Market
167 Masterman Road, London, E6 3NW
www.friendsofqueensmarket.org.uk

Villages

Campaign to Protect Rural England
128 Southwark Street, London, SE1 0SW
020 7981 2800
www.cpre.org.uk

Mebyon Kernow
Lanhainsworth, Fraddon Hill, Fraddon, St Columb, Cornwall, TR9 6PQ
www.mebyonkernow.org

Orchards

Tenbury English Mistletoe Enterprise
www.teme-mistletoe.co.uk

Marcher Apple Network
www.marcherapple.net

Bernwode Plants
Kingswood Lane, Ludgershall, Buckinghamshire, HP18 9RB
01844 237415
www.bernwodeplants.co.uk

Dragon Orchard
Dragon House, Putley, Ledbury, Herefordshire, HR8 2RG
01531 670 071
www.dragonorchard.co.uk

Other Organisations

Common Ground
Gold Hill House, 21 High Street, Shaftesbury, Dorset, SP7 8JE
01747 850820
www.commonground.org.uk

New Economics Foundation
3 Jonathan Street, London, SE11 5NH
020 7820 6300
www.neweconomics.org

Campaign for an English Parliament
Office 1, Margarethe House, Eismann Way, Corby, Northants, NN17 5ZB
07071 220234
www.thecep.org.uk

Notes

Chapter 1

1. Bluewater website: http://www.bluewater.co.uk.
2. See Paul Kingsnorth, *One No, Many Yeses: a Journey to the Heart of the Global Resistance Movement* (London: Free Press, 2003).
3. J. B. Priestley, *English Journey* (London: Mandarin, 1994), p. 22.
4. H. J. Massingham, 'The Monotonous Landscape', 1946, in H. J. Massingham, *A Mirror of England: Anthology of Writings (1888-1952)* (Bideford: Green Books, 1988), p.176.
5. Ian Nairn, *Outrage*, 1955, quoted in 'The British Landscape', *The Ecologist*, November 2006, p. 25.
6. 'Not In My Back Yard': the derogatory acronym applied by government and big business to those who oppose their projects at local level.
7. George Orwell, *The Lion and the Unicorn: Socialism and the English genius* (London: Penguin, 1982), p.63.

Chapter 2

1. Silk Tork, 'Regional Breweries of Britain, Part Two', *Ratebeer Weekly*, 28 January 2004. See www.ratebeer.com/Story.asp?StoryID=273.
2. Peter Haydon, *Beer and Britannia: An Inebriated History of Britain* (Stroud: Sutton, 2001), p. 306.
3. Roger Protz (ed.), *Good Beer Guide 2007* (London: CAMRA Books, 2006).
4. Campaign for Real Ale, February 2007. See http://www.camra.org.uk/page.aspx?o=232930.

5. 'Investment in rural services can pay dividends', Countryside Agency, 6 November 2001. See http://www.countryside.gov.uk/LAR/archive/presscentre/investment_rural_services.asp.

6. Campaign for Real Ale, February 2007. See http://www.camra.org.uk/page.aspx?o=232930.

7. Campaign for Real Ale, Pub Heritage – Historic Pub Interiors. See http://www.heritagepubs.org.uk/home/nationalinventory.asp.

8. Hilaire Belloc, 'On Inns', 1948, in Hilaire Belloc, *Selected Essays* (London: Methuen, 1948), p. 119.

9. Haydon, *Beer and Britannia*, p. 3.

10. R.V. French, 'Drink in England', quoted in Haydon, *Beer and Britannia*, p. 8.

11. *Pub Companies: Second Report of Session 2004–05* (London: House of Commons Trade and Industry Committee, 2004), p. 8.

12. The UK's three biggest pub companies at the time of writing are Punch Taverns, Enterprise Inns and Mitchells & Butlers. They own 9304, 7809 and 2000 pubs respectively: a total of 19,113.

13. *Pub Companies*, p. 12.

14. See www.thespiritgroup.com.

15. George Orwell, 'The Moon Under Water', *Evening Standard*, 9 February 1946.

16. *Ibid.*

17. *Ibid.*

18. Christopher Hutt, *The Death of the English Pub* (London: Arrow, 1973), p. 131.

19. *Ibid*, p. 157.

20. Mike Bell, personal correspondence.

Chapter 3

1. 'British Waterways – Fast Facts', factsheet (Watford: British Waterways).

2. 'British Waterways – Business', factsheet (Watford: British Waterways).

3. *2004/05 Annual Report and Accounts* (Watford: British Waterways, 2005).

4. *Ibid.*

5. See British Waterway's website: www.britishwaterways.co.uk/home.

6. Oliver Tickell, 'Coasting erosion', the *Guardian*, 12 October 2005.

7. *2004/05 Annual Report and Accounts* (Watford: British Waterways, 2005).

8. See www.saveourwaterways.org.uk.

9. Mark Milner, 'Grant squeeze threatens to cut Britain's canal keeper adrift', *Guardian*, 26 May 2007.
10. 'New Inquiry Announced: British Waterways', press release, Environment Food and Rural Affairs Committee of the House of Commons, 1 December 2006.

Chapter 4

1. See www.burysteds.org.uk/why_develop.html#.
2. See http://moreheart.info/cattlemarket/.
3. *High Street Britain: 2015* (London: House of Commons All-Party Parliamentary Small Shops Group, 2006), p. 27.
4. 'Local Works' newsletter, summer 2005. See www.localworks.org.
5. Andrew Simms, Julian Oram, Alex MacGillivray and Joe Drury, *Ghost Town Britain* (London: New Economics Foundation, 2002), p. 23.
6. Anthony Barnes, 'Farewell then, second-hand bookshops' *Independent*, 30 October 2005.
7. *High Street Britain: 2015*, p. 10.
8. Simms *et al*, *Ghost Town Britain*, p. 37.
9. Andrew Simms, Petra Kiell and Ruth Potts, *Clone Town Britain: the Survey Results on the Bland State of the Nation* (London: New Economics Foundation, 2005), p. 25.
10. See, for example, the activities of Tesco in Withernsea: *High Street Britain: 2015*, p. 25.
11. Andrew Simms, Petra Kiell and Ruth Potts, *Clone Town Britain* (London: New Economics Foundation, 2004).
12. Simms *et al*, *Clone Town Britain* (2005).
13. Which might explain why they filed for bankruptcy while I was in the middle of writing this chapter. Failing utterly to change with the times, Little Chef stuck with fry-ups, sausages and big mugs of tea while the people of England were apparently demanding pan-fried wholemeal lattes and decaf skinny bruschettas.
14. 'UK grocers face competition probe', BBC News Online, 22 January 2007.
15. *Ibid.*
16. Simms *et al*, *Clone Town Britain* (2005), p. 13.
17. Paul Brown, 'Secret deals with Tesco cast shadow over town', *Guardian*, 22 January 2004.

18. Patrick Barkham, 'Secret deal behind a Norfolk town's mystery U-turn on new supermarket', *Guardian*, 29 April 2006.
19. *High Street Britain: 2015*, p. 71.
20. *High Street Britain: 2015*, p. 66.
21. Simms *et al, Clone Town Britain* (2004), p. 23.
22. See Paul Kingsnorth, *One No, Many Yeses* (London: Free Press, 2003), Chapter 8.
23. Simms *et al, Clone Town Britain* (2005), p. 25.

Chapter 5

1. The source for this quote was the Countryside Agency's website – which, like the CA itself, no longer exists (it was merged into 'Natural England' during the writing of the book). See http://en.wikipedia.org/wiki/Countryside_Agency.
2. *The State of the Countryside 2020* (London: Countryside Agency Publications, 2003).
3. *Agriculture in the United Kingdom 2005* (London: DEFRA, 2005), Chapter 3: 'The Structure of the Industry'. See http://statistics.defra.gov.uk/esg/publications/auk/2005/default.asp.
4. For the tax year ending 5 April 2005 the median gross annual earnings for full-time men were £25,100, and for full-time women £19,400: a mean of £22,250. Source: 'Corrected: 2005 Annual Survey of Hours and Earnings First Release', Office of National Statistics, 30 November 2005. See www.statistics.gov.uk/StatBase/Product.asp?vlnk=14203.
5. *Agriculture in the United Kingdom 2005*, Chapter 2: 'Farming Income', p. 12.
6. Helen Carter and Polly Curtis, 'Hill farms teetering on the breadline', *Guardian*, 21 January 2004.
7. Hansard, House of Commons Written Answers, 21 July 2004: Column 243W. http://www.publications.parliament.uk/pa/cm200304/cmhansrd/vo040721/text/40721w02.htm.
8. 'Factsheet: Suicide', (London: Mind). See www.mind.org.uk/Information/Factsheets/Suicide/.
9. William Cobbett, *Rural Rides* (London: Penguin, 2001), p. 185.
10. Robin Page, *The Decline of an English Village* (Barton: Bird's Farm Books, 2004), pp. 195–6.
11. Graham Harvey, *The Killing of the Countryside* (London: Vintage, 1998), p. 7.

12. 'A Real Future for our Countryside – A Green Alternative to Countryside Alliance', press release, Friends of the Earth, 28 February 1998.
13. Oliver Tickell, 'Paradise postponed', *New Scientist*, 17 January 1998.
14. Tim Radford, 'Warning sounded on decline of species', *Guardian*, 19 March 2004.
15. Oliver Rackham, *The History of the Countryside* (London: J. M. Dent, 1999), pp. 25–6.

Chapter 6

1. Tania Branigan, 'Development casts shadow on Chinatown', *Guardian*, 22 November 2004. See http://society.guardian.co.uk/urbandesign/story/0,11200,1356675,00.html.
2. From Rosewheel's website – www.rosewheel.co.uk – which has now been disabled.
3. 'The people behind Legacy', *Guardian*, 13 January 2001. See www.guardian.co.uk/dome/article/0,,421686,00.html.
4. 'Dome bidder's gift to Labour', BBC News Online, 6 January 2001. See http://news.bbc.co.uk/1/hi/uk_politics/1103614.stm.
5. David Hencke, 'Ministers ignored advice on Dome bid', *Guardian*, 12 January 2005. See www.guardian.co.uk/dome/article/0,,1388295,00.html.
6. See http://en.wikipedia.org/wiki/Sunday_Times_Rich_List_2005.
7. Paradise Project information sheet, issued by www.liverpoolpsda.co.uk.
8. See http://quiggins.has.it.
9. Anna Minton, *What Kind of World are we Building? The Privatisation of Public Space* (London: RICS, 2006), p. 3.
10. *Ibid*, p. 20.
11. *Ibid*, pp. 3–4.
12. See www.stmodwen.co.uk.
13. Mike Phillips, 'Market Stalls', *Property Week*, 19 January 2007.
14. *Ibid*.
15. See www.no2id.net.

Chapter 7

1. 'The Big Picture. Census 2001 – benchmark for the 21st Century', press release, Office of National Statistics, 13 February 2003.
2. 'The Big Number. Census 2001 reveals UK population is 58,789,194', press release, Office of National Statistics, 30 September 2002.
3. See www.cpre.org.uk/campaigns/housing-and-urban-policy/housing-supply/housing-supply-what-is-the-problem.
4. *Regional Planning Guidance for the South East (RPG 9)* (London: Government Office for the South East, 2004), Chapter 12 – Ashford growth area.
5. *Ibid.*
6. *Regional planning guidance for the South east (RPG 9)* (London: DETR, 2001).
7. Ronald Blythe, *Akenfield* (London: Penguin, 1969), p. 13.
8. Craig Taylor, *Return to Akenfield: Portrait of an English Village in the 21st Century* (London: Granta, 2006), p. xv.
9. *Ibid*, p. 225.
10. *State of the Countryside 2006* (London: Commission for rural communities, 2006). See www.ruralcommunities.gov.uk/files/SoTC06_Complete.pdf.
11. Quoted in Julia Goldsworthy, 'Homeless at Home: a Report on Cornwall's Affordable Housing Crisis' (Liberal Democrat team for Cornwall, April 2005), p. 3.
12. Cornwall County Council. See www.cornwall.gov.uk/index.cfm?articleid=12689.
13. Paula Demarzio, 'Cornwall records highest house price growth, says Halifax', abcmoney.co.uk, 14 April 2006. See http://www.abcmoney.co.uk/news/1420062313.htm.
14. 'Land registry: residential property price report, January–March, 2006', http://www.landregistry.gov.uk/assets/library/documents/rppr_q1_2006.pdf.
15. Peter Kingston 'Closed for business', *Guardian*, 10 May 2005.
16. *State of the Countryside 2006*, p. 30.
17. Quoted in Julia Goldsworthy, 'Homeless at Home', p. 3.
18. 'Give Cornwall what it wants', thisisthewestcountry.co.uk, 22 January 2004. See http://archive.thisisthewestcountry.co.uk/2004/1/22/21396.html.
19. See www.dti.gov.uk/regional/regional-dev-agencies/index.html.

20. Regional Development Agencies Act 1998, Part One: 5 (1).
21. The map is online at www.thecep.org.uk/news.shtml.
22. 'Scathing report throws future of regional assemblies into doubt', www.thisislondon.co.uk, 5 March 2007.
23. *State of the Countryside 2006*, p. 28.
24. Craig Taylor, *Return to Akenfield*, p. 32.
25. Home Builders Federation Press Release, 'Social Housebuilding Drops', 29 April 2003. See Paul Kingsnorth, *Your Countryside, Your Choice* (London: CPRE, 2005), p.17.
26. See www.postwatch.co.uk/custinfo/CustInfo.asp?id=18.

Chapter 8

1. Sue Clifford and Angela King, *England in Particular* (London: Hodder and Stoughton, 2006), p. 14.
2. John Vidal, 'Ancient apple orchards face bonfire as blight of farm payments bites', *Guardian*, 29 March 2004.
3. Clifford and King, *England in Particular*, p. 310.
4. See http://news.bbc.co.uk/1/hi/programmes/politics_show/ 3190854.stm.

Chapter 9

1. Richard Mabey, *The Common Ground* (London: Arrow, 1981), p. 153.
2. See the website of the Campaign for an English Parliament: www.thecep.org.uk/.
3. See Paul Kingsnorth, *One No, Many Yeses: a Journey to the Heart of the Global Resistance Movement* (London: Free Press, 2003), Chapters 7 and 8.
4. See www.localworks.org.
5. George Orwell, *The Lion and the Unicorn: Socialism and the English genius* (London: Penguin, 1982), p.64.

Acknowledgements

Thanks are due to many. To my patient agent, Patrick Walsh, and my excellent editor, Laura Barber. To my brother, Simon Kingsnorth, who is responsible for my websites: www.paulkingsnorth.net and www.realengland.co.uk. To my friends Mark Lynas and George Monbiot, who commented critically and sometimes even helpfully on much of what I have written here. To Stuart Paterson, whose patient nudging over several years has taken me and my writing to some necessary places. To my ever supportive and wonderful mother and family, who have been through so much this last year and survived it all. To my dog, Quincy, who insisted on dragging me out of the house on a regular basis, thus possibly preserving my often crumbling sanity.

To the K Blundell Trust of the Society of Authors and to the JMG Foundation, for financial assistance which kept food on my table during the writing of these pages. To Zac Goldsmith in particular, for his continued support for my work. To the team at the *Ecologist*, where some of this writing first appeared in various forms, particularly Harry Ram and Jeremy Smith. Variations on some of this book's contents have also appeared in the *Daily Telegraph*, the *Guardian* and the *New Statesman*.

Then, my two greatest debts. First, to all the people I met during the course of researching this book, who gave me their time, showed me their life's work, fed me dinner and their thoughts, and made it all possible. I hope I have done them justice. Secondly, and most of all, to my beautiful wife Jyoti, who makes everything worthwhile, who keeps me going and who inexplicably puts up with me, whatever I do or fail to do. It couldn't have happened without her.

Finally, to my late father, who didn't live to read what I have written here. I would have liked him to. I hope he has found peace.

Index